Plain Madeleine

Mrs. John Jacob Astor in Bar Harbor

Mac Smith

Down East Books

Camden, Maine

Down East Books

An imprint of Globe Pequot, the trade division of The Rowman & Littlefield Publishing Group, Inc.
4501 Forbes Blvd., Ste. 200
Lanham, MD 20706
www.rowman.com

Distributed by NATIONAL BOOK NETWORK

British Library Cataloguing in Publication Information available

Library of Congress Cataloging-in-Publication Data

Names: Smith, Mac, 1964– author.
Title: Plain Madeleine: Mrs. John Jacob Astor in Bar Harbor / Mac Smith.
Other titles: Mrs. John Jacob Astor in Bar Harbor
Description: Lanham: Down East Books, 2024. | Includes bibliographical references.
Identifiers: LCCN 2023054168 (print) | LCCN 2023054169 (ebook) | ISBN 9781684752133 (paperback) | ISBN 9781684752218 (epub)
Subjects: LCSH: Fiermonte, Madeleine Force Astor Dick, 1893–1940. | Astor family. | Socialites—United States—Biography. | Widows—United States—Biography. | Astor, John Jacob, 1864–1912. | Bar Harbor (Me.)—Social life and customs—20th century. | Bar Harbor (Me.)—Biography.
Classification: LCC CS71.A85 2024 (print) | LCC CS71.A85 (ebook) | DDC 974.1/45 [B]—dc23/eng/20231221
LC record available at https://lccn.loc.gov/2023054168
LC ebook record available at https://lccn.loc.gov/2023054169

∞™ The paper used in this publication meets the minimum requirements of American National Standard for Information Sciences—Permanence of Paper for Printed Library Materials, ANSI/NISO Z39.48-1992.

This book is dedicated to cousin Christy McKeen for teaching us about having a big heart, generosity, strength, and a youthful spirit.

Contents

Introduction 1

Chapter 1: White-Winged Visitors 3
Chapter 2: Dark Horses 23
Chapter 3: Winter's Buds 53
Chapter 4: No Friendly Glance 87
Chapter 5: Tragic Sights 97
Chapter 6: The Girl Widow 121
Chapter 7: Plain Madeleine 153
Chapter 8: Debs of Other Days 177
Chapter 9: This Terrible Thing 203
Chapter 10: Little to Tell. 251

Conclusion 281
Bibliography 285

Introduction

We will never know the true Madeleine Talmage Force Astor Dick Fiermonte. For someone whose name has been splashed across the headlines for more than one hundred years, Mrs. Astor safeguarded her privacy as best she could in a world full of prying eyes.

The Madeleine Astor that emerges from her biography is a woman very symbolic of the times in which she lived, the world of society, an artificial institution that has gone by the wayside, much like ancient traditions such as rating a woman's worth by the amount of her bridal dowry or wearing exclusively black clothing in widowhood, both changes directly influenced by Madeleine Astor.

John Jacob Astor owned the world, or at least enough New York real estate to make him the third richest man in America, worth billions in today's dollars. Madeleine Talmage Force had not much more than looks, charm, and a formerly prominent last name. She also had determination.

This book starts by outlining the Golden Age of Bar Harbor, Maine, where Madeleine arrived for her entrance into a higher society. To know the largeness of this intimidating new world, which had largely been built by the Astor family, is to know the challenge that Madeleine Force faced when she arrived there as a fourteen-year-old girl, a world she ultimately conquered before triumphantly walking away.

The only apt comparison between the romance of John and Madeleine Astor and any later couple would be that of Prince Charles and Princess Diana in the 1980s. This comparison is apt not only because of the intense press pursuit of the Astor story but also because Princess Diana's great-grandparents were one of the few prominent families to welcome the socially exiled John Astor and Madeleine Force into their home during their shocking courtship.

As a girl, Madeleine Force's parents were able to buy her a very small chair at a very large table, the chair being membership at the Bar Harbor Swimming Club and the large table being Bar Harbor itself. Young Madeleine's natural drive and her determination to find her own spot in that higher society would combine with one of the largest events in society's history—the divorce of John Jacob Astor—to pull Madeleine from her small chair at the corner of the table to the center throne of society, with all the world watching.

Though Madeleine Astor would walk away from it all with her second marriage, she never left center stage, the world always watching, especially when she tried to return to society as a woman in her forties on the arm of a handsome, penniless boxer nearly half her age.

This is also the story of Madeleine Astor's legacy through her children, especially John Jacob Astor VI, born four months after *Titanic* sank. This includes young John Astor's legal fight with his half brother, Vincent Astor, over the immense Astor fortune (of which John received a disproportionately small share) and the ultimate loss of the Astor fortune.

As dramatic and influential as the *Titanic* chapter of Madeleine's life had been, it would be only the first of many dramatic chapters in her short life.

No part of this book has been fabricated.

Note: Though the correct spelling of Madeleine Force's first name contained two e's, before she became an Astor her first name was often misspelled by reporters, a practice that continued until the end of her life.

Chapter 1

White-Winged Visitors

Among the white winged visitors in our harbor none has attracted more attention or been the object of greater interest than the Nourmahal, John Jacob Astor's beautiful steam yacht, which is the finest private yacht afloat.

—*Bar Harbor Record*, August 1, 1894

Bar Harbor, Maine, had been the Astors' territory long before the young Madeleine Force landed on its rocky shores. The head of the family, Colonel John Jacob Astor IV, had been part of Bar Harbor's summer colony many years before his future second wife, Madeleine Talmage Force, had even been born. His first wife, Ava, served as Bar Harbor's honorary leader during their yearly summer visits there.

Colonel John Jacob Astor's first recorded visit to Bar Harbor was in 1888, along with his parents, aboard his father's grand yacht, the *Nourmahal.* Not yet a colonel, John Jacob Astor was then a twenty-four-year-old bachelor, the youngest of five children and the only son, whose parents were among the wealthiest of Americans and the leaders of society. Colonel Astor's four sisters, all older, were married well by that era's social standards.

John Jacob Astor was living a life of leisure. His generation of Astors was a good one in which to be born. His grandfather, the original John Jacob Astor, had made the family fortune in fur trading. The family invested that money into a young New York City's real estate. The Astor family had avoided the extreme ups and downs of the stock market on Wall Street, on which many of their colleagues depended; instead, the Astors *bought* Wall Street, or at least several properties along it, as well as major holdings on Broadway and other parts of the ever-growing city. "There is scarcely a ward, street or avenue in the city in which Mr. Astor does not own real estate," wrote the *New York Times*.

Astor family tradition was in Colonel Astor's favor. The tradition was for the oldest son to inherit the entire fortune, which was always kept intact. Being the only son of the current head of the Astor family was indeed good news for John Jacob Astor in that regard.

For the man who seemed to have everything, being the son of the leaders of New York society had developed the introverted Colonel Astor into an unusual person. Though he was considered a socialite, he seemed uncomfortable around people. On June 30, 1888, the year of Colonel Astor's first recorded visit to Bar Harbor, the *Portland Daily Press* reran a story from the *New York Morning Journal* that described the bachelor heir to the Astor fortune as "being of rather quiet and retiring disposition. Although blessed with wealth incalculable, in appearance he is far behind even the mediocre. Six feet high, thin and awkward, big-boned, lantern-jawed, possessed with hands and feet he doesn't know what to do with, he generally creates the impression on the mind of an observer that he would give a good deal to be 'out of it.' This is especially noticable in a ballroom, where he is at his worst, yet all the marriagable daughters, from the innocent debutante to the rounder of twelve years' experience, shower their most fetching smiles upon his head, invariably without success. He spends nine months in the year and nine-tenths of his money abroad, so New York sees less of him than its fashionable matrons with unmarried daughters would like."

John Jacob Astor was a man of leisure who disliked having nothing to do. His mind was active, and he used it for creating inventions, which were generally donated to the public for the general good rather than profit. Colonel Astor enjoyed travel, and whenever the newest mechanical means of travel was announced, it seemed to captivate his interest. He would be fascinated by the newly invented automobile, owning several hundred thousand dollars' worth of them in his short lifetime. He also was fascinated by the brand-new invention of the airplane, as well as the inner workings of steamships.

Though Colonel Astor was a religious man, supporting many churches generously, he also believed in the facts of science. These beliefs were reflected when, at age thirty, Colonel Astor wrote a book, *A Journey in Other Worlds: A Romance of the Future*, which drew on his scientific interests and his keen, introverted imagination. The book was published in 1894.

"The protracted struggle between science and the classics appears to be drawing to a close, with victory about to perch on the banner of science, as a perusal of almost any university or college catalogue shows. The classics had been thrashed out, but science was just beginning," wrote Colonel Astor in the book's introduction. "Next to religion, we have most to hope from science."

The story was set in the year 2000. The plot of the book involves the Terrestrial Axis Straightening Company working to straighten the axis of the Earth's rotation in an attempt to combine the extreme heat of summer with the intense cold of winter and produce a uniform temperature for each degree of latitude year-round. In doing so, characters voyage to the different planets of the solar system in a spaceship named the *Callisto.*

Colonel Astor describes the future New York City, with avenues two hundred feet wide containing shade and fruit trees, a bridle path, broad sidewalks, and open spaces for baby carriages and bicycles. The masts of ships carried windmills instead of sails to supply their own power. Disease was detected with a wave of special paper in the air. Most disease and illness had been eliminated with the knowledge of proper diet. Railroad trains were propelled by magnetic energy, with large magnets placed in the rails at fifty-foot intervals.

"This period—A.D. 2000—is by far the most wonderful the world has as yet seen. The advance in scientific knowledge and attainment within the memory, of the present generation has been so stupendous that it completely overshadows all that has preceded," wrote Colonel Astor.

* * *

Unlike the first of Colonel Astor's recorded yearly visits to Bar Harbor in 1888, John Jacob Astor was a different man during his 1893 trip. His father had died the year before, and now Colonel Astor was in control of the Astor estate, along with the money and social position that came with it. He was the third richest man in the United States of America, estimated to be worth between $90 million and $100 million. Colonel Astor would be considered a multibillionaire today, worth $2 billion when adjusted for inflation.

Colonel Astor was also a married man on his 1893 visit, having wed Ava Willing, a socialite from a prominent Philadelphia family. Their marriage, the social event of the season, was done in grand style. John and Ava Astor's February 17, 1891, wedding was the first item on the front page of the *New York Times* that day. Because the wedding was held in Philadelphia, the couple arranged for a special train to carry the four hundred New York guests to Pennsylvania. The guests formed a parade as they traveled from the train station in Philadelphia to the Willing home and the two fashionable hotels where they stayed.

"New York practically took Philadelphia by storm today," reported the *New York Times*. "Its 400 invaded the fashionable quarter of the town, and it capitulated."

John and Ava's wedding gifts were described as magnificant, costly, and as beautiful as any given at any wedding in America. This was not an overstatement. Among the gifts received by the couple were a furnished house on Fifth Avenue in New York City (the most fashionable home address in the country) and a summer cottage in Newport (the most fashionable address in summer colonies).

The yearly seasonal visits from the head of the Astor family were important to the social prominence of Bar Harbor and to the ongoing competition the popular Maine summer resort had with Newport, Rhode Island. John Jacob Astor's mother, *The* Mrs. Astor, was still the head of New York society. John Jacob's wife, Ava, was expected to ascend to that throne at the point when John Jacob's mother passed, and the continuation of Astor's traditional visit was important to Bar Harbor's reputation and standing in the overall social community. The previous season, 1892, in their first year as a married couple, John and Ava had not made the yearly visit, in part owing to the death of Colonel Astor's father. Because Ava Astor's choice of summer destination was just as important as that of Colonel Astor, the appearance of the Astors in 1893 was especially important. The arrival of the newly married Astors that summer drew much attention in Bar Harbor. "Among the white winged visitors in our harbor none has attracted more attention or been the object of greater interest than the Nourmahal, John Jacob Astor's beautiful steam yacht, which is the finest private yacht afloat," wrote the *Bar Harbor Record*.

Along with seven guests, the Astors arrived on the *Nourmahal* in late July that season. The Astors would draw attention not only because of who they were but also because Colonel Astor's yacht contained the newest form of water transportation available—a launch boat, used to ferry passengers back and forth from the yacht to the mainland. Though launch boats were not uncommon, Colonel Astor's was, as it was run by battery power. Named the Corcyean, Colonel Astor's electric launch was only the second built in the world at the time.

The Astors made the most of their ten days anchored in Frenchman Bay that season. The *Bar Harbor Record* reported on a party given by Ava Astor aboard the *Nourmahal* during that time: "The reception given by the Astors on board the Nourmahal Friday was a delightfully pleasant affair despite the rain and was attended by the elite of the cottage contingent and the visiting diplomats. Mr. Morton sent bushels of flowers aboard in the morning, and the yacht presented a magnificent scene with the beautiful summer gowns of the guests amid the floral surroundings."

Ava Astor's name would also head the list of subscribers to a dance being held at the fashioinable Louisburg Hotel, near the center of Bar Harbor and a few blocks from the water. The event was charitable in nature, with proceeds donated to a local school.

The Astors' 1893 visit was rounded out as the guests of honor at a picnic hosted by the US minister of Belgium, who was vacationing in Bar Harbor. The outing was held on Bar Island but was interrupted by a hard rain. The party quickly moved to the inside of the nearby Bar Harbor Canoe Club and continued the festivities.

* * *

Just as John Jacob Astor's life was in a state of change in 1893, so was Bar Harbor itself. Many years previously, Mount Desert Island had been discovered by self-described "rusticators," a few artists and other free spirits from places such as New York City and Pennsylvania. The visiting artists captured on canvas the rugged natural beauty of the island. The more these paintings, and the stories of the Maine island they represented, made their way into the mansions of society's leaders, the more there grew a curiosity about Mount Desert Island itself.

One obstacle to large-scale visitation to Mount Desert Island for the elite of society in the second half of the 1800s was the trip to get there. The same rugged beauty that was drawing more and more people also made the voyage difficult. A trickle of society visitors started to arrive from New York and Philadelphia, a trip that necessitated several changes of trains and catching the ferry, which ran only a few days a week and whose running was spotty. Members of society had ample financial resources for a convenient trip to Mount Desert Island, if only one were available.

All that changed in the year 1884 with the construction of Mount Desert Ferry. The small train and ferry station was located on the mainland at Hancock Point, near Ellsworth. This arrangement enabled visitors from as far away as Philadelphia to board a train and stay on that train all the way to Mount Desert Ferry, where they would transfer to the elegant steamship *Sappho*, with only a forty-minute ride across Frenchman Bay to reach Bar Harbor and the other beautiful towns.

Until this time, local boarding houses were utilized by the rusticators and the first of the people they drew to Bar Harbor. As the trickle grew, however, the boarding houses grew into large hotels, with the level of elegance increasing with the level of society staying there. By the year 1893, when John and Ava first arrived as a married couple, Bar Harbor was realizing that it was not a flash-in-the-pan summer resort, as had been so many others along the Maine coast. People began to think of Bar Harbor not in terms of the present, but rather of the future. Bar Harbor was now well into its Hotel Era and the beginning of its Golden Age.

By now the passenger and freight traffic to Mount Desert Island was growing so rapidly that the Maine Central Railroad was forced to take trains from other routes during the summer to put them on the Mount Desert Ferry run. With the ease of importing building supplies not offered on the island, cottages started to appear, with many more built every season. Bar Harbor was beginning to rival the more traditional and popular society summer resort of Newport, Rhode Island. The businesses dependent on the summer colony were expanding all across the island. According to the *Bar Harbor Record*, 1893 was a period of prosperity in Bar Harbor. "It isn't a 'boom' now," the paper wrote as the 1893 season came to a close.

* * *

The evolving Bar Harbor was feeling its growing pains. One public concern in Bar Harbor was the fast driving of horses on public roadways, the rash of accidents it caused, and the need to stop the accidents. Bicycles were also making their first appearance on the island. The two-wheeled contraptions were initially seen as a fad. Sherman's, a store that sold stationery and just about everything else (and which is still in existence today), was one of the original bicycle dealers in Bar Harbor.

The length of the summer season in Bar Harbor was growing. By March a few of the famous names were beginning to appear in the anticipated pages of the Cottage Directory of the *Bar Harbor Record*, which the newspaper ran weekly every summer season. In 1894, the *Bar Harbor Record* proudly boasted that thirty-five new cottagers had changed their summer addresses from other prominent seasonal resorts such as Newport. The newspaper briefly went to a Saturday edition to handle the increasing social news and to afford quicker availability of the Cottage Directory.

The newspaper was also popular for its Hotel Directory, listing the weekly and seasonal guests at the large hotels in Bar Harbor. The newspaper would also list the latest yacht arrivals in every edition. In 1894, the year after Colonel Astor's first visit as a married man, Bar Harbor was visited by Lord and Lady Randolph and Jeanette Churchill (parents of Sir Winston Churchill) and a Russian prince, their names mixing with the other international diplomats and notable names that were already there. "Bar Harbor is feeling its oats this week," wrote the *Bar Harbor Record.*

* * *

The Newport cottage of Beechwood would be the summer base of John and Ava Astor, but they would continue their extended summer visits to Bar Harbor. Both the Bar Harbor summer colony and the local villagers who depended on that colony looked for the *Nourmahal* every season. The Astors would choose Bar Harbor's elegant hotels for some of their entertaining while there, but their yacht was their home base. The Astor ballroom on Fifth Avenue in New York held four hundred while the *Nourmahal* held considerably fewer guests, making an invitation to a function on the *Nourmahal* much harder to get.

In 1894, John and Ava Astor would arrive in Frenchman Bay in late July with a large party of guests. Among the functions that season was a dinner hosted aboard the *Nourmahal* for nineteen. The yacht was adorned with exceedingly attractive floral decorations provided by the noted florist F. H. Moses of Bar Harbor and Bucksport. The dinner table was a mass of pink and white sweet peas in crystal dishes. The arrangements were described as unique and elaborate. "Both the captain and Mr. J. H. Hormer, Mr. Astor's private secretary, treat visitors with the utmost courtesy," wrote the *Bar Harbor Record.*

The *Nourmahal* (which meant "the fairest of women") was built in Wilmington, Delaware, in 1877 for Colonel Astor's father. She was 246 feet long, 30 feet in breadth, with a hold depth of 30 feet, 6 inches. The *Nourmahal* carried forty-five officers and crew, the captain and first mate both being Maine men.

That August, Ava Astor attended the weekly hop at the Malvern Hotel, a large and fashionable hotel on Kebo Street conveniently located near the Kebo Valley Club, another favorite location of the summer colony.

"The extreme heat of Saturday did not prevent a large gathering at Kebo Valley in the evening. The pleasant nooks and corners with which the piazzas of the club house abound were filled by the dancers between the fairy waltzes and also by others who could keep cool and also hear the strains of the exquisite music as it was wafted to them. Handsome women, beautiful gowns and an exceptionally large number of dancing men made this dance the most brilliant thus far this season. Mrs. John Jacob Astor was effectively gowned in a light gray satin with festooned lace ruffles and lace, and was also draped on the bodice. A beautiful cluster of red roses was worn and were in striking contrast to the sober tints of her gown," noted the August 1, 1894, edition of the *Bar Harbor Record*.

* * *

During the cold-weather months in Maine, when Bar Harbor was a much emptier and different place, the people of Bar Harbor continued to follow the Astors' personal movements and developments through the local newspapers. The members of society were the celebrities of their day, in a time before television, movies, or the internet. The only real medium of mass communication was the newspaper, and alongside the news stories were the stories of the members of society, the wealthy elite. The society pages basically acted as part of the entertainment section of the newspapers, as close to television or the internet as possible for the times. The stories of society's elite were fascinating in a time when a lax income tax favored the ultra-wealthy, who had become incredibly well off harnessing the vast resources of a young United States of America. With difficult economic times being the norm for the average person in the general public, the stories of the lavish lifestyle and unimaginable adventures of the members of society were fascinating and helped sell newspapers, especially when a little scandal crept into a story. Men like John Jacob Astor were often followed by reporters as a matter of course, especially during controversial periods of their lives. Colonel Astor and his second wife, Madeleine, would take on the celebrity quality seen in this era by the coverage of Prince Charles and Lady Diana Spencer of England.

After two summer seasons in Maine, in 1895 the people of Mount Desert Island followed with interest the news of Ava Astor's father, seventy-three-year-old Edward Shippen Willing, who was reported to be ill in France and too sick to travel back to the United States. A trip to Europe by the Astors during the summer to visit the ailing Astor in-law would take their name from the Bar Harbor headlines for the 1895 season. The Astors, however, would continue with tradition and travel to Bar Harbor that season. The *Nourmahal* arrived with a number of guests that year, with Mrs. Astor receiving daily cablegrams while on the island, updating her on her father's condition. The Astors and their guests socialized at the Kebo Valley Club, with John Jacob Astor playing golf and his wife hosting a dinner party before one of the the club's nightly dances. Those dances were described by the newspapers as being popular with the Bar Harbor summer colony's younger set and a "jolly" time.

* * *

When the Astors' summer season was over that year, they chose not to head to France to be with Ava's father, instead continuing with a much-anticipated social obligation in New York. A housewarming was planned for that fall for what was being called the Astor "palace" on upper Fifth Avenue, New York City. The Astor family owned two side-by-side mansions there. John Jacob Astor, the bachelor, had lived in the mansion on the left, and his parents lived in the mansion on the right. With the passing of John Jacob's father, along with his marriage to Ava, the Astors planned a formal combination of the two homes into one. Extensive construction was begun, the result being one large palace with plenty of room for the home's three occupants and their large household staff. Other than the Vanderbilt mansion just down the street, the Astor mansion was the largest residence in Manhattan.

The Astor mansion at 840 Fifth Avenue was the center of New York society. It was the home of the leader of society, Colonel Astor's mother, Caroline, known as "*The* Mrs. Astor." The *New York Times* referred to Caroline Astor as "the acknowledged leader of society." The Astors' Fifth Avenue home (commonly called "Eight-Forty") was the equivalent of Windsor Castle.

The Astor mansion was central to New York society. In January of every year, Caroline Astor would host a grand ball. With the ballroom of the Astor mansion able to accommodate four hundred guests, those guests invited every year were known as "The Four Hundred," a simple term with so much importance in a different time.

Caroline Schermerhorn and William Backhouse Astor were from old money, but barely, being just two generations removed from the first John Jacob Astor, fur trapper and trader. Caroline was the acknowledged leader of society, having assumed the title on the death of her mother-in-law. Caroline's role as leader was to protect the overall reputation and importance of the old families of society by keeping out the newly rich families until they had proven themselves. With a few families falling out of Mrs. Astor's favor every year for one social infraction or another, there was always room for a few new families, and Caroline Astor's invitation to the Astor ball, one of the Four Hundred invitations sent every year, served as the ticket into that sacrosanct society.

* * *

Mr. and Mrs. John Jacob Astor continued their annual summer visit to Bar Harbor aboard the *Nourmahal* for the next fourteen years as a married couple. During this time, John Jacob Astor IV would earn the military title of colonel with his equipping of a military battalion for the Spanish–American War, as well as his service in battle in the Philippines with that battalion. Colonel Astor's official role was as a military inspector.

"Mr. John Jacob Astor has equipped at his own expense a battery of artillery and presented them with his compliments to President McKinley, promising to maintain them during the war," wrote the *Daily Kennebec Journal*. "One is glad to see that American millionaires are to some extent doing their share toward helping the country that made and preserves their riches for them."

In the early 1900s, Mainers would be enthralled by Colonel Astor's fascination with automobiles. Cars were just coming into use in Maine and were still rare. The *Bar Harbor Record* reported in 1905 that Colonel Astor owned twenty-two automobiles, noting that William Vanderbilt, another prominent Bar Harbor summer colonist, owned fourteen.

"John Jacob Astor is the largest private owner of automobiles in this country," wrote the *Daily Kennebec Journal*. "They number 24, the average cost of each is about $5,000, making a total of $120,000 invested in his machines." (The value of the twenty-four automobiles would be worth $4 million when adjusted for inflation.)

* * *

John Jacob's Astor importance on Mount Desert Island can be seen from a performance by local Bar Harbor residents in April 1907. The recurring skit was called "The Old Deestrict Skule [School]" and was an extremely popular part of a program held by the young people of the Bar Harbor Baptist Church over the winter. The programs were held at the Casino, a popular Bar Harbor summer colony building on the corner of Bridge Street and Cottage Street. Despite its name, the Casino was not a house of gambling but instead a place of live entertainment.

The Casino was packed, and the series was popular. A local orchestra furnished live music featuring a male quartet, which received an encore. The premise was simple: A skit would be performed in which prominent real-life people were portrayed by the Bar Harbor residents as students on their way to school. Characters in this particular performance of the skit included Lydia Pinkham, who was famous for her cure-all medicines; Brigham Young, president of the Church of Jesus Christ of Latter-day Saints; outlaw Jesse James; millionaire Cornelius Vanderbilt; and Bar Harbor's own Colonel John Jacob Astor, played by a young local man named Robert W. Martin.

"The Old Deestrict skule is always a popular entertainment and Monday evening's performance was no exception," wrote the *Bar Harbor Record*. "The costumes of the entire school, including the school committee, were ludicrous in the extreme."

The newspaper noted that Robert Martin's portrayal of Colonel Astor was "highly amusing." "There was not a dull minute from start to finish and the entertainment was highly popular," according to this account.

* * *

In the summer of 1893, when Colonel John Jacob Astor and his wife, Ava, were visiting Bar Harbor for the first time as a married couple,

Colonel Astor's future second wife, Madeleine, had just turned one month old back in the New York borough of Brooklyn.

Madeleine Talmage Force arrived in Bar Harbor as a fourteen-year-old girl along with her older sister, Katherine, and their mother, also named Katherine. History suggests that it was the future of daughter Katherine that had brought the Force family to Bar Harbor in 1907. Katherine had just turned sixteen and would soon be a debutante about to be introduced, along with the other female members of her circle of New York society, to the eligible young men of that social circle of marrying age. Though Madeleine was still two years away from her debutante year, ironically, she would marry first, twelve years before Katherine's first and only marriage.

The traditional society saying had been that if one was not prepared to make it socially in Newport, they should start at Bar Harbor. Bar Harbor was considered a second-tier resort, with the first tier being Newport, Rhode Island. Bar Harbor was a natural choice for Brooklyn's Force family, themselves a second-tier society family.

The Force family was making a decided transition when they arrived in Bar Harbor for the summer of 1907. The Force family fortune was mainly nonexistent, though Mrs. Force's Brooklyn social ancestry was strong. During this time, the family moved their year-round residence from Brooklyn to a newly purchased town house in New York City, and their social activities began to increase in social prominence, from Brooklyn's Riding Club to Bar Harbor's Swimming Club.

Bar Harbor itself was in a state of transition when the Force family arrived, now well into its Cottage Era, marked by the glamorous multistory cottages, which were truly mansions, being built by the social elite as their summer residences. This was Bar Harbor's "Golden Age." That Golden Age is now gone, as is Madeleine Force Astor and the world of society she represented. In the summer of 1907, however, society and its importance were very much alive as Mrs. Force and her two daughters checked into the Newport House.

* * *

Madeleine Talmage Force was the second and youngest daughter of William H. and Katherine Talmadge Force. Her parents were of society. Had it not been for the scale on which the Astors socialized, the Force family would have stood out in their own right. And they did stand out—in Brooklyn society.

Madeleine's mother had provided the social prestige to the marriage. Katherine Talmage was from a socially prominent, political, and long-established Brooklyn family. The Talmage family had descended from William the Conqueror and was one of the oldest families in English history. The Talmages are reported to have come to Brooklyn and other locations in America as early as the 1600s.

Katherine's grandfather, Thomas Talmage, had served as mayor of Brooklyn. A great-uncle had served for sixteen years as a congressman, representing the state of New Jersey, and another as a US minister to France. It was through her father, Tunis, however, that Katherine Talmage came into her own social prominence.

Tunis Talmage had been educated in the Brooklyn public school system. At age seventeen, he traveled to California as part of the Gold Rush. He would return to Brooklyn in 1852, where he became a contractor, grading many of the dirt streets and avenues in the growing city. With the money he earned from those projects he would start a retail coal business, which quickly developed into a wholesale trade.

Finding business and financial success, Tunis would make his start in New York politics in 1860, where he served as supervisor of the Eighth Ward for two years. In 1862, he was elected alderman of that same ward, and during his second term he served as the president of the board. Tunis Talmage went on to represent the Fourth District in the New York State Legislature in 1874 and 1875.

Tunis Talmage was described as generous, kindly, and beloved. He made his mark in New York politics during a heated debate over a popular park. Prospect Park was Brooklyn's version of Central Park and served the same essential purpose in the built-up city. Tunis's father, former Brooklyn mayor Thomas Talmage, had been the chief promoter of the building of Prospect Park and had carried through with the necessary legislation to have the park created. Thomas Talmage was credited with building Prospect Park.

Tunis's challenge with Prospect Park was to change the way the taxes on the park would be paid. Under Tunis Talmage's proposal, the burden of paying the taxes would shift to all taxpayers in the city of Brooklyn, not just the few property holders contiguous to the park. Though Tunis's idea was not popular, he would rise in political stature due to his overall handling of the entire situation during a controversial and angry time.

"Mr. Talmage claimed the whole city was equally benefited by the park, and by his strenuous efforts to overcome the stormy opposition to the measure made many friends in both parties," wrote the *Brooklyn Daily Eagle*.

* * *

While Katherine Talmage brought the respect of Brooklyn society to the Force marriage, Madeleine's father, William, brought industriousness and hard work, which helped finance the family's social advancement. William H. Force was born in Brooklyn, the son of William and Mary Emmons Force. Educated at the Poughkeepsie Academy, William Force spent most of his young life in Brooklyn. As a young man, he helped start the trucking firm of Force and Glover and later established the firm of William H. Force & Co. after his business partner's death. The business rapidly grew from trucking to forwarding and shipping, specializing in the commodity of coffee.

On July 16, 1889, William Force and Katherine Talmage were married in Brooklyn at the fashionable town house of Katherine's grandfather, Thomas. Katherine was twenty-five, William was thirty-seven. William and Katherine Force's first child, Katherine Emmons Force, was born in Brooklyn on March 12, 1891. Two years later, on June 19, 1893, their second and youngest daughter, Madeleine, was born in the same city.

* * *

The events of society and its clubs were different on the other side of the Brooklyn Bridge. Where the Astors were noted for their private box in the "Golden Horseshoe" at the Metropolitan Opera in Manhattan, Mr. and Mrs. Force spent time at the Riding and Driving Club of Brooklyn. Part of this difference in social activities seemed to come in part through more of an enjoyment of the outdoors and physical social activities held by the Force family in comparison to the social activities of John and Ava Astor.

Katherine and William Force were very active in the Riding and Driving Club of Brooklyn, which was organized in 1889, the year they were married. The original idea of the club was met with much negative response, with people saying Brooklyn could not support a society-driven club for horse riding. Soon after being built, however, the club was thriving.

The clubhouse was a spacious building, three stories high, built of brick with sandstone trimmings, and occupying more than half the block on which it was situated. The clubhouse's mahogany interior was handsomely furnished. The first floor housed a parlor and reception rooms. There was enclosed glass on the ring side of the clubhouse to view the horse racing and shows, through which there was a fine view of the arena. On the second floor were the women's dressing rooms, with every convenience. The third floor was used as a dining room and kitchen. In the basement were the men's dressing rooms, lockers, and a large plunge of artesian water.

"The club takes a leading part in Brooklyn's fashionable clubdom and its series of equestrian entertainments every winter are a popular feature of society," wrote the *Brooklyn Daily Eagle.*

* * *

The Riding and Driving Club would soon embrace the "fad" of bicycles, which seemed a natural fit for the athletically oriented club. Mr. and Mrs. Force were sponsors of the Cycle Club of Brooklyn, an offshoot of the riding club. The Friday Evening Ride soon became popular among club members.

Still, horse riding was the main activity at the Riding Club of Brooklyn. The horse ring itself was enclosed in a building that was 200 feet by 150 feet. The arena was naturally well lit during the day, with elongated windows along the sides of the rectangular building, and at night by electric light. Along the inside walls on both long sides was a narrow balcony on the ground floor. When there was not racing, club members could use the ring for walking.

"Perhaps one of the main reasons for the great success which the former horse shows have met with is the particularly strong hold which the club has, not only upon its members, but upon their families and even the outside public," wrote the *Brooklyn Daily Eagle*. "One of its unique and salient features is that the wives and daughters, unmarried sisters and minor sons of the members are entitled to all the privileges of the club, so that women are oftener seen and in larger numbers in the club house than the men."

* * *

With the new Riding and Driving Club of Brooklyn thriving, the idea for an annual show there was proposed the year Madeleine was born. William Force, who often served on the organizing committees for various riding club events, offered money and a plate as championship prizes, as did other members. With Mrs. Force seven months pregnant with Madeleine, the *New York Times* reported that Mr. and Mrs. Force were "noted spectators" at the event.

Three years later, in 1896, it was decided to make the horse show bigger and better. The show would last for a week that year, with day and evening entertainment provided. William and Katherine Force were noted to be in attendance at almost every event during the week. Mr. J. Clinch Smith (a future *Titanic* survivor) was a judge that year, also serving as the patron of coaching.

The spirit of being active in social functions rather than just watching them may have been what drew the Force family to invest their time and effort in the Riding and Driving Club of Brooklyn. The *New York Times* noted that one feature of the show, "and one peculiar to Brooklyn," was the number of society girls who drove or rode in the show. On the more fashionable side of the Brooklyn Bridge, the members of society simply watched while their horses were displayed by people hired to do so.

One newspaper did find imperfections with the show and the size of the clubhouse in Brooklyn.

"Society is present, but for lack of space to form a promenade, must remain tucked away in boxes or seats the entire evening," wrote the *Brooklyn Daily Eagle*. "This is undoubtedly the reason why handsomer gowns are not worn at the show. Brooklyn women have been criticized for not making the occasion more dressy, but there is little incentive to wear elaborate frocks. Seats are crowded too loosely together, and the voluminous folds of a smart dress are sure to suffer when sat upon for three consecutive hours."

Despite the criticisms, the *Brooklyn Daily Eagle* deemed the well-attended horse show an overall society success: "Whoever predicted the abolishing of the horse in favor of that popular steed the bicycle should have visited the Riding and Driving Club last week."

* * *

While the Astors summered in Newport and Bar Harbor, the Force family chose Long Island for their summers. They stayed at rented cottages and hotels in Lawrence and Bayport there. Long Island was a fashionable location but not as high on the social scale as Bar Harbor and Newport.

One location that seemed special to the outdoor-loving Force family was the Robins Island Gun Club. The Robins Club was located in Peconic Bay, off Long Island, and inhabited 435 acres of wilderness well stocked with wildlife. The private, exclusive club's purpose was "improving and elevating the character of field sports," and it was popular with the sportsmen of Brooklyn society. The club was not easy to get into, however, with a membership limited to twenty-five persons. Mr. Force was an officer in the club.

* * *

William and Katherine were socially prominent enough that their attendance at an event, either together or separately, would be noted along with the other prominent guests in New York's society pages. A few examples follow: In February 1896, Mrs. Force was a subscriber, and her presence was noted, at the Cinderella Dance, a charitable hospital benefit held by the members of Brooklyn society. This was the third in the season's series of Cinderella dances, given in the assembly rooms of the Pierrepont, one of Brooklyn's leading hotels. The ballroom was decorated with a large red and yellow heart that was suspended from the center of the bay window in the ballroom. A bow and flaming torch were attached to the heart. The event was described by the *Brooklyn Daily Eagle* as "distinguished by the pleasantness which is characteristic of these dances. . . . The favors were uncommonly pretty and artistically arranged at one corner of the room, and lent a charming touch of color. The fixtures were picturesque. The souvenirs were a handsome collection of posters . . . and tiny gaily colored hearts for the fair participants, with large, bright tinted balls of crepe paper and dainty quotations for the men."

In 1896, Mr. and Mrs. Force were guests at a large card party at the Hotel Margaret. Progressive Euchre was played in the hotel's dining room, and a few simple prizes were provided. All proceeds were for charity, benefiting the children's ward of a local hospital. "Refreshments also of an unpretentious order were served later, and the whole affair proved most enjoyable," wrote the *Brooklyn Daily Eagle.*

In 1897, Mr. Force hosted a table at a library fundraiser. Four days later, Mrs. Force assisted in receiving at the social debut of a young cousin. In April 1899, Mrs. Force served on the organizing committee selling tickets for a Euchre benefit for a sick young Brooklyn woman. The following month she would help organize, along with two other people, a benefit called "Aunt Jane's Circle" to aid the Home for Aged Colored People.

The turn of the century would find Mr. and Mrs. Force at the Hotel St. George, in winter of 1900, as subscribers to a series of dances in the hotel's ballroom. The Hotel St. George was the largest building in Brooklyn at the time. On October 18, 1903, the *New York Times* noted Mrs. Force's presence at a large luncheon at the Dyker Meadow Golf Club in Brooklyn given by Mrs. Francis E. Dodge of Normandy Park, New Jersey, a cousin of Mrs. Force. In 1904, Mr. Force would be appointed to the Committee on Terminal Facilities of the New York Board of Trade and Transportation.

* * *

The year was now 1907, the year that the Force family first arrived in Bar Harbor, Maine. Summers would no longer be spent on Long Island or on Robins Island but in the summer colony that was rivaling the fashionable Newport, Rhode Island. Bar Harbor was a natural choice for an active, outdoorsy, socially prominent family such as the Forces when they were making plans for their introduction into a higher society.

Mrs. Katherine Talmage Force had come from a society background and had grown up in that system, and she continued those traditions with her two daughters. With no real options for support open to women of the time, how well a young woman married was of vital interest to her future. Being in society's eye, the selection of a spouse took on extra importance.

In the search for socially suitable husbands for her daughters, Mrs. Force's timing was impeccable.

Chapter 2

Dark Horses

The second round of the ladies' tennis doubles championship tournament to-day brought forth surprises, some of the strongest pairs being put out of the running by "dark horses."

—*New York Times* describing Madeleine Force's tennis tournament play in Bar Harbor, August 31, 1910

The year 1907 marks the first recorded visit of the Force family to Bar Harbor, who arrived on Saturday, July 13. The arrival of Mrs. Katherine Force and her two daughters, Katherine and Madeleine, at the Newport House was noted in the *New York Times*. Mr. Force would join them later in the season, which would become the Force family tradition during their time on Mount Desert Island.

The Newport House, where the Force family stayed that first season, was the only hotel on the Bar Harbor waterfront at the time and the first hotel seen by arriving visitors at Bar Harbor, situated atop a small hill across from the steamboat wharf. The Newport House was large and modern, but it was not built for glamour like other hotels, instead catering to comfort with an eye on economy. The building was four stories high, running parallel to the shore, affording a commanding view of Frenchman Bay. The hotel also offered the Annex (which featured apartment-type rooms) and a few separate cottages for rent while still enjoying the hotel's amenities.

The grounds of the Newport Hotel were well-kept green lawns with flowering shrubs. The hotel featured a spacious covered veranda, generously supplied with rocking chairs, that ran along the shore side of the building and wrapped around the sides. The cooler air from the water allowed for escape from the summer heat at the Newport House better than most hotels more inland.

Inside the Newport Hotel were spacious public rooms that were handsomely but comfortably furnished in light tints designed to rest the eye. The dining room was lofty and well ventilated, and the music room featured tapestried walls, a large fireplace, and many cozy corners. There were writing desks and worktables along with ample easy chairs and lounges. The hotel's kitchen turned out meals made from food sourced locally from island farms and market gardens. Many guests at the Newport Hotel had been summering there for years.

* * *

The Golden Age of Bar Harbor in which the Force family was arriving was also noted for the high societal institutions that had been formed by the summer colony in Bar Harbor, and the elaborate buildings erected for the elegant social activities those clubs offered. There was the Building of Arts among the crown jewels of high entertainment in the rural Maine town. There was the Casino, with its misleading name, offering some of the finest entertainment that could be found in the country. The Astor family, and their Bar Harbor cousins the Kane family, had been instrumental in the building and continued support of these summer colony institutions, seemingly out of place in an otherwise rural Maine fishing and farming community. There were clubs for every activity desired by the island's summer visitors. These clubs were so popular and exclusive, and people so eager to get into various functions, that tickets given to guests of members had the year of the summer season printed on them so that previous seasons' tickets could not be used again by uninvited guests.

* * *

The most popular summer colony club in Bar Harbor, and one of the first clubs joined by the Force family, was the new swim club, located on the shore of Frenchman Bay, in the center of the village, just a short walk away from the Newport Hotel.

The Bar Harbor Swimming Club joined together the desire of summer colonists for physical activity with the necessity of social functions. In existence for only four years when the Force family arrived, the original clubhouse boasted as its showpiece a saltwater pool built into Frenchman Bay with a large float in the center and room for canoeing. A large, covered, wooden grandstand with seats on the second story was provided to watch the water activities and also offered a beautiful view of Bar Harbor's natural scenery. The facility boasted a bathhouse and private dressing rooms as well as rooms for socialization.

Close to the shore sat the clubhouse, a large, three-story, rectangular building with pink and white awnings adorning the first-floor windows. A large American flag sat proudly on the center of the building's slanted roof. Between the back of the clubhouse and the water grandstand ran a wooden boardwalk along the middle of the wide lawn. On one side of that boardwalk stood the fenced-in tennis courts. Tennis was very popular in Bar Harbor at this time. Swim club members and their guests sat in folding wooden chairs or stood on the lawn to watch the tennis matches. Men in white pants and sports coats—many with straw hats, some with walking sticks—adorned the lawns in the summer. The women dressed in white or light-colored dresses, frilly, that ran from neck to ankle, with full sleeves, many with umbrellas shading their already amply hatted heads.

Most of the activities at the swim club, both physical activities and social functions, were accompanied by a live orchestra. Every year the people of Bar Harbor eagerly anticipated the arrival of the Boston Symphony for the season's accompaniment at the Bar Harbor Swimming Club.

* * *

It has always been argued that Mrs. Katherine Force groomed her daughters to find socially suitable husbands. The timing of the change in the Force family's summer locations, coinciding with the age of social introduction for her two daughters, could argue that the change was for that purpose. The physically active Force family had every opportunity for athletics combined with socialization back in Brooklyn and on Long Island.

Even if Mrs. Force's summer move to Bar Harbor grew from a desire for socially appropriate marriages, this motive does not necessarily make her a bad person as we look back a century at different times. A good marriage was the best way for a young woman to succeed in the early 1900s, at a time when there were few opportunities for self-support. The social traditions had been going on for generations by then. Ironically, Madeleine Force's marriage to Colonel John Jacob Astor would help change some of those now-antiquated traditions.

* * *

Much like Bar Harbor's transition from the Hotel Era to the Cottage Era, the Force family would transition from the Newport House into a cottage the following season. Their name first appears in the *Bar Harbor Record*'s Cottage Directory in 1908 in the July 15 edition: "Force, Mrs. W. H.—New York—Pinehurst, Eagle Lake. Misses Force." Their cottage was much farther inland than had been the Newport Hotel, though still within easy traveling distance. The cottage would afford the Force family a better opportunity to entertain, which they did.

The athletic pursuit of choice of the Force sisters was tennis, and they excelled at the sport. Within days of arriving in Bar Harbor that season, both Madeleine and Katherine had signed up for the Bar Harbor Swimming Club's annual season-long tennis tournament. Within two weeks of arrival Madeleine Force's name would appear in the *Bar Harbor Record*, having won the first round of the mixed doubles tournament at the Kebo Club, which was closer to the Force's cottage that season. Tradition held that most of the ladies' tennis was held at the swim club, while the men's tennis and mixed doubles were played at the Kebo Club. The Force sisters were noted for their appearances at both clubs during the season.

The time spent on the tennis courts at the Bar Harbor Swimming Club was getting the Force sisters noticed by Bar Harbor's more established summer colony. Madeleine and Katherine were in a group of a dozen young society women who were the first to appear in a vaudeville program at the popular Casino that August. The name of their part in the program was "The Bells," in which they "charmingly" played a melody on bells. Other features of the program, performed by other young society men and women, were a satirical one-act play, impersonations, and other skits.

Less than a week after the vaudeville show, Madeleine and Katherine's names were the first on the list of names of young women who hosted an annual fair in benefit of the town's new hospital. Held on the lawn of the summer cottage known as Saltair, located along the historic and fashionable West Street, the annual event raised $500. The group hosting the sale was a coterie of young female summer colonists who had been holding the fair for several years, raising several thousand dollars for the hospital during that time, "reflecting great credit upon the young ladies who had it in charge," noted the *Bar Harbor Record*, "and they are certainly deserving of the thanks of the community for the good that they have accomplished."

The newspapers noted that the Force family had entertained extensively at their cottage during their 1908 visit. Early that fall they headed to Europe, presumably for the daughters' Grand Tour. They would return to the United States at the beginning of October and head for a new home that Mr. and Mrs. Force had purchased on East Forty-Ninth Street in New York City. They were no longer a Brooklyn family; now they were of New York society—far from the Four Hundred, but at its doorstep. At the end of the year Mrs. Force would entertain a party of her daughters' friends in their new home to see the old year out.

* * *

The Bar Harbor that the Force family arrived at for the first time in 1907 was a different Bar Harbor than the one Colonel Astor and his wife Ava had come to on their first visit as a married couple in 1893. Over the ensuing fourteen years, the rivalry between Bar Harbor and Newport had continued.

"The New York papers are devoting a little more space to Bar Harbor this year if we are not mistaken," wrote the *Bar Harbor Record*. "They can well afford to for in the past they have been particularly niggardly with the resort. Newport and Lenox and all the many small resorts have come in for generous notice, while Bar Harbor has been out in the cold."

Bar Harbor's growth continued over those years. There were now telephones on the island, with a record nine hundred active telephones at the peak of the summer season. Plans were being made for the building of the Jesup Library. The Jordan Pond House was still in its infancy.

When the Astors first visited Bar Harbor, the concern had been the rash of accidents with the horse and buggy. Now the argument was over automobiles: whether they should be allowed on Bar Harbor's narrow horse paths that served as public roads, and what to do with the occasional summer colonist showing up for the season with their automobile. A state law recently passed permitted the individual towns on Mount Desert Island to decide whether to allow automobiles. Bar Harbor was a holdout, denying permission despite the automobile's growing popularity.

* * *

Among the changes in Bar Harbor since John and Ava Astor's first visit was the building of the first Astor summer cottage in that town. "Breakwater" was an imposing building located along the socially desired Shore Path.

John Kane and his wife, Annie, were the owners of Breakwater. John Innes Kane and Colonel John Jacob Astor were second cousins. John Innes Kane's grandmother, Dorothea Astor Kane, was a sister of Colonel John Jacob Astor's grandfather, William Backhouse Astor Sr. John Innes Kane was just as much an Astor as Colonel John Jacob Astor; they simply had different last names.

John Innes Kane was one of six children, but he and his wife, Annie C. Schermerhorn, had no children of their own. They had been married twenty-six years when Breakwater was built in 1904. Visits by the Kane family are noted in Mount Desert Island newspapers as far back as 1882, six years before Colonel Astor's first recorded visit. In the *Mount Desert Herald*, the island's weekly newspaper at the time, there is a listing of Mrs. DeLancey Kane and family staying at "The Old Rectory"—a cottage either on Mount Desert Street or in the immediate vicinity, in the center of Bar Harbor's village. Eleanora Iselin Kane (Mrs. DeLancey

Kane) was John Innes Kane's sister-in-law, and she and DeLancey Kane had one child, DeLancey Iselin Kane, who would have been five years old in 1882. At the same time, John and DeLancey's brother Walter and his wife, Mary, of New York were staying Bar Harbor's Nickerson Cottage.

The Kanes were members of Bar Harbor's Hotel Era who had made the transition to the Cottage Era. John and Annie Kane originally had a summer cottage in Newport but had always made visits to Bar Harbor before building Breakwater and making Bar Harbor their permanent summer home. In 1884, John I. Kane was listed as being at the Malvern, along with his sister-in-law, Mrs. DeLancey Kane, and Miss Sybil Kane, twenty-six, his unmarried sister. In 1887, Mrs. DeLancey Kane and family are listed as staying at Arcadia Cottage on the south side of Eagle Lake Road. Walter Kane and his family, from Newport, were staying at the Mainstay Cottage on Eden Street or in the immediate vicinity. John Innes Kane was listed as staying at the Malvern, a hotel popular with the Astor family.

In 1888, John I. Kane was noted as being a guest at a party given by Commodore Elbridge T. Gerry, head of the New York Yacht Club, aboard his steam yacht, the *Electra*. Kane, along with his brother Walter (and presumably the men's families), was part of a large party of yachtsmen and summer residents of Bar Harbor who enjoyed a sailing excursion during the event. "The menu was in accordance with the elegance of the yacht," wrote the *Mount Desert Herald*.

The *Bar Harbor Record* noted on July 6, 1893, that Mrs. DeLancey Kane, wife of John Innes Kane's brother, and her daughter, Mrs. Jay, were expected to arrive at the Malvern. "Mrs. Kane will entertain a great deal this summer, as usual," wrote the *Record*.

* * *

John Kane and John Astor had many similarities. Like his more famous cousin, John Innes Kane had always taken a keen interest in scientific matters, especially those dealing with discovery and exploration. He was also fond of art and travel. His year-round home in New York City, on West Forty-Ninth Street, was simple in its elegance, decorated with furnishings bought all over Europe.

There were differences between Colonel Astor and his cousin, however. John Innes Kane took no interest in business dealings, and he was not as sought after by newspaper reporters as Colonel Astor, though his movements and social activities did make the social columns. He also was not part of Caroline Astor's Four Hundred, though many of his siblings were.

Another difference between the cousins, and one of the reasons Mr. Kane did not take an interest in business, was that he did not have nearly as much of the Astor money as his cousin, even though he had the same Astor blood. John I. Kane had not yet been born when his great-grandfather, the original John Jacob Astor, had died. Though his siblings received a share of the fortune, John did not. John Innes Kane was worth less than half a million dollars, equivalent to approximately $17 million today. John's wife, Annie, had a larger fortune than did her Astor husband.

* * *

Though not as rich as his cousin, John Innes Kane was more involved in the social fabric of the Bar Harbor summer colony, eventually spending his entire summer there, compared to Colonel Astor's two-week visits. In 1903, the John Innes Kane family began their transition from Newport to Bar Harbor by breaking ground on their summer cottage, Breakwater. The Kanes' move out of their Newport summer home was a coup for Bar Harbor.

Located on Hancock Street, within the boundaries of the busy village, the large Tudor-style Breakwater mansion boasted stables and a greenhouse. The first year that Breakwater was being built, the Kanes took the cottage Am Meer for the season. Mrs. Ann Schermerhorn (Mrs. Kane's mother) accompanied them. The following year, with Breakwater not yet complete, they stayed at Reef Point, the cottage of Mrs. Mary Cadwalader Jones.

Yearly, readers of the *Bar Harbor Record*, and later the *Bar Harbor Times*, would read of the arrival of the Kanes early in the season and cousin John Jacob Astor later in the season aboard the *Nourmahal*. John

Innes Kane had a small, engine-powered, open pleasure craft, a naphtha boat, called the *Tramp*.

"The domestics of John Innes Kane have opened their beautiful house, The Breakwater, Shore Path, and are busy filling window boxes, placing awnings, etc., against the arrival of the family, who are at present in another of their country houses," announced the *Bar Harbor Record* in its May 31, 1911, edition, typical of the annual announcement of the Kanes' summer arrival.

The Kane family was quite civic minded in the Bar Harbor community. The same year that Breakwater was built, land was being purchased by the Bar Harbor Medical and Surgical Hospital for a needed expansion, which doubled the size of the hospital, adding nine new ward beds, seven private rooms, an emergency and isolation ward, an X-ray room, an eye clinic, a pathology lab, and a nurses' dining room. The Kanes contributed to the building fund.

Because Breakwater was located along the Shore Path, Mr. Kane was a member of the Bar Harbor Village Improvement Association's Shore Path Committee. John and Annie Kane would become incorporators of the Kebo Country Club of Mount Desert, one of the oldest clubs in Bar Harbor, and would sponsor many events there, with John Kane playing in the annual golf tournaments. John and Annie Kane also were donors of championship cups for the annual Bar Harbor Horse Show.

* * *

John Innes Kane was fifty-four years old when Breakwater was built. He would enjoy Breakwater for less than ten years, dying on February 1, 1913, less than a year after *Titanic* sank.

* * *

The Force family had only been Bar Harbor summer colonists for two years when one of the most monumental events in society's history occurred with the death of Caroline Astor, leader of the society and of the Four Hundred, which Mrs. Force wished for her family to enter.

When the Force family first arrived in Bar Harbor in 1907, there were already rumors about Caroline Astor's health, which was described as precarious that season. Mrs. Astor was not as socially active that winter, and the following season Colonel Astor announced that his mother's Newport estate, Beechwood, would not be opened for the season, which had been society's first true indication that there was serious trouble with Mrs. Astor's health. By October 1908, Mrs. Astor would be confined to her bed in the Fifth Avenue mansion, attended to by three physicians. Caroline Astor died on October 30, 1908.

"Long Leader of New York Society," read the *New York Times* subheadline announcing Mrs. Astor's death.

"Mrs. Astor at the time of her death for more than twenty years had been the acknowledged leader, with almost absolute power to make or mar the social destiny of those who sought her patronage. Her visiting list was the index of the socially select. She ruled with strong hand, and there was none to dispute her way, though her frinds were wont to say that the most compelling thing about Mrs Astor was her kind and winning smile.

"Tradition, wealth, and social accomplishments combined to enable her to hold her position as the head of New York society, when that society was passing through a perplexing era of transition which came with the rapid growth of fortunes in new hands and the newly rich clamoring at the gates."

The *Times* noted how Mrs. Astor had been at the debut performance of the Metropolitan Opera every season. Her daughter-in-law, Ava, had traditionally been her guest. "She made her appearance at 9 o'clock almost to the minute, and the arrival of Mrs. Astor, wearing all her magnifiicant jewels, was regarded as a proclamation that the New York season had been formally opened. Every lorgnette in the house and opera glasses as well were trained on the Astor box, where, as an enthusiastic foreigner once expressed it, she sat looking 'like a veritable Duchess and grand dame.'"

The newspaper noted how Caroline Astor insisted on rejecting the social norm of being identified by her husband's name, Mrs. William Astor. She would become offended if she were referred to as anything other than Mrs. Astor. Still, she seemed to know that even she was replaceable, as seen in her quote to the *New York Times* a month before her death: "I am not vain enough to think New York will not be able to get along without me. Many women will rise up to take my place, but I hope my influence will be felt in one thing, and that is, discountenancing the undignified methods employed by certain New York women to attract a following. They have given entertainments that belonged under a circus tent rather than in a gentlewoman's home. Their sole object is notoriety, a thing that no lady ever seeks, but, rather, shrinks from."

The death of Mrs. Astor caused concern among the members of society, and the newspapers who covered them, not about who would fill Mrs. Astor's role but whether the role needed to be filled at all.

"There are many who believe that with Mrs. Astor has passed away the last leader of New York society. No one, they say, will ever be able to occupy the place she filled, for the condition in New York's upper set, which justified the term leader, with all it implied, and rendered the position almost as well established as though it had been provided for by the Constitution, have changed materially since this gifted and tactful woman ascended to it," wrote the *New York Times*.

* * *

Though the death of Mrs. Astor caused shockwaves, there seemed little question as to who would ascend to her position as the acknowledged leader of society. Caroline Astor had set the tradition herself.

Caroline's husband, William, was the second son of William Backhouse Astor Sr. and younger brother to John Jacob Astor III. Following the death of John Jacob Astor III, some thought that his daughter-in-law would become the new social leader; however, Caroline Astor assumed that leadership instead. Under the unofficial rules of ascension, the current Mrs. John Jacob Astor, Ava Willing Astor, seemed the natural choice as society's next leader. She had the ancestral and social background and, more important, the name of Mrs. John Jacob Astor. John and Ava Astor were already tenants at the Astor mansion on Fifth Avenue, society's headquarters. The death of Mrs. Caroline Astor, and her replacement in that role by her daughter-in-law, should have been a mere blip on society's radar. Instead, it set in motion a chain of events that would change and eventually end the institution of society as it was known.

Ava Astor had long wanted a divorce from Colonel John Jacob Astor, but she also appeared to want the social position that his name and the death of his mother would provide. Rather than choosing between staying with a man she did not love and losing her desired position in society, Ava Astor chose to attempt both. Society would be stunned when it was announced that Ava Astor had filed for divorce from Colonel John Jacob Astor shortly after the death of his mother.

* * *

By now John Jacob and Ava Astor had two children: a son, William Vincent (seventeen), and a daughter, Ava Alice Muriel (six). During the summer season of 1909, the first season after Mrs. Astor's death, the Astor family did not spend their time together. Instead, Ava Astor and her daughter Muriel sailed to Europe while Colonel Astor and his son stayed behind in Newport, where Vincent was preparing for entrance into Harvard. On returning to New York with her daughter that fall, Ava Astor made the shocking announcement: She was suing her husband, John Jacob Astor IV, for divorce.

"The news that her [Mrs. Caroline Astor's] daughter-in-law was suing for a separation caused no end of talk in social as well as business circles in New York," reported the *New York Times*.

This was not the first divorce to hit the Astor family. In 1892, newspapers were printing stories suggesting that Colonel Astor's sister Charlotte, who was married to a man named James Drayton, was having an affair during her time in England away from her husband. The two would eventually divorce and Charlotte would remarry, causing great scandal for the Astor family.

The 1909 divorce had long been expected among intimate friends of the Astors. According to the rumors, Colonel and Mrs. Astor had had a serious fight while they were in Europe the previous summer, the same time that she filed for the divorce. The entire matter was kept secret until Ava's announcement in 1909, when the divorce was about to be granted. Though the divorce had been rumored among some in society, the general public knew nothing of what was about to happen.

It would appear by the timing of Ava's filing for divorce that she had been waiting for the death of the first Mrs. Astor before pursuing this course. The divorce suit would allegedly include the naming of women with whom Colonel Astor reportedly had been intimate during his marriage to Ava. Had she filed for divorce and damaged Colonel Astor's reputation while Mrs. Astor was alive, the wrath of Colonel Astor's mother could have resulted in the banishment of Ava Astor from the society that she was expected to lead on Caroline Astor's death. Apparently staying married to Colonel Astor and taking the social throne by rights was worth the sacrifice for Ava Astor. By divorcing him after Caroline Astor's death, not before, and without invoking Caroline Astor's wrath, Ava Astor would still have a shot at the title of leader of the Four Hundred.

Through a series of legal maneuvers, the divorce proceedings were dealt with under the utmost secrecy, which would create resentment and hostility against Colonel Astor by the general public. Because the case was sealed, the curious public had to rely on rumors for the reasons of the divorce. Generally it was believed that one (if not more) co-respondents had been named by Mrs. Astor. One of those identified was "The Belle of Sheepshead Bay."

According to a story that ran in newspapers across the country at the time of the divorce announcement, rumors in circulation associated the name of Colonel Astor with that of a scandal-ridden young socialite whose divorce had resulted in her social exclusion from the summer colony of Newport. In 1901, eight years before the Astor divorce, "Belle" had eloped at age sixteen. Because of her age, her new husband was arrested on the grounds of abduction. Though "Belle" was of Newport society, her new husband was from Brooklyn. The arrest was sensational. "Belle" was soon disinherited by her father.

Four years later, "Belle" again appeared in Newport, a married and yet unaccompanied woman renting a fashionable cottage there. Disinherited by her father, "Belle's" means for affording this Newport cottage were unknown. However, Colonel Astor was a frequent visitor to that cottage. "Belle" and Colonel Astor were often seen riding in Astor's big, red automobile along Newport's popular Surf Avenue. "The circumstance caused considerable comment on the part of the exclusive natives," reported one newspaper.

The episode ended with "Belle" abruptly leaving Newport, where it was said that she had been asked to vacate her cottage. "Belle" and Colonel Astor's names were brought into further controversy that year when she accused two of her household staff of stealing diamonds and rubies valued at $50,000, worth $1.75 million when adjusted for inflation. In return, the servants accused "Belle" of having originally received the jewels as a gift by one called "Colonel." They went on to accuse their employer of having "lost" the jewels on another occasion, that time in England, and claimed that a certain New York millionaire had redeemed them with a reward of $25,000. The servants said that despite her report of a theft, "Belle" currently knew the location of the jewels. They went on to say that "Belle" had complained to them that her husband had threatened to sue for divorce, mentioning the "Colonel" as co-respondent.

"Belle" and her husband divorced later that year; she went to Europe, where she met and married an English war veteran, whom she divorced the year before Colonel Astor's divorce, after having taken an apartment in Manhattan.

Three days before Ava Astor arrived back in the United States and made her startling divorce announcement, Colonel Astor and his son, Vincent, embarked on the *Nourmahal* and headed for Cuba and the West Indies. It was said that Colonel Astor had taken Vincent from the United States to spare him the humiliation of the announcement. They were at sea when the divorce news broke. According to Colonel Astor's secretary, William Dobbyn, they were due back in November.

Vincent's health, described as not being robust, required attention, no doubt escalated by the loss of his grandmother, the deteriorating Astor marriage, and the stress of his upcoming entrance to Harvard University. With the sailing of the *Nourmahal*, immediately gossip began about Colonel Astor's current activities. Three weeks before Ava announced the divorce, "Belle" took a hasty trip to Paris. Friends of "Belle" said that they did not doubt that "Belle's" hasty trip to Paris might mean that she intended to join Colonel Astor on his yacht. They rumored that she had been a guest on similar trips for the last three years.

* * *

Immediately after Ava arrived in America and made the divorce announcement, she would retreat to a fashionable and yet secluded spa at French Lick Springs, Indiana. She registered on the evening of October 30 under the name "Mrs. Austin" of Red Bank, New Jersey. She attempted to hide her identity, and employees of the hotel denied knowledge of her presence to reporters. Mrs. Astor spent much of her time in her room but frequently would appear on the veranda of the hotel, where she was the center of silent attention.

Society gossiped about where Mrs. Astor would ultimately end up living after the divorce. She would return to New York City, stopping at the Astors' Fifth Avenue mansion, telling reporters she was overseeing a remodeling project there. Ava's brother, J. D. Barton Willing, arrived in New York from Philadelphia to help his sister with her legal action. The announcement of the divorce and the rumor about the co-respondents would gain Ava Astor sympathy, and the scandal did not seem to be jeopardizing her role as the presumed new leader of the Four Hundred.

"Mrs. John Jacob Astor, Leader of New York Society, Who Is Suing for Separation," read the headline of one syndicated newspaper story.

"The beautiful and queenly leader of New York's Four Hundred, who succeeded the late Mrs. William Astor as recognized leader of the New York society. She has won besides the social triumphs of England and America an enviable reputation for her wise charities and her persistent philanthropic efforts. With a firm though gentle hand she has upheld the standards of society in accordance with her own high ideals. She has always found time to devote her truest efforts to the care of her own home and of her children.

"She is a typical American woman, but exceptional in beauty. Tall, regal and willowy, her movements are very graceful Seen at a ball in one of the wonderful Paris creations which she is said never to wear twice, she is a figure never to be forgotten. Her gowns are wonderful creations, and have been the subject of numerous articles in newspapers and magazines. There are many beautiful portraits and photographs of Mrs. Astor in existence, and these have been published scores of times on both sides of the Atlantic."

* * *

Ava Astor would stay in New York until the divorce was granted on November 8, 1909, a month after she had made her announcement. There was a small gathering of spectators in the courtroom when the divorce case was called. Because no names were used, the spectators were unaware of what they were witnessing. Henry W. Taft, brother to then president William Taft, appeared for Mrs. Astor. Shortly after the case was called, Mr. Taft quietly arose.

"I have a motion with which you are familiar, and would like to have the judgement signed and an interlocutory decree granted," said Mr. Taft to the court.

The judge replied, "I have read very carefully the report of the referee in this matter, and am of the opinion that the evidence presented justifies the findings of the referee. I shall, therefore, sign the judgement and grant an interlocutory decree if there are no objections."

Mr. Lewis Cass Ledyard, Colonel Astor's lawyer, arose and said there were no objections. The papers were signed, whereupon Mr. Taft made a second motion, asking that all papers in the case be sealed. The motion was granted.

The court found in favor of Mrs. Astor, and she was granted an absolute divorce. She received custody of Muriel, while Colonel Astor had custody of Vincent. She received an outright cash settlement but lost use of any of the Astor homes and facilities. It was reported that Colonel Astor made a settlement with Ava of $10 million in lieu of alimony.

Soon after the divorce was granted, Ava was making plans to sail back to Europe with Muriel to spend the winter season there. Ava Astor's time in London had won her personal friends among the members of society there as easily as she had in New York, including a friendship with the royal family, and England was becoming her second home.

* * *

With the divorce complete, Colonel Astor was soon headed to sea again aboard the *Nourmahal*, this time in part to let the headlines of the divorce die down. The headlines a week later, however, would throw the divorce story back into the news and ultimately lose more public sympathy for Colonel Astor when it was announced that the *Nourmahal* had disappeared and Colonel Astor and Vincent were thought to be lost at sea.

From 4:00 p.m. on November 13 through 8:00 p.m. the following night, a storm ravaged the West Indian Ocean. When the storm cleared, with inquiries being made as to the safety of the *Nourmahal*, no responses were heard. No one had seen the very visible, internationally famous John Jacob Astor or heard from his almost equally famous yacht, the size of a small warship. Anxiety for the Astors' safety grew by the hour and then by the day. Over the following week ships were arriving in port and telling stories of how violent the storm had been, with still no word from Colonel Astor. "Every added hour of uncertainty deepens the anxiety felt for Colonel John Jacob Astor and his son, Vincent," wrote the *New York Times*.

The United States Treasury Department dispatched the revenue cutter *Algonquin*, which was directed to make a search for the missing yacht in the West Indies. A steamer from the Turks Islands and the British cruiser *Sovila* were also sent in search of the missing *Nourmahal*.

Concern was heightened when the German steamer *Wotan*, arriving in Tampa, Florida, and unaware of the missing yacht, relayed a story that the ship had sighted a submerged wreck sixty miles due north of Matanzas, off the north coast of Cuba. Captain Hans Seldalkier reported that his ship did not approach the wreck close enough to make a thorough investigation, and he could not say whether the ship was the *Nourmahal*.

The location of the wreck would have been off course for the *Nourmahal*, which had been bound from Kingston, Jamaica, for San Juan, Puerto Rico. Many maritime experts agreed that the powerful storm could have blown the yacht off course and that there was a good chance the wreck was the *Nourmahal*.

The US revenue cutter *Yamacraw*, which was at Charleston, South Carolina, received the new information by wireless. Her captain wired back that he would leave at once for the wreck site, joining two tugboats already put out from Key West, Florida, on the same mission. The president of Cuba dispatched a naval vessel to the scene of the wreck as soon as he received word of the sighting. In addition, orders were issued to all captains of ports and commanders of all naval vessels to report promptly any sightings to Washington, DC.

In New York, William Dobbyn, Colonel Astor's secretary, continued day after day without contact from his employer and friend. The *Nourmahal* carried no wireless equipment. The storm had broken onshore communication cable lines in many areas, only being restored a week later, and many hoped that Colonel Astor and his son were safe but unable to communicate for those reasons. With the addition of the report from the *Wotan* of the wreck suspected to be the *Nourmahal*, Mr. Dobbyn grew concerned, as did Astor's friends and business acquaintances.

"Col. Astor's secretary, William A. Dobbyn, would not admit yesterday that there were any grave fears for the safety of the yacht, but there was a report yesterday that a conference of the trustees of the Astor Estate would be held soon," reported the *New York Times*.

With the divorce final, Ava Astor and her daughter were about to leave the United States aboard the *Lusitania* when she was told of the disappearance of the *Nourmahal*. Ava Astor continued her travel plans but kept in touch with Astor estate trustee Nicholas Biddle by means of wireless messages. Mr. Biddle promised to wire any new developments. While the ocean search continued, the implications of John Jacob Astor's disappearance and possible death were being discussed. Some speculated that because Colonel Astor had left New York before the final divorce decree was issued, Ava Astor might not get her divorce settlement or the divorce might not be considered final and she might, ironically, inherit part of the Astor estate, which she had just rejected along with the man who controlled it.

* * *

The wireless search for Colonel Astor and Vincent was led by Douglas Robinson, Astor estate trustee and brother-in-law of Theodore Roosevelt, who had just left office. Mr. Robinson immediately sent out an SOS to all ships and stations equipped with the new invention of wireless radio. The use of SOS was so new that the newspapers covering the story explained specifically what SOS stood for: "It is the call for instant attention and means that each operator must stand by to receive the message. And that he must at once transmit it along the line and without delay. All other business has to give way for an SOS message."

Mr. Robinson sent the following message: "Wireless, telegraph, or cable any report whatever concerning yacht *Nourmahal* and her location to . . . Robinson . . . NYC. Make every effort to obtain such information, and also report to this company."

"The sending out of this general call for help shows that Mr. Astor's associates regard his disappearance as alarming," wrote the *New York Times*. "The dispatch of such a message as that sent out by wireless is a costly affair, for it not only interferes with the company's business in giving it the right of way, but puts every United station at the service of the Astor trustees."

By now the amount of taxpayer money being spent on the search for Colonel Astor and his yacht was $2,000 a day, approximately $70,000 when adjusted for inflation. Soon the United States Navy was saying what was on many people's minds—that Colonel Astor's silence seemed to be deliberate.

* * *

On November 22, the *New York Tribune* let the world know that Colonel John Jacob Astor and his son were alive: "Nourmahal Safe at Puerto Rico."

Colonel Astor had sent a cable the day before announcing that he, Vincent, and the yacht were fine. He said they had arrived safely in Puerto Rico aboard the *Nourmahal* on November 14, the day after the storm, but the country's cable line had been out of repair until November 20. Colonel Astor's secretary, William Dobbyn, immediately sought confirmation of the cable, at the same time cabling Mrs. Astor, still aboard the *Lusitania* for England.

Regarding the reason behind his voyage, Colonel Astor said he had gone to Puerto Rico to get away from "meddlesome people." The United States Congress looked into the disappearance of the *Nourmahal* and passed a resolution to investigate the costs of the search. Back in Bar Harbor, the potential loss of one of its most prominent summer colony members was noted with the dry Down East wit: "Col. John Jacob Astor is back, and if he will enquire at any well-regulated newspaper office he will find that there is no dust on his obituary," wrote the *Bar Harbor Record.*

* * *

The Astor divorce would have its impact on Bar Harbor. With the distractions of the death of Caroline Astor and the deviation from the normal summer travel traditions associated with the Astor divorce, there is no record of the Astors visiting Bar Harbor in 1908 and 1909. Instead, the island newspapers ran the stories of the divorce from larger newspapers. There was concern that the Astor name would be lost forever to the Bar Harbor summer colony amid the turmoil.

One name that did emerge in 1909 was that of Madeleine Force as she made the Bar Harbor Swimming Club her own territory—via their tennis courts.

"The Forces were prominent entertainers last season and will take a prominent part in the summer's gaieties," wrote the *Bar Harbor Record* after the Force name was added to the 1909 season's Cottage Directory in the June 23 edition.

That year the Force family changed their summer home to Buena Vista on Eden Street, much closer to the Bar Harbor Swimming Club than the previous season's cottage. The swim club was described by the *Bar Harbor Record* as "one of the social centers of Bar Harbor," and it was especially popular with Mrs. Force and her two pre-debutante daughters. Though members of the summer colony of all ages enjoyed the club, it seemed to be especially popular with the members of the younger colony set in general. All activity levels were accommodated with facilities for physical activities and facilities for dinner and dancing, including a broad veranda "for those who did not dance." For those who did swim, a live orchestra accompanied their aquatics.

Mrs. Force and her daughters were there at the opening ball for the Bar Harbor Swimming Club's 1909 season, held on Saturday, July 12. A live orchestra provided accompaniment for dancing that night.

* * *

Madeleine and Katherine Force played tennis on the courts at both the Kebo Valley Club and the Bar Harbor Swimming Club, though it was at the swim club that they received the most attention. At both clubs that year, Madeleine and Katherine soon entered the women's tennis tournaments, both mixed and single. There were eighteen entrants into the Kebo's women's singles tennis tournament that year.

The 1909 season was described by the *Bar Harbor Record* as the best season on the tennis courts that Bar Harbor had ever enjoyed, "according to those who have followed the sport closely here for years." As the 1909 season was winding down, the tennis courts were heating up with tournament play in front of great crowds.

"The tournaments played on the courts of both the Kebo Valley club and the Swimming club have been entered by many players, and the aspirants for hours in every case have furnished exciting tennis, playing strongly before large galleries," reported the *Bar Harbor Record.* "The final matches have been for the most part very close and interesting, the successful ones in the survival of the fittest . . . players having played the game for all it was worth and never losing hope until the end."

The *New York Times* reported that the tennis play "brought forth surprises, some of the strongest pairs being put out of the running by 'dark horses,'" including Madeleine Force. Madeleine would earn her way to the finals in the mixed doubles tennis tournament at the Kebo Valley Club, but she and her partner Reginald Waterbury were defeated by a score of 7–5, 8–6, 6–4.

Madeleine would have better luck on the tennis courts of the swim club. In the semifinals of the ladies' singles tournament, she defeated Miss Elizabeth Wells 6–3, 6–0. In the finals, Madeleine Force would earn the title of tournament champion at the Bar Harbor Swimming Club by winning two out of three sets from her opponent.

"Miss Madeline Force of New York established her title as women's tennis champion of Bar Harbor Friday," wrote the *Bar Harbor Record.*

The story was picked up by the *New York Times.* "Miss Force Wins Maine Tennis Title," read the September 4, 1909, edition. "BAR HARBOR, Me., Sept. 3: Miss Madeline Force of New York won the tennis championship of the State of Maine in ladies' singles this afternoon on the Swimming Club courts, defeating Mrs. Martin L. Feary of Boston, a daughter of Bishop William Lawrence, 6–5, 6–3."

Through her play on the courts of Bar Harbor, Madeleine Force earned not only her first championship but also her first headline as a member of her family's new, higher society.

* * *

The more established summer colonists of Bar Harbor must have liked what they saw in the Force sisters on the tennis courts. Late that summer, they were asked to play parts in a production at the Building of Arts, one of the crown jewels of Bar Harbor's summer colony. They would appear in a production of *The Bridal Veil,* a play written by Mrs. A. Clifford Barney of Washington, DC. The Greek-themed production was performed amid the trees in the amphitheater behind the Building of Arts. Madeleine and Katherine Force were given parts as priestesses of the god Apollo. Proceeds from the production would be donated to the Bar Harbor Medical and Surgical Hospital.

The initiation to the Building of Arts was an important milestone for the Force sisters. The Building of Arts had opened the same season the Force family first arrived in Bar Harbor, just two years previously. Built and supported by the more established summer colonists, including the Astors and the Kanes, the ornate building was a copy of an old Grecian temple finished to represent Parian marble. The roof was red tile. The stage inside was built to compete with the most professional stages in the world. The building was located near the Kebo Valley Club amid a beautiful grove of trees. The building boasted a seating capacity of 380 summer colonists.

"Some of the most prominent girls and men of the summer colony were in the choruses, including . . . Katherine and Madeleine Force," wrote the *New York Times.*

* * *

After returning to New York at the end of the 1909 summer season, Mrs. Katherine Force prepared for the social debut of her oldest daughter, Miss Katherine Emmons Force, at their New York home. Miss Katherine Force was to host a dance. Society columns at the time, including the *New York Times*, noted that Mrs. Force "was Miss Talmage," the name of her father, the former mayor of Brooklyn, indicating that Mrs. Force still held social prestige in New York.

On the day after Christmas, Katherine Force's formal debut photograph, taken by famed society photographer Aime Dupont of New York, was the first of seven debutante portraits featured in a special society page in the *New York Times.*

"It has been the custom of Mrs. Force to take her two beautiful daughters to Bar Harbor every Summer. There they were greatly admired and were the recipients of much attention from young men of wealth and social rank. Mrs. Force was always socially ambitious, it was said, and had set her heart on her daughters making what is called 'good matches,'" wrote the *Hudson Columbia Republican* a year later at the time of Madeleine Astor's engagement to Colonel Astor.

Interestingly, though this was Katherine Force's debut season, it was younger sister Madeleine who would appear at the Bal Masque in February 1910, society's farewell to the debut season, held on the eve of Lent.

The masquerade ball was the annual closing event of society's winter season and was incredibly popular among the members of society. "The fame of the Bachelors' Bal Masque has grown so rapidly in the very few years it has existed that there are not half enough invitations to supply the demand," wrote the *Philadelphia Inquirer.* "From New York, Virginia, Washington and far-off Paris come guests to join in the frolic, and last night's was the gayest and merriest ever given by the far-famed bachelors."

The elaborately elegant Horticultural Hall on the New York City fairgrounds had been under preparation for weeks, being transformed into an apple orchard in full bloom. The invited guests had only a moment to admire the elaborately decorated hall before the lights briefly went out, coming back on at a dim shade. A dance troupe began a performance in the shadows, which signaled the beginning of a program of entertainment.

"With a wild whoop a crowd of merry sailors, grasping a Chinaman by the pigtail, executed a wild dance on the ballroom floor and the fun was on. In a second a rollicking two-step crowded the ballroom, men without partners grasped the nearest lady. A monk danced with a saucy French maid in scarlet tartan, a dashing captain's sword cut a yard of flouncing off a summer girl's frock; a Dutch girl lost a sabot and a Chinaman gallantly offered one of his, and everybody merrily joined in the frolic."

The program was followed by supper and dancing, but not in the usual stiff style of society. The event's organizers had arranged for snow to be brought into the hall, resulting in an hour-long snowball fight. "Disarranged, torn costumes, dented fancy headgear and wigs decidedly awry were mute evidence of the hotness of the battle," wrote the *Philadelphia Inquirer*.

The unmasking was at midnight. At some point the debutantes were organized into a formal receiving line. At 3:00 a.m., the hosts let loose three hundred balloons in the hall's ballroom, all marked "Bal masque." "Like small children, the guests scrambled wildly for the balloons, for three hundred meant only one here and there amid eleven hundred guests." Realizing the disappointment of the eight hundred guests who did not secure a balloon, the organizers quickly dispersed a number of fancy valentines among the ballroom, "and the scramble began again."

* * *

While the Force family was officially presenting older daughter Katherine, Colonel John Jacob Astor was beginning his life as a divorced man. Some of his time was spent planning a large dinner for the newly renovated Fifth Avenue Astor mansion. The event was supposed to have taken place as a housewarming for his and Ava's family home, with Ava at his side. Instead, the socially awkward John Jacob Astor was assisted in receiving his guests by his sister Caroline Astor Wilson. Despite the scandal of his divorce, Colonel Astor was still invited to social functions, including ones hosted by Fifth Avenue neighbor Cornelius Vanderbilt, who was an Astor in-law through Colonel Astor's sister Caroline.

Colonel Astor would also find himself the butt of public jokes. Though the exact number of co-respondents listed in the Astor divorce action was not known, it was agreed that Colonel Astor had not lived up to the gentlemanly conduct his social position required. This lapse was made fun of by an actress during a theatrical production that winter. Colonel Astor was in attendance at the Herald Square Theatre on the evening of February 25, occupying two right-hand box seats with a party of friends. The play was *The Yankee Girl*. The principal actress of the play, after making her first entrance in a white duck sailor suit, was supposed to say her line, which was that she was "just off the yacht *Pansy*." Learning that Colonel Astor was in the audience, instead she delivered the line as "just off the yacht *Nourmahal*," at the same time looking over at the box that Colonel Astor occupied. He was reported as looking rather startled, but the women in the party applauded heartedly.

Colonel Astor and Vincent spent part of the spring that year sailing to Europe, returning to the United States in the middle of May. They headed straight for their country estate in Rhinebeck, New York, where they planned to stay for a few weeks before heading to Newport for the summer. With a new life ahead of him, Colonel Astor also had a new yacht with the commissioning of the *Noma*. Her headquarters was in Newport Harbor during the summer, as had been the *Nourmahal*'s.

* * *

In 1910, Bar Harbor was described as having the coldest and most backward spring that ever had visited the coast of Maine. The weather set back the arrival of the cottagers and hotel guests, of which there were still many. When they did finally arrive, however, they seemed to be there to enjoy the season for all that it was worth. Guests in Bar Harbor that year included Winston Churchill and his wife, Clementine, who were entertained along with international diplomats on the Pulitzer yacht.

The name of the Force family first appeared in the Cottage Directory in July of that year. The residence of Mrs. William Force and the Misses Force was again different from the previous year, this time in a cottage named Bierkas, also known as Studio in the Field, located on Stephens Lane in the center of the village, not far from the Newport Hotel and again close to the Bar Harbor Swimming Club.

Immediately the Force women headed to the Bar Harbor Swimming Club, which featured a newly constructed second outdoor tennis court, necessary because of the popularity of the sport at the club. Madeleine Force, now Bar Harbor's tennis champion, was immediately back on the tennis courts. People wanted to see whether this social outsider would win a second time in a row, which would entitle her to ownership of the championship cup. Madeleine's arrival back on the tennis court attracted the attention of the *Bar Harbor Record*: "Miss Madeleine Force, winner of the ladies' singles tournament, is here, as are other good racquets among the ladies, including . . . Katherine Force."

The following week, the newspaper would record Madeleine's victory, along with Reginald Waterbury, over Miss Susette Davis and W. Davis, 6–4, 6–3, in the mixed doubles tournament at the Kebo Valley Club. The playing was described as close and lively. In the semifinals, Miss Force and Mr. Waterbury beat Miss Blair and Mr. Blair 6–4, 6–4. The finals were ultimately won by Miss Winthrop and Mr. Rogers, who beat Miss Force and Mr. Woodbury 7–5, 5–8, 6–4.

With the increased popularity of the sport of tennis among the summer colony, the Bar Harbor Swimming Club was now holding its own mixed doubles tournament rather than sharing it with the Kebo Club. The same week of Madeleine's loss in the Kebo Club's mixed doubles, she began in the preliminaries in the mixed doubles lawn tennis tournament on the swim club courts. With a large crowd of spectators watching, she and M. Taylor Pyne Jr. defeated Miss L. Knowlton and N. Rae 6–1, 6–2. The following week, with scores of 6–3 and 6–1, Madeleine and Mr. Pyne became the mixed doubles champions.

"New Yorkers Win Maine Title," read the *New York Times* headline in the August 6 edition. "Madeleine Force and Taylor Pyne of New York, in a hard-fought contest, 6–3, 6–5, on the Swimming Club courts. The play was watched by a large gallery and was close throughout."

"The largest number of members and subscribers of the season were at the Swimming Club Friday and many witnessed this match," wrote the *Bar Harbor Record.*

After the playing of tennis that day, many of the club members took a swim, and "the large pool presented an animated picture for several hours at mid-day. The Boston Symphony Orchestra played a special program, which was listened to by scores of men and women, young and old of the summer colony," reported the *Record.*

* * *

With Bar Harbor very busy in the summer season of 1910, Newport, Rhode Island, was also full, and a little too full for John Jacob Astor. He and Vincent had arrived there and planned to spend the entire summer at Ferncliff. Soon, however, news spread across the country that Ava Astor and Muriel would be making a visit to Newport in August. Ava reportedly was engaged to be married.

Sailing under the name Mrs. John Astor on the passenger list, Ava Astor and Muriel would arrive in New York aboard the White Star Line steamship *Oceanic.* Her son Vincent would arrive on the Astor yacht *Noma* to meet his mother. The use of Colonel Astor's yacht would seem to indicate some spirit of cooperation from Colonel Astor in the visit.

At the pier in New York, Ava Astor was detained as customs inspectors examined her many pieces of luggage. She told inspectors that because she owned no property in the United States, she should not have to pay a duty. She would send Muriel and her nanny away in a taxicab and apologize to her son for the delay before assisting customs officials with the opening of her many trunks. She explained that the pearls she wore as a necklace and the diamond cross pendant were imitations of the very valuable originals. In the end, she was required to pay a $500 duty.

The delay while the trunks were inspected gave waiting reporters a chance to ask questions of Ava Astor. She refused to discuss her plans, other than to say that she expected to go to Newport after a stay at the Gotham Hotel in New York. When asked by customs officials her address in the United States, she said Newport.

When Mrs. Astor was questioned concerning the reports that Lord Curzon, former viceroy of India, had been paying her attention, Mrs. Astor exclaimed, "I do not intend to marry Lord Curzon, nor do I intend to marry anyone else. As to my plans? I do not want to discuss them any further."

Mrs. Astor would travel on to Newport with Muriel, along with a regiment of servants and two wagons full of shipping trunks. They went to the summer home of her brother, Barton Willing, where Mrs. Astor was expected to spend the rest of the summer. Barton was described as having spent a large sum of money improving the cottage for his sister's comfort. Mrs. Astor was described by reporters as "looking handsomer than ever and in the cheeriest of moods."

On hearing the news that his first wife was to arrive in Newport, Colonel Astor announced plans for an extended cruise aboard his yacht. Because Ava Astor would arrive five days ahead of schedule, however, a meeting between the divorced couple in Newport was a real possibility. "Newport is agog tonight over the news of Mrs. Astor's arrival before the departure of her former husband," wrote the *Syracuse Post Standard*.

Colonel Astor's hastily planned exit on his cruise did not take place in time. The warships of the North Atlantic Fleet had come for their annual visit to Newport a little early that season. A party was given in honor of the officers of the fleet. Everyone of social importance in Newport was there, including Colonel John Jacob Astor and his former wife, Ava.

Ava Astor arrived wearing her famous low-cut gown of black, adorned with her rope of pearls. Colonel Astor arrived separately along with a date (recent debutante Roberta Willard) and Vincent. "The son and mother were most cordial and the boy danced several times with her," reported the *Syracuse Post Standard*.

Being in Newport at the same time had not been entirely bad for Colonel Astor, as it afforded him the opportunity to reunite with his daughter, Muriel. They were both out in automobiles when they saw each other for the first time.

"They stopped to chat and seemed extremely happy at the meeting," reported the *Syracuse Post Standard.* "What took place is known only by father and daughter, and all the Astors refuse to talk on the subject of their domestic relations, which is the gossip of all Newport."

* * *

Four days later, with his ex-wife commanding Newport, Colonel Astor closed Ferncliff. Along with Vincent and a party of friends, Colonel Astor boarded the *Noma* and headed to Bar Harbor.

The scandal of Colonel Astor's divorce did not seem to have hurt him socially in Bar Harbor. He was soon being entertained at dinners there and hosting dinners of his own, mainly at the Bar Harbor Swimming Club, where Madeleine Force was commanding the tennis courts, in the heat of tournament play, defending her new position in society there.

"Had Mrs. Ava Willing Astor not arrived in Newport at the time she did, society folk here [Bar Harbor] were pointing out today her former husband would have remained in Newport and consequently would not have met his present fiancée, who was not known in the Rhode Island set," reported the *Utica Herald Dispatch* a year later, after the formal engagement announcement of Colonel John Jacob Astor and Madeleine Force.

Chapter 3

Winter's Buds

Winter's buds are guests.

—*New York Times* headline announcing the activities of Madeleine Force and other society debutantes during New York's 1911 debut season

Madeleine Astor's first recorded date with John Jacob Astor would be on Monday, August 29, 1910, at the Bar Harbor Swimming Club.

Colonel Astor and his party, including his son, Vincent, had arrived in Bar Harbor only a few days before, sailing from Newport shortly after Ava Astor's arrival. Colonel Astor soon found himself at the Swimming Club, so close to the wharf. Large crowds were there daily now watching the popular sport of tennis. This particular day was the opening day of the ladies' doubles tournament.

According to other Swimming Club guests who were there when the couple first met, Colonel Astor immediately went to the club's tennis courts, where he first saw Madeleine and Katherine Force. "Col. Astor was at once impressed with both the beauty and the athletic skill of the young New York girls and sought immediately to be presented," reported the *Utica Herald Dispatch*.

By that afternoon, Colonel Astor and Madeleine were playing an informal game of mixed doubles tennis on the Swimming Club's courts against son Vincent and sister Katherine. From that point on, the guests of the Bar Harbor Swimming Club described Colonel Astor's devotion to Madeleine as "constant and intense." That evening Madeleine was a guest of Colonel Astor at a dinner party at the swim club.

"Col. Astor a Host at Many Dinners," read the *New York Times* headline. "Col. John Jacob Astor, who with his son, Vincent, has been here for some time, has been both host and a guest at a number of affairs. Col. Astor has entertained nearly every day at the Swimming Club, giving various small and large parties, and several dinners have been given in his honor. On Monday he entertained at dinner, his guests including the Misses Madeleine and Katherine Force, Mrs. W. H. Force, A. E. Gallatin, and Vincent Astor. The party enjoyed a theatre party in the evening. On Tuesday he entertained small parties."

The listing of Madeleine's name first in the *New York Times* story suggests she was the guest of honor. In the *Bar Harbor Record*'s account of the dinner, the young Force girls are not mentioned—only Colonel Astor, Mrs. Force, Vincent, and Mr. Gallatin.

Colonel Astor would return to the Bar Harbor Swimming Club the day after his first date with Madeleine, where the popular tennis tournaments were continuing. Among the many hosts of luncheons at the active clubhouse that day was Colonel Astor, who also gave an informal dinner that evening.

Colonel Astor would continue to be entertained at other Bar Harbor functions without Madeleine's name mentioned. He would leave Bar Harbor after his brief visit, headed back to Newport. There, Vincent would go to Hot Springs with his mother, while daughter Muriel would spend a month at Ferncliff with her father. The Force family stayed in Bar Harbor until the end of September. Madeleine and her sister, Katherine, continued their participation in the tennis tournaments. Ultimately, two days after her first date with Colonel Astor, Madeleine and her partner would be defeated in the ladies' doubles semifinals.

While Colonel Astor spent his time in Bar Harbor entertaining a select few of the summer colony, his ex-wife spent her time reinforcing her social position in Newport. "No social event of importance has been given in Newport this summer, since Mrs. Astor arrived from Europe, without Mrs. Astor being present," wrote the *New York Times*.

Ava and Muriel would sail back to England that fall, and Colonel Astor and Vincent would return to Ferncliff, the Astors' New York country estate; from there, Vincent would return for the new school year at Harvard. However, young Madeleine was not far from Colonel Astor's mind.

"From the moment he was presented to Miss Madeleine Force the colonel seemed to be fascinated by her charms," wrote the *Hudson Columbia Republican* several months later. "He found opportunities to be in her company daily, and later in the fall he entertained her and her family at his magnificent country estate at Rhinebeck. In the winter Miss Force, with her sister and her mother, was a frequent occupant of the famous Astor box in the 'golden Horseshoe.'"

* * *

Though Colonel Astor and Madeleine Force did not publicize their relationship, neither did they seem to be taking pains to hide it. Colonel Astor would arrive at some events alone, and at other functions he and Madeleine would be seen together. One notable society event at which they were prominent was their luncheon during New York Aviation Week, a time during which many of the Four Hundred indulged their interest in the newest travel innovation, hosting luncheons and dinners on Long Island.

"Col. John Jacob Astor and his son, Mr. Vincent Astor, were present Wednesday for the first time," reported the October 28, 1910, edition of the *Washington Post*. "They had luncheon at the Turf and Field Club, and in their party were Mrs. William H. Force and the Misses Katherine and Madeline Force."

Colonel Astor and Madeleine Force were being seen together enough that members of society were starting to gossip about the nature of their relationship. Though their relationship was truly no one's business, those who lived by society's sword died by society's sword. No one truly thought that Colonel Astor would stay single after his divorce from Ava Willing Astor. Whomever he remarried would be the presumed leader of society but would also receive competition from Colonel Astor's first wife, who was still using his prestigious name. Anyone with whom

Colonel Astor was romantically linked would be privately scrutinized by the members of the Four Hundred, on many levels.

Madeleine Force would be of concern to the members of that society. The two largest problems were Madeleine's age and her social position. She was seventeen years old, legally still a child, and she was less than half the age of Colonel Astor and younger than her presumed future stepson, Vincent.

In addition, she was from Brooklyn. Even the Force family's move across the bridge to Manhattan two years earlier could not make up for that fact, nor could Mrs. Katherine Talmage Force's Brooklyn social pedigree. Though the social difference might be overlooked, the age difference combined with Colonel Astor's messy divorce made Madeleine Force's ascendance to Mrs. Caroline Astor's position problematic. One function of society's leader was to help keep out "new money." The Force family was barely able to claim that otherwise undesirable title. There was no way a teenage girl from Brooklyn could have the background to serve as social dictator and gatekeeper to the established New York names that filled out the list of the Four Hundred. Madeleine had not even made her social debut. She was a mere poor girl in the eyes of society, and the gossip surrounding her relationship with John Jacob Astor was scandalous, unsettling, and soon would have the attention of the world!

* * *

The winter's season of debutantes and debuts began just after Thanksgiving in 1910. Katherine Force had come out the winter before, and this was Madeleine's season. By now she had been dating Colonel Astor for three months and was being discussed in society circles.

The Force sisters were what the *New York Times* called "Winter's Buds." They were young society women of an age that made them presentable for marriage. These young women would entertain at their own coming-out party with the help of that season's other "Winter's Buds." In exchange, that circle of young women would attend and assist with the debut functions of each of the other girls in the circle. Traditionally a formal function would be held at the young woman's home, with the home afterward opened to socially acceptable young bachelors of the circle invited for dancing.

Madeleine's debut season was noted for cotillions, weddings, and dances. Members of society hosted special receptions regardless of whether they had children of debut age. With the start of the 1910 winter season marked by heavy snow, the debut season's activities that year also included sleighing and sledding parties. With Christmas just two weeks away, many of the events were charitable in nature. Madeleine Force was noted at many of these activities.

"Winter's Buds Are Guests," read the *New York Times* headline describing the events that season. "With the approach of the Yuletide season social festivities are becoming more varied and increasing in number. All sorts of amusements are being planned for the holidays for the young folks, who, so far, have simply dominated the early Winter season," wrote the December 11, 1910, edition of the *Times*. "Last week was a most strenuous one, especially for the debutantes, and while the older folks were attending the opera, or giving small dinners, the younger ones were hurrying about in motors from one coming-out reception to another, and on two notable occasions during the week dancing the cotillion at Sherry's."

Immediately after that story in the society pages, the next story read "Col. John Jacob Astor and his son, Vincent, who returned last week after a six weeks' stay abroad, will make a cruise in the West Indies in the yacht Noma late this Winter."

* * *

Madeleine's debutante season began with the debut of Miss Katherine Shaw at Ms. Shaw's residence at 31 West Fifty-First Street. Madeleine Force was in attendance, as were Madeleine Olga Roosevelt (niece of President Theodore Roosevelt) and Julia Dick (sister to Madeleine's future second husband, William). There was a reception and dinner accompanied by the presence of several young, eligible men. A week later, Madeleine was a guest at the same sort of function for Miss Lydia Butler, which began with a tea in the afternoon followed by dinner for the receiving party. An equal number of young men were there for the informal dancing that followed the dinner.

The cycle would repeat itself for the next month, sometimes nightly, sometimes weekly. On December 3, 1910, Madeleine was a guest at the debut of Miss Henrietta Thaw, who was presented in the afternoon at her Fifth Avenue home, followed by dinner and then dancing with the invited young men. On the afternoon of December 12, Madeleine assisted in the receiving at the debut of Miss Margaret Mackay at the home of Mrs. Archibald Mackay on West Thirty-Ninth Street. On December 21, four days before Christmas, Madeleine and her sister, Katherine, attended a dance given at the Plaza for Miss Jeannette McAlpin. Under the Christmas decorations, there was dancing throughout the evening and a buffet dinner at midnight.

* * *

Madeleine Talmage Force made her debut into society on December 22, 1910, at her East Thirty-Seventh Street home in New York. The event was noted, as were the other society debuts, in the *New York Times*, the *New York Tribune*, and other newspapers.

"Miss Madeleine Force a Debutante" was the headline in the December 23, 1910, edition of the *New York Times*.

The event started with a reception at the Force home, where the seventeen-year-old Madeleine was presented. Madeleine was assisted in receiving by her mother, her sister, and the girls whom she helped receive at their own coming-out parties that season. Among the guests was Beryl Kane, a cousin to Colonel Astor.

By now Madeleine Force had been through two finishing schools, Miss Ely's in Greenwich and Miss Spence's in New York, where she was described as an especially brilliant pupil. Immediately after her debut, Madeleine was invited into the clique of debutantes known as the Junior League.

"When she was made a Christmas present to the exclusives of New York on December 22, 1910, she attracted but little attention," wrote the *Washington Times* several months later. "[S]he was a perfectly finished product. She danced well, conversed well, could take boot and saddle with the rest of them. Her ease and poise were remarkable, and because she did as well as anybody else, there was no cause for the critical society names to comment upon her.

"She has ridden some of the hardest mouthed jumpers that have ever 'topped timber' on the courses of the Riding and Driving and the Hamilton clubs of Brooklyn. Horsemanship, aviation or any one of a dozen out door sports, as well as the art of social chatter and how to sail triumphantly through a long society dinner, are alike open books to Madeline Talmage Force.

"And in her father's craft at the New York Yacht Club the dainty Miss Madeleine has often gone out into weather that made supposedly stouter hearts than hers remain on the flat and join the rocking-chair commodores.

"All of these accomplishments which look better on a background of turf or sea may make it appear that the 18-year-old girl has been something of a hoyden [tomboy], but those who tell about her out of door accomplishments just haven't gotten around to the cultured Miss Madeline.

"If she can swing a knee over a saddle leather just a bit better than most men are supposed to be able to do, she also has gained for herself a reputation for being mentally alert and a dangerous opponent with the sugar-coated barb of drawing-room repartee."

* * *

Though Madeleine and Colonel Astor's names had been unofficially linked since their first date in Bar Harbor, nothing was printed in the press about their relationship. Hints to Madeleine Force's growing social importance due to those rumors were in evidence.

In describing the fashions seen during the beginning of the debut season that winter in New York, the *Washington Post* listed Madeleine Force's name second. Until then, unless the story was about Bar Harbor tennis, Madeleine's name was generally found buried toward the bottom of a news story, if found at all.

"Miss Madeline Force wore a blue frock, with a silver lace top and flame-colored girdle, and as she is a blonde the effect was excellent," wrote the *Washington Post* on December 14.

* * *

The same night as Madeleine's debut, Colonel Astor was hosting a dinner at the elegant St. Regis Hotel. A week later, no longer considered a child in society's eyes but instead a woman of marriageable age, the seventeen-year-old Madeleine Force was officially his guest at the same popular hotel dining room.

"Col. John Jacob Astor entertained at dinner last evening at the St. Regis, having has his guests Mrs. William H. Force, Miss Force, E. M. Moore and Vincent Astor," reported the December 30, 1910, edition of the *New York Times*.

* * *

By now the fact that Colonel Astor and Madeleine Force were in some sort of relationship was an open secret among the members of society. They were seen together frequently in the Astor box at the Metropolitan Opera House, which was significant. The Metropolitan Opera was the unofficial clubhouse of New York society, with almost every notable name owning a box there. In the past, the tradition for opening night had been for Mrs. Caroline Astor to be in attendance, with Colonel Astor's first wife, Ava, as her guest. Now Colonel Astor sat in the same box, with young Madeleine Force in Ava Willing Astor's seat. Now the same people who trained their opera glasses on the Astor box every season for the acknowledgment from *The* Mrs. Astor that the season had begun saw instead saw a forty-six-year-old man and a seventeen-year-old girl. They saw scandal, and they saw insecurity for their society and all that it stood for, including its leisurely way of life, a life of elegance, of privilege. In Madeleine Force, they saw the unimportance of their institution.

Colonel Astor continued the Astor family tradition of the great Astor mansion ball at the beginning of each new year. The fact that Madeleine Force was in attendance seemed to reinforce the rumors that were circulating through society from her attendance at the opera.

The Astor ball held on February 6, 1911, was described by the *New York Times* as "one of the smartest dinner dances of the season at his town house." Colonel Astor invited 280 members of society, with an additional three hundred invited for dancing after dinner. Colonel Astor was seated at a long, narrow table in the center of the dining room. Mrs. Force, Madeleine, and Katherine were his guests. Vincent Astor was the host of the eight dining tables in the mansion's central hall.

The ball was described by the *New York Times* as the most decorative seen that winter in New York. An orchestra played music for dancing, which went on until well past midnight. Colonel Astor gave several gifts to his guests, including Chinese fans of white feathers for the women, walking sticks for the men, and electric flashlights for both.

* * *

Before Colonel Astor's arrival at the Bar Harbor Swimming Club in the summer of 1910, the names of the Force sisters had generally escaped the notice of the press. With their continued presence with John Jacob Astor, this situation was quickly changing.

Madeleine and Katherine Force were invited to participate in a society event held January 10, 1911. The event was a tableau, in which Madeleine and Katherine, along with twenty-one other people from society, impersonated heroes and heroines of poetry and other art. The event was held in the large ballroom at the Plaza in New York as a charity benefit for the Lincoln Hospital and Home in the Bronx. After the event, the ballroom was cleared for dancing. Madeleine and Katherine Force's parents were also in attendance.

Colonel Astor and Madeleine Force were being received by society to some extent, as seen by the dinner party and dance hosted by Mrs. Burke Roche on March 10, 1911. Held at the Hotel Gotham, the dance was for her sons, Francis and Maurice. Colonel Astor and the Force sisters were among the one hundred guests, predominantly of the younger set, who sat at twelve tables beautifully decorated with flowers. Mr. Roche was the great-grandfather of Diana, Princess of Wales, whose sensational, short life Madeleine's was starting to mirror. After this dinner, the Astor–Force relationship began to be talked about openly. By the end of the month, newspapers started printing the rumor.

"It is reported in social circles here that Colonel John Jacob Astor, who was divorced in 1909, is soon to marry Miss Madeline T. Force," reported a syndicated news story with the dateline in New York. "Miss Force is a popular society girl and has been seen much in the company of the millionaire recently." The story was accompanied by a side portrait of "Miss Madeline Force, Who May Become Bride of Colonel John Jacob Astor."

Another newspaper used the headline "ASTOR TO MARRY? Smart Set Interested."

"New York and London society is much interested in the report that Colonel John Jacob Astor is paying marked attention to Miss Madeline T. Force, a beautiful young woman well known in the metropolitan smart set. This bit of gossip seems to set at rest the constantly recurring rumor that there is to be a reconciliation between the Colonel and his first wife, who divorced him in 1909."

Madeleine Force, accompanied by her sister Katherine, again attended the Bal Masque, now held in a large private New York City studio that had once served as a stable. This year, rather than having her name buried in the extensive guest list, Madeleine Force's picture and name were part of the two-page story's headline: "Miss Madeline Force, the Next Mrs. John Jacob Astor, It Is Said, Who Went to the Ball as 'Folly.'" Together, Madeleine and Katherine Force, along with two other sister debutantes, were costumed as "The Follies of 1911."

The largely ignored Madeleine and Katherine Force now had the attention of society—and of the newspapers.

"The 'two graces,' that is what New York society calls the Misses Katherine and Madeleine Talmage Force, the two lovely daughters of Mr. and Mrs. William H. Force," wrote the *Rochester Catholic Journal* in its April 28, 1911, edition. "The younger of the two, Miss Madeline, has received so much attention from Col. John Jacob Astor that gossip hints at the probability of an engagement. . . . Should Miss Force, who is also 20 [actual age seventeen] years old, wed Mr. Astor, she will succeed to the leadership of New York society, which the Astor women have always held, and to the splendid Astor collection of jewels. Besides, she will be mistress of the Fifth Avenue mansion, the Newport villa and the splendid country house at Rhinebeck on the Hudson, where Mr. Astor built a half million-dollar gymnasium for his former wife. The Forces are interested in yachting and all forms of outdoor sport. Their home is at 31 E. 49th Street, NY. William H. Force, the father of the two beautiful girls, is a member of the New York Chamber of Commerce and is prominent in the business world. Their mother was Miss Katherine Talmage."

* * *

As the summer season of 1911 got under way in Bar Harbor, all society talk turned to the relationship of Colonel Astor and Madeleine Force. Bar Harbor's 1911 summer season was slow that year, in part because it was competing with the coronation of King George V and Queen Mary in England. The Jesup Library was dedicated and opened. An airplane had been brought in for a week to give residents a chance to purchase a sightseeing ride. Some summer colonists were threatening to leave the resort if a road for automobiles were to be built in Bar Harbor.

The Force family did not spend their summer season in Bar Harbor that year, instead staying in New York City. The family's absence, and the reason for it, caused more talk than if they had been there. For the people of Bar Harbor, there was special significance in whoever would serve as the next Mrs. Astor, for the name brought with it the role of society's leader. That person would have great influence over where the family spent their summer season. The thought of a new Mrs. Astor was earthshaking, and Bar Harbor knew its grasp on the actual name of Astor was always tenuous from season to season. Yet Madeleine had embraced Bar Harbor, whereas Ava used to visit for short periods every summer and had not been seen since her divorce.

* * *

On August 1, 1911, from his Front Street office in New York, with wife Katherine at his side, William H. Force made the official announcement of his daughter Madeleine's engagement to Colonel John Jacob Astor.

Nearly a year had gone by since the first date of Madeleine Force and John Jacob Astor, a year full of gossip and speculation. Mr. Force said he was making the announcement for the protection of his daughter's reputation. He said he had called Colonel Astor on the telephone the day before on Colonel Astor's arrival in New York from Newport. After that call, said Mr. Force, he decided it was time to make the formal announcement. His statement suggested conflict between Colonel Astor and Mr. Force on the issue of the announcement.

"The engagement has been rumored in social circles for several months. Therefore I insisted on making the formal announcement. I called Col. Astor on the telephone today and we discussed the matter. For reasons of his own he had not desired so early an announcement, but he accepted my point of view and it was agreed between us that I should make the announcement," said Madeleine's father.

Madeleine's mother spoke highly of her prospective son-in-law. She did clarify the timeline of the engagement, denying the rumor that the couple had been engaged for some time. "That is not so," Mrs. Force asserted. "The engagement dates back only a few days. My daughter and Col. Astor met at Bar Harbor last summer for the first time."

Mrs. Force said that her daughter would probably have as quiet a wedding as possible. She added that there had already been too much talk about the matter. Following the announcement, reporters soon descended on the Force home in New York City. Madeleine, who had just received a big box of flowers that lay on a chair in the front hall of the house, seemed in a pleasant state of excitement over the great diamond ring on her finger. She said it was true that she and Colonel Astor were engaged but that a date for the wedding had not yet been set. "It may be this fall, and it may be later," Madeleine told the gathering reporters.

Later in the day, Colonel Astor confirmed Mr. Force's announcement.

* * *

Though Mr. Force might have thought the official announcement of the engagement would have a calming effect on the rumors and talk of his daughter's reputation, instead he had taken the story from rumor to fact, which gave permission for criticism from all corners. There was still much public resentment over the secrecy involved in Colonel Astor's recent divorce from his first wife and the sense that he had received special treatment because of his family name and his wealth. There was also concern that remarriage for Colonel Astor would be considered illegal under the divorce laws of the State of New York. For a man in Colonel Astor's social position to be committing an act that could be considered illegal was unthinkable.

The condemnation was swift and sharp and took the form of both outright denouncements and small jabs. One of the first denunciations was quick and personal. It came from Miss Clara B. Spence, from whose private finishing school Madeleine had just graduated. Miss Spence wrote to the *New York Evening Post*, "Not only should we be indignant with the arranged marriage of a young girl with a 'notorious roue,' but the so-called leaders of society who, perfectly understanding the terms of the marriage, continue to send flowers and congratulations must share with parents the responsibility of encouraging a marriage which can lead only to unhappiness and scandal."

As a result of the engagement announcement, there was an immediate call for a change in divorce laws across the country. Soon committees in different state governments were meeting to discuss the subject. In the beginning of September, New York state senator Franklin Delano Roosevelt, whose cousin, Theodore, was an in-law to Colonel Astor, announced that he would introduce a resolution calling on the representatives of the New York State Congress to initiate action looking toward the enactment of a uniform federal divorce law.

From Las Vegas, Nevada, came news that citizens planned to establish a divorce colony there, which would be a fashionable colony such as Bar Harbor and Newport. Their desire was to cater to the wealthy families of society, such as the Astors, who were seeking divorces.

* * *

With the announcement of the engagement, it was time for Colonel Astor to formally introduce his fiancée to his level of society. This being August, that society would be found in their summer colony of Newport. This would be society's chance to meet the woman they had been gossiping about for the past year. Until the announcement, Madeleine Force being the replacement for Caroline Astor had just been a matter of speculation; now it was fact.

In early August, Colonel Astor, along with the Force family, left New York for Newport aboard the *Noma*, staying at Astor's Beechwood cottage. Mr. and Mrs. Force would spend some of their time there looking for a summer cottage of their own before Mr. Force returned to New York to resume business. Madeleine's mother and sister would stay in Newport with Madeleine.

"The eighteen-year-old girl, daughter of the senior member of a forwarding firm, whose family, although admitted to the best of Brooklyn society, never stepped through the sacred portals of wealth and culture until her meeting with Colonel Astor," wrote the *Washington Times* a few days into Madeleine Force's introduction to Newport. "When her engagement to Colonel Astor was announced, this 18-year-old girl was lifted from the comparative seculsion of the 'younger set' in New York society to the eminence of a girl whose future as a social leader is assured. In the full glare of publicity the women who now are the arbiters of New York society since the death of Colonel Astor's mother have scrutinized her.

"The society of Newport and New York will judge Miss Force along the strictest standards, it is said, and the record established by the mother of her future husband will be one of the last obstacles she must overcome. So the question is not so much, will she make good, as 'Can she become Mrs. Astor the second?' Madeleine Force's eighteen years of education and winsome girlhood may not lift her to the social eminence of women of greater experience."

Colonel Astor was asked by a reporter, "Will she make good?"

"That will be up to her," responded a smiling John Jacob Astor.

Before leaving for New York, while waiting to board the launch for his yacht, John and Madeleine were confronted by reporters. Colonel Astor said that he was very happy and there was nothing left to say.

* * *

The arrival of the Astor–Force party in Newport coincided with the start of the yacht races there, an especially popular time at the summer resort. Ruth Livingston Mills, cousin to Colonel Astor and a leader in the Newport summer colony, acted as Madeleine's unofficial social sponsor during the visit. Colonel Astor would arrange for a large reception at Beechwood for his fiancée and her family, though it never took place.

The first social event for Madeleine Force on the arm of her new fiancé was at a large dinner given by Ruth and her husband, Ogden Mills, on August 6, shortly after their arrival. The dinner was in honor of their titled daughter, Beatrice Forbes, Countess of Granard. Madeleine would meet two hundred leaders of society there. Another night they would be the guests of honor at a dinner hosted by Mr. and Mrs. Paulding Fosdick.

Over the first few days in Newport, Colonel Astor and Madeleine spent their time at the Newport Casino, known for its athletic facilities. There, the couple both played and watched tennis at the club. In a mixed tennis match, they would play against Astor cousin Miss Beryl Kane and Mr. Lawrence L. Gillespie. The latter pair won. Madeleine would wear a white linen suit and a large Panama hat for the outdoor tennis court and then a long white polo coat for socializing afterward. Colonel Astor and Madeleine continued their tennis playing at the Casino the day before the start of the yacht races. They were also hosted at a luncheon given in their honor by Mr. and Mrs. Charles F. Hoffman, Fifth Avenue neighbors of Colonel Astor. Mr. Hoffman's father was an Episcopal minister and rector of the All Angels Episcopal Church of New York. The Astors were also Episcopalians. That evening they were the guests of honor at a dinner hosted by Mr. and Mrs. William Starr Miller, also Fifth Avenue neighbors. The father of Mrs. Starr, Edith Caroline Warren, was a founder of the Metropolitan Opera.

The yacht races were a lively event. Colonel Astor entertained aboard his yacht, watching teams fight for the Astor Cup, which he traditionally provided to the winner. On board the *Noma* were Madeleine, her sister and parents, and Vincent Astor. The evening after the races, the colonel and Madeleine attended one of the most elaborate dinner dances that had taken place in Newport that summer, at the summer home of Mr. and Mrs. James and Arleigh Haggin. There were one hundred guests there. The reception room was treated with American Beauty roses, Madeleine's favorite flower.

* * *

The *New York Times* ran a file photograph of Colonel Astor's Newport cottage, Beechwood, "where Miss Madeleine Force and her parents have been entertained." The *New York Times* ran pictures, which were rare at the time, of Colonel Astor, Madeleine, her family, and the rest of the party arriving at the yacht club dock in Newport. Soon a formal, commissioned portrait of Madeleine was released to the newspapers, which appeared on the front page of publications across the world.

* * *

The invitations extended in Newport did not outweigh the criticism coming from churches across the country. Concern over the possibility of an immediate wedding seemed to prompt a stinging action by the Newport Minister's Union, which adopted a resolution two days after the official engagement announcement that none of its members should perform a marriage when one of the parties has been divorced. Though Colonel Astor was not mentioned by name, the resolution was passed just as John and Madeleine were arriving for her introduction to society there.

Many other churches across the country were not as polite as those in Newport, attacking Colonel Astor personally. The sermon of the Reverend Charles Chalmers Richmond, rector of St. John's Episcopal Church, located in the socially prominent Philadelphia, was particularly savage. In covering the story, the *Chicago Examiner* also went after Madeleine's mother:

"Can Mothers Sell Their Daughters for Money?"

"Is Discussed, the Question Raised by Astor–Madeleine Force Engagement."

The story reported on the denouncement of the engagement from church pulpits across the country, singling out that of Reverend Dr. Charles Chalmers Richmond, who said that because of the Astor–Force engagement, American maidenhood and motherhood were on the auction block. He compared Madeleine's mother to Simon Legree, whipping her daughters to the "Babylonian Marriage Mart."

"She is being sold! She is being sold," said Reverend Richmond. "White slavery is not now restricted to the limits of our great cities. The mothers of beautiful girls are in direct competition. The difference is in the terms, conditions and price, but not in the effect, so far as morality in the modern conception of ultra-social life is concerned.

"In the marketplace of fashion ambitious and designing women who have beautiful girls of marriageable age assemble their wares just as the Oriental huckster displays his rugs and gems, and with surpassing daring deck out these maids, of tender years so that their charms may be displayed—and sold.

"These young women are not given in marriage—they are sold into marital slavery.

"The world of fashion is a mere marriage mart like that of old Babylon, in which the most beautiful of our American girls are set on show.

"The sanctity of the Church is invaded by these social criminals, who call down, in fact, the wrath of God, while they pretend to seek His blessing.

"Honest love is barred by a well-trained door-keeper, and much-vaunted and much-decried society agrees with moral rot.

"The time has come when the law must interfere to protect the youth of the country."

The *Chicago Examiner* itself found the entire romance ridiculous. "This being the silly season, enter the satirical skit called the Astor–Force wedding!" wrote the *Examiner*. "And here is the entire public watching the performance, and most of them crying upon it."

However, the newspaper did criticize Mr. and Mrs. Force, as well as a hypocritical public: "Young cannot be expected to see clearly through a glittering rain. . . . And then, like the crystal gazer, she has looked so far into the white fire of her diamond engagement ring perhaps she has become self-hypnotized. With mamma and pappa pouring adulations into her ears, she moves in a kind of daze. . . . Sisters, of the thousands of you who are crying out, some of you are sincere, but there are more of you, any one of whom would split her hobble skirt in her wild race to the alter and Col. Astor—if he only asked you!"

* * *

In Madeleine's home city of Brooklyn, her engagement, which might have been seen as a success for a Brooklyn girl of the time, was instead criticized at the Roman Catholic Church of Our Lady of Lourdes by Reverend James F. Donahue, who said Mr. and Mrs. Force were using Madeleine as "a marketable commodity."

"Instead of teaching children to pray for the success of their future life, mothers place their children, and especially their daughters, in the market as the slave holders in the South sold their slaves to the one who gave the highest price. Our forefathers looked upon marriage as a sacred obligation and the father taught his son how to look forward in the path of righteousness. Today the mother puts her daughter forth as a marketable commodity. Today the young man is no longer found in the church pew with his father, but on the contrary the church is a torture to him and his best sermon is found in the yacht club, and every man of experience can give a synopsis of those yacht club sermons."

Not all criticisms were large; some were just small enough to give editorial writers a chance to hone their humor skills. "Miss Madeleine T. Force, Colonel Astor's bride-to-be, rejected a $400 gown and took one for $100," wrote the *Syracuse Herald* on August 16. "We thought '400' was her lucky number."

In Bar Harbor, the remarks felt personal. They mainly came in the form of editorials reprinted from other newspapers. In its August 9, 1911, edition, the *Bar Harbor Record* reprinted an item from the *Boston Globe*. "But Never A Bit Does Society Care," read the headline.

"The 18-year-old beauty who is to marry Colonel John Jacob Astor, now in his 48th year, has the comfort of knowing that only three correspondents were named in the complaint when the colonel was divorced—Boston Globe."

Two weeks later, the *Bar Harbor Record* reprinted an item from the Philadelphia press:

For it's off with the old love, and on with the new;
Divorces are easy and we all draw a few.
The Lady is "cute" and she's only eighteen.
But whether the new Force'll hold him is yet to be seen.

A week later, the *Record* reprinted another piece from the *Boston Globe*, this time bringing Colonel Astor's son and Madeleine Force's sister into the controversy: "If Col. Astor's son Vincent is to marry the sister of his father's fiancée, he will become his father's brother-in-law, and the complications of relationship in the third generation will be too appalling to predict."

* * *

Madeleine's father, William Force, returned to New York from Newport while the rest of his family stayed behind. A reporter for the *Meriden Morning Record* in Connecticut traveled to Mr. Force's office at 78 Front Street to ask about the accusations that he and his wife had "sold" their daughter.

William Force's desk was situated in the corner of the old-fashioned suite of offices, and he was visible to the reporter before the reporter's arrival had been announced. The reporter watched as William Force took his attention away from the papers on his desk, swinging his chair around and gazing out the window "in quiet reflection for several moments." The reporter watched as a clerk entered Mr. Force's office and presented the reporter's calling card.

"Turning quickly to his desk again, he delved into his papers again with busy activity," noted the reporter.

"Spare, clean-shaven, and with a determined jaw, Mr. Force looks like a solid business man, to whom the glories of social advancement would not particularly appeal. His face certainly did not beam with satisfaction, the expression being one akin to disgust."

The reporter described Mr. Force as being visibly annoyed by the attacks from the Episcopal Church. Through the clerk, he sent word that he was too busy to be interrupted. He said he had returned today from his Newport visit with his daughter and was so busily engaged with business that had accumulated during his absence that he could not spare the time to see anyone.

* * *

During the visit of Colonel Astor and Madeleine Force to Newport, the summer colony there had expected a wedding at any time. Instead, they received a cancellation of the further social obligations that had been made by the couple. Madeleine was not a full two weeks into her reception by the Newport summer colony when the announcement was made that she and Colonel Astor would have to withdraw from the events to which they had been invited. Colonel Astor announced that the strain of all the socialization had been too much for Madeleine. The attacks on the Force family at the same time that they were being introduced to society's elite were blamed.

Colonel Astor, Madeleine, and the Force family boarded the *Noma* and returned to New York, with Vincent Astor staying behind at Beechwood. Because notice had been given about the *Noma*'s expected movement from Newport to New York, a crowd of people, including a battery of news cameramen, was awaiting their arrival at the East Twenty-Third Street New York Yacht Club. Colonel Astor gave the crowd the slip, however. Instead of landing there, he sailed to a landing at the foot of East Twenty-Third Street, where an automobile was waiting. From there the party went to the Force residence on East Thirty-Seventh Street. Several hours later, word reached the crowd awaiting the *Noma* that the yacht had landed at another spot. The tired-looking crowd was disappointed, with some of them having been waiting since sunrise to get a glimpse of the couple.

The reporters and cameramen quickly headed from the wharf to the Force home in the city, and Colonel Astor appeared at the door. They asked about his future plans. To all inquiries, the colonel replied that he had nothing to say.

Though Madeleine was exhausted from the social rounds in Newport, she felt well enough to go out with Colonel Astor that afternoon to take luncheon at the St. Regis at a table decorated with orchids. She wore a blue gown and a black hat trimmed with blue.

* * *

Madeleine would not be seen out for the next three days. The *New York Times* ran a headline in the August 17 edition regarding her condition:

"Col. Astor's Fiancée Ill."

"Miss Force's Nerves Give Way Under Strain of Engagement Publicity."

"The condition of Miss Madeleine Talmage Force, the fiancée of Col. John Jacob Astor, who has been ill for the last day or so at the home of her parents, 37th Street, was said to be unchanged. It is said that her nerves have given away under the strain of publicity and the discussion which her engagement has aroused.

"Dr. Lewis A. Conner, a physician for the Astor family, is attending Miss Force. Col. Astor was an early caller at the home of his fiancée, and there were many messages of inquiry received during the day from Col. Astor's friends at Newport regarding her illness.

"The attending physician would make no statement regarding her condition, but it was said at the house that she was able to sit up and had done so several times during the day. Col. Astor himself is reported as saying that her indisposition was nothing serious, but a state of nervousness on account of the tremendous strain to which she has been subjected.

"For the last two weeks she has been entertained a great deal, especially at Newport, where she entered into the outdoor activities such as tennis with great vim and also attended many of the dances and dinners. Her last public appearance was last Tuesday, when she took luncheon with Col. Astor at the St. Regis."

* * *

Madeleine's recovery came at the same time that the newspapers announced that her dowry settlement had been reached. On Thursday, two days after her luncheon at the St. Regis, Madeleine was well enough to go out with Colonel Astor and do a little shopping. The following afternoon, she found herself at the Astor estate offices on Twenty-Sixth Street, just west of Broadway. She was accompanied by Colonel Astor and her father. It was rumored that the details of the dowry were settled that day and that Colonel Astor had settled $2 million cash on his fiancée. In actuality, it would be revealed years later that Madeleine Force had received two trusts from John Jacob Astor. The first, which was revokable on her remarriage or death, was worth approximately $1.5 million, not adjusted for inflation, the interest of which was hers to keep. The second trust belonged to Madeleine outright and could not be revoked. The value of that trust fund was $300,000.

When the trio emerged from the office, Colonel Astor was described by reporters as "in the 'love all the world' mood which had engrossed him all day," according to the August 18, 1911, edition of the *New York Evening World*. After leaving the office, they headed for the New York Yacht Club, where the *Noma* lay in wait at the pier, coaled, provisioned, and awaiting Colonel Astor's orders. Mrs. Force and Katherine would soon join them. A passing storm delayed their embarkation on the yacht for half an hour. The nose of the yacht was pointed toward Long Island Sound.

At 4:00 p.m., the party left the yacht club for their automobile for the trip to the pier. This gave reporters a chance to ask Colonel Astor questions. When he was asked whether he were to be married aboard the *Noma*, as was being rumored, Colonel Astor replied, "No, not just yet. Not for some time."

Colonel Astor refused to say where they were going but said that he would return the early part of the next week. His private secretary accompanied him.

"How long are you to be gone, Colonel?" asked an *Evening World* reporter.

"Don't know. Couldn't say really, you know. Miss Force hasn't been well. Doctor says she needs a change. We'll stay out until she's better. That's all. Until she's better."

Colonel Astor was asked about the trip that he, Madeleine, and the rest of the party was undertaking. He replied that they might go fishing, saying the trip was on the advice of Madeleine's physicians.

"Just to get away from everything and get a rest," said Colonel Astor. "Don't know yet where we shall go. Couldn't say, honestly."

"All this time Col. Astor was smiling affably, winking at times at Miss Force, but failing to get her to reciprocate his amiability," noted reporters.

By this time the party were seated in Colonel Astor's automobile. The chauffeur went around to the hood to crank it up. The automobile would not start. While the Force family, not used to reporters, was undergoing a very trying time with the news stories attacking them, John Jacob Astor was accustomed to engaging in familiar, yet casual, repartee with the necessary journalists who followed him everywhere even during ordinary times. Reporters noted that wrath was added to contempt on the facial features of the Force family.

"Are you going to be married?" Colonel Astor was asked while his chauffeur continued to try to start the car.

"Oh, my dear Colonel," gasped Mrs. Force, "this is really terrible. Tell your man to start at once."

* * *

At the pier, a small crowd of curious had assembled as the automobile arrived. As Madeleine walked to the pier to the awaiting yacht, she was leading a terrier. As she passed along the boardwalk, a mongrel ran along side of her. The vagabond dog looked as if it had not eaten for several days, and when Madeleine saw the dog, she stooped and petted it, exclaiming as she did, "Poor little doggie."

Having seen off Colonel Astor, Madeleine, and Mr. Force, Mrs. Force and Katherine headed on a separate trip, to Connecticut. There were many rumors regarding the destination of the *Noma*, one report being that the yacht would proceed to the high seas, where the marriage of the couple would take place in international waters, or to France. Another rumor had it that the party would travel to the Connecticut shore, where they would be joined by Mrs. Force and Katherine, and the marriage would take place in some small town in that state. Friends of Colonel Astor speculated that the yacht might be headed to the private Robins Island for a fishing excursion, where Mr. Force was a trustee and active member of the island's sportsmen's club.

Instead of escaping the public and the press, however, with true Astor misfortune, they found themselves in the middle of another news story.

The wind was strong and the sea stormy during the *Noma*'s voyage from New York. That night, while making her way through the rough seas, with Colonel Astor, Madeleine, and Mr. Force all retired for the evening, Captain Richard Roberts heard the faint cries of desperation off the *Noma*'s port bow. The yacht *Zingara* had been disabled in the passing storm. The five men of the yacht, all bank clerks from New York, were clinging to the wreckage, over which the sea was breaking. The *Zingara*'s flag was upside down in a signal of distress.

Captain Roberts slowed the *Noma*'s speed and turned on the searchlight, illuminating the scene just a short distance away. The *Noma*'s lifeboat was swung out and manned. Meanwhile, disturbed by the stopping of the engines and the scurrying of many feet, Colonel Astor dressed and ran on deck. Learning the facts, he summoned Madeleine and her father.

Madeleine arrived on deck wearing a heavy polo coat. She was on the bridge with Colonel Astor and her father in time to see the *Noma*'s lifeboat lowered and a volunteer crew sent off to the wrecked sloop.

"Hurry and save the men," cried Madeleine.

They watched the skillful maneuvering of the lifeboat as it came under the lee of the wreck, taking all the endangered men aboard.

"Beautiful, boys! Nobly done!" cried out Madeleine Force.

As the lifeboat returned to the *Noma*, Madeleine was the first to take hold of the ropes as Captain Roberts ordered the lifeboat brought aboard and, along with her fiancé and father, assisted in the hoisting of the rescue boat. As soon as the men were onboard, Madeleine poured them hot coffee and offered them sandwiches. She added a cheery word for each of the men as she served them.

Colonel Astor ordered that warm clothing be provided for the men and that all that could be done for them should be. Madeleine remained on deck for an hour and only went below again after saying goodnight to the rescued young men and thanking Captain Roberts and the *Noma*'s crew for their efforts. The men were landed back in New York the next morning. Again, Colonel Astor, Mr. Force, and Madeleine began their trip on the *Noma*, destination unknown.

Ironically, while she was standing on the bridge watching the rescue of the men, Madeleine exclaimed that she had many times heard and read of rescues at sea, but this was her first sight of such a thing and she would never forget it.

* * *

The newspapers' pursuit of the wedding story continued for the next three weeks. Every time the *Noma* sailed, they speculated that Colonel Astor and Madeleine Force were headed to one spot or another to get married.

The story heard in Fairfield, Connecticut, was that the Bridgeport Yacht Club had been notified that the *Noma* would be arriving there. The story that a wedding was imminent in Connecticut was given support by the arrival of Madeleine's mother and sister. Mrs. Force had gone to visit Mrs. Harry S. Glover, a cousin, in Fairfield. Katherine joined her mother after a brief visit to Sea Bright, New Jersey.

"The town of Fairfield was thrown into some excitement this afternoon over the rumor that Col. John Jacob Astor and his fiancée were due to arrive in the afternoon to get married at the home of Mrs. Harry S. Glover, where Mrs. Force and her daughter, Katherine Force, had been stopping for the past two or three days," reported the August 21, 1911, edition of the *New York Times*. "The Town Clerk of Fairfield said tonight that no application for a marriage license had been made by Col. Astor here, and that, so far as he knew, none was to be applied for."

No wedding would take place during that three-week period. The *Noma*, with Colonel Astor, Madeleine, and Mr. Force aboard, would spend time anchored off Robins Island. The party would take their meals on the yacht and spend time fishing and touring the game preserves of the island in a carriage. The *Noma* would return to New York on August 22, anchoring off the New York Yacht Club. Colonel Astor, Mr. Force, and Madeleine went directly to the Force residence, where Mrs. Force and Katherine awaited them. The following evening, Colonel Astor and Madeleine motored to Long Beach, New York, and dined at the Hotel Nassau, returning to the city later in the evening.

"The arrival of Col. Astor and his fiancée at the hotel caused quite a flutter among the guests, as it was unexpected," reported the *New York Times*. "Miss Force seemed in splendid spirits, and had a healthy tan on her face, and seemed much improved in health after the cruise, which was taken merely for her benefit. . . . As soon as John Astor arrived in town yesterday he was met with a bombardment of inquiries regarding the date of his coming marriage, and even while the party was fishing and bathing in Peconic Bay, it is said, he did not escape from the same question. But he was unwilling to make any comment on his approaching marriage. Instead, he said they had all had a splendid trip and had spent most of their time after entering Peconic Bay bathing and fishing."

* * *

A week after Madeleine's dowry had been arranged, the paperwork was signed by all parties. The now-antiquated tradition of the dowry was a strong Astor family tradition, as it was among many members of society at the time. The aim was to protect the family fortune by keeping it all together. To do so, any time someone married into the family, they were given either cash or a trust fund in lieu of any future claims on the family fortune. The intended bride generally owned the interest of the trust fund but lost the trust fund entirely on death or remarriage. The amount settled on a young lady was of importance to the curious members of society and could serve as a ranking. A similar settlement had been made for Colonel Astor's first wife.

"The marriage settlement made by the head of the house of Astor is always the last act before his marriage," wrote the *New York Times*. "The amount is known only to the principals and their representatives in the negotiations."

This signing of the dowry paperwork was the last act looked for by Colonel Astor and Madeleine Force before a wedding would take place. The wedding could be at any time now. First, however, would be Colonel Astor's trip with his son, Vincent, back to Boston, where Vincent would enter his junior year at Harvard. Colonel Astor assisted his son in finding living quarters there for the school year. On Colonel Astor's return to New York, the chase for the wedding story continued.

* * *

On arriving back in New York, fresh wedding rumors began circulating on September 2 when reporters saw Mrs. Force and her daughter Katherine leave the Force family home in a taxicab, along with a large amount of baggage. They were taken to the *Noma*. Shortly after their departure from the home, Colonel Astor arrived there in his automobile. He ignored the reporters' questions as he ran briskly up the steps and into the house. He reappeared a few minutes later, accompanied by his fiancée.

With Madeleine at his side, Colonel Astor was in good humor and had patience with the reporters' questions. A reporter asked him whether he was going away to be married. Colonel Astor's only answer was a hearty laugh.

"Will you be away over Labor Day?" the reporter asked.

"I really cannot say," replied Astor.

"Will you be married before you return to New York?" the reporter asked.

"I hope you boys will have a good time," was Colonel Astor's only answer, followed by further laughter. A moment later, he and Madeleine were speeding away from the Force home and arriving at the wharf.

The luggage taken from the Force home to the *Noma* consisted of two trunks, seven bags, and a number of small hand pieces. It was said that four men, friends of Colonel Astor, had boarded the yacht and were of the party that were to spend the Labor Day weekend at Ferncliff.

At his country home in Rhinebeck, Colonel Astor showed his fiancée and guests the estate, part of the tour being given in one of colonel's automobiles. The party motored to Poughkeepsie one afternoon, taking luncheon there. In their free time back at Ferncliff, the party swam or played tennis, taking advantage of the large, recently renovated private gymnasium and the athletic field, which was put in perfect condition for their arrival. Their only real disturbance during the visit was the blasting of rock by the New York Central Railroad for track improvements at one corner of the estate.

Colonel Astor and his fiancée did entertain over the weekend, having about a dozen friends as guests. Colonel Astor skipped his well-known custom of visiting Kingston Point Park in New York over the Labor Day weekend in his launch of the *Zyllaphone*, and yet everyone was so anxious to get a glimpse of the couple that a large crowd had formed there anyway.

* * *

Whether a wedding had been planned for the weekend at Ferncliff is unknown. Every day, the public awaited news of a ceremony, and every day resulted in disappointment. The Astors and the Force family returned to New York early the following week. Eventually, it was revealed that the marriage license was dated August 29, closer to the date of the formal signing of the dowry agreement. This timing might suggest that a wedding had been planned for the Labor Day weekend but an obstacle was encountered.

The sticking point now seemed to be finding a minister to perform the ceremony. There had been almost complete rejection of the engagement, and churches across the country banned their clergy from performing the ceremony. On September 7, after no wedding ceremony had materialized over the Labor Day weekend, the *New York Times* reported that Colonel Astor was offering $1,000 through an attorney to any minister who would marry him and his fiancée. Reports also said the offered fee eventually increased to $10,000 before an active clergyman could be found. The newspapers were soon filled with the stories of ministers who had been offered a grand sum and rejected it on principle.

The day before the actual ceremony, Reverend Edwin S. Straight of Providence, at one time a Free Baptist minister but now a carpenter, announced that he had been requested to perform the ceremony and had consented. The headline in the September 9 *New York Times* was "Carpenter to Marry Astors." Reverend Straight was interviewed by reporters but did not discuss the specific arrangements.

A former minister, it was reported, was not good enough for the Force family. It was reported that the couple insisted on being married by a clergyman who was in good standing and who was in charge of a parish. The level to which the marriage was accepted by society would depend largely on the legitimacy of the ceremony. The person performing the ceremony, along with the setting, was important. A simple city hall marriage would not suffice. Astor's Fifth Avenue home in New York could not be used for the ceremony because Astor's remarriage was illegal under the divorce laws of that state. The second choice would be Beechwood at Newport. The problem was the resolution adopted by the Newport Minister's Union forbidding any of their clergy from performing a wedding ceremony in which one of the parties had been married.

Ultimately, an active minister was found and the retired Reverend Straight's services were dismissed. After his dismissal, Reverend Straight talked to reporters, saying he had gone to Newport and stayed at a hotel there believing that he was to officiate at the wedding. Before he could leave for Beechwood, he said, he received word early in the morning that his services were not required. Reverend Straight said he felt hurt and humiliated and that "a thousand dollars would not compensate for the injury done" to his feelings.

Reverend Straight was asked whether Colonel Astor had still paid his expenses. "That is only what any gentleman would be expected to do," the reverend replied.

* * *

Reporters seldom left the outside of the Force home in New York City for the week after Labor Day. They watched as Colonel Astor made visits and Madeleine and Katherine shopped, bringing home boxes from some of the most fashionable shops in New York City. On one particular day, Colonel Astor arrived to find no one home. During his wait, Colonel Astor was seen to come out to the home's front stoop several times, gaze up and down the street, and then go back inside. Madeleine and Katherine arrived an hour and a half late. Colonel Astor greeted his fiancée enthusiastically. He called for a taxi, and soon he, Madeleine, and Katherine were heading down the street, with a squadron of taxicabs filled with reporters and photographers following them. Katherine was dropped off at the Grand Central Station subway station, and Colonel Astor and Madeleine continued to the St. Regis, where they had tea. Colonel Astor escorted Madeleine back home afterward.

Shortly after 8:00 p.m., he called again and took his fiancée out in a taxicab. They were gone for two hours. On their return, Colonel Astor stayed about twenty minutes. When he came out, he was asked what arrangements had been made for the wedding.

"As yet," he replied, "we have made no definite arrangements in regard to our marriage. In fact, matters stand just as they did yesterday."

Colonel Astor went to his town house at 840 Fifth Avenue, where it was said he would spend the night. The *Noma*, lying off Eightieth Street, had been coaling during the day and was taking on provisions until late into the evening. The captain and both mates later went ashore, indicating to reporters that the yacht would not be sailing immediately. It was rumored, however, that the intention was that the *Noma* would leave in the morning, with her prospective destination still unknown.

* * *

On September 9, reporters were again in pursuit of Colonel Astor and Madeleine after he picked her up at her home.

"Where are you going?" one reporter was so bold to ask.

"Follow me and find out," replied Colonel Astor good-naturedly.

The reporter and his colleagues followed the couple, ending up at the New York Yacht Club, where the *Noma* had been taking on coal. A fresh group of reporters was on hand to receive them. The reporters even helped open the doors of the cab and carry the luggage down to the float. Then the questions began.

"Have you been married?" asked one reporter.

"I have not," replied Colonel Astor.

"How silly," added Madeleine.

Colonel Astor and Madeleine went aboard the *Noma*, but the ship did not immediately leave. Instead, they waited for Mr. Force.

The loss of privacy and the constant insulting of his family seemed to have gotten to William H. Force. He had lived in the relative anonymity of Brooklyn society before his daughter met Colonel Astor. Now Mr. Force's name and those of his wife and two daughters were on the front page daily, and he and his wife were being accused of selling their child. The constant encampment of reporters and photographers outside of his home the past few days waiting for the wedding story was too much. The morning before, Mr. Force had left the family house to go for his morning walk. Immediately the photographers started following him. Mr. Force noticed the photographers maneuvering to take his picture, turned around, and made a gesture indicating that he would not be photographed. One man continued to pursue Mr. Force but stopped when Mr. Force raised his cane and rushed at him. The photographer fled, with Mr. Force pursuing, shaking his cane and declaring loudly that he would have the photographer arrested.

The photographer had no trouble in keeping ahead of the irate fifty-nine-year-old William Force, who, it would turn out, was in the last six years of his life. Suddenly the photographer turned, halted an instant, got a good snapshot of the angry William Force, raised cane and all, and then ran off. Mr. Force, disgusted, walked back home. There were no arrests.

When arriving at the wharf to join his family the following day, Mr. Force was accompanied by a bodyguard, who was described by reporters as "burly."

"This man escorted him down on to the float and shielded him from the eager cameras," said one of the reporters there.

* * *

The Astor party—Colonel Astor, his fiancée, her sister, and her father—arrived at Beechwood in Newport aboard the *Noma*, from New York, early in the morning of September 10, 1911. Vincent joined the party at 8:00 a.m. for breakfast aboard his father's yacht, and Madeleine's mother joined them onshore later.

In the way that fate had a way of turning the Astors' life fortunes into misfortune, this was also true on the wedding day. After breakfast aboard the yacht, the wedding party was prepared to leave the *Noma* for the ceremony at Beechwood. Madeleine was dressed in a semi-hobble skirt of blue cloth, with a peach basket hat to match. Her sister, Katherine, wore a steel gray dress and a black picture hat. Colonel Astor wore a dark sack coat suit, straw hat, and carried a cane.

Instead of leaving the yacht, however, the wedding party was met by the Newport sheriff, Frank P. King, who had boarded the *Noma* with a writ of summons in a suit brought against Colonel Astor by two women whose brother had been killed at Beechwood the previous summer while repairing telephone lines in the cellar. The family was suing for a financial settlement for damages. The sheriff was asked whether Captain Roberts or Colonel Astor's attorney (who was present) could receive the legal document, but the sheriff said he had to deliver it personally. He was escorted to the personal quarters of the yacht and delivered the paperwork to Colonel Astor.

For most brides, such an event would have ruined the day, but with all that John and Madeleine had gone through over the past year, this was but a small inconvenience. Once the unpleasantness of serving the papers was behind them, the yacht's motor launch was brought to the gangway. With Colonel Astor at the wheel, the wedding party was carried ashore quickly. On landing at Newport's Wellington Street pier, automobiles carried them to Beechwood, where they were met by Mrs. Force and other witnesses for the ceremony. Mrs. Force wore a black empire gown of crepe de chine with a string of pearls around her neck.

* * *

Beechwood's grand white and gold ballroom was filled with American Beauty roses, Madeleine's favorite (as well as the favorite of Colonel Astor's mother). This was the sole flower of the ceremony's floral decorations. The ballroom's windows offered a backdrop of a choppy sea blowing the gathering gray rain clouds into shore. As the wedding couple met in front of the ballroom's beautiful white marble fireplace, Colonel Astor almost jumped to take Madeleine's hand. Clasping hands, they turned to face the minister, who stood on a red rug underneath a great cut-glass chandelier.

Madeleine Astor was described as appearing radiant with happiness. Colonel Astor was described as having recovered from a nervousness he had exhibited earlier in the day, appearing calm and self-possessed. According to the *Syracuse Herald*, the wedding scene impressed the witnesses with the belief that Colonel Astor and Madeleine Force were devoted to each other.

The ceremony was short. Katherine Force was the maid of honor, Vincent Astor the best man. Mr. Force gave his daughter in marriage. Mrs. Force stood near her husband and the bridal couple, while around them were Astor's attorney; Astor's personal secretary, William Dobbyn; and Thomas Hade, the superintendent of Beechwood, who had served both Colonel Astor and his parents there for many years. As Colonel Astor slipped the ring on Madeleine's finger, he reportedly lost his composure, slipping his arm about her girlish figure, clasping her tightly, and kissing her.

After the ceremony, Madeleine was given a kiss by her parents and sister, and the couple received the congratulations of their guests. Colonel Astor then led the party to the dining room, where a hasty wedding brunch was served and toasts to the newlyweds given. Madeleine took an American Beauty rose for her corsage on her way out of the ballroom.

Colonel Astor's son, Vincent, was reported to be extremely happy during and after the wedding. He gave the newlyweds the heartiest congratulations after the ceremony and again later when bidding them goodbye. After the newlyweds left Beechwood, Vincent would take Mr. and Mrs. Force to a local Newport hotel for luncheon before leaving for New York.

After the hastily arranged wedding brunch, the handful of guests stood at the doorway and bade John and Madeleine goodbye as they walked down the hall of Beechwood and out the door to start their new life together as Mr. and Mrs. John Jacob Astor IV. Because of the suddenness of the ceremony, the Astor chauffeur was not available to take the newlyweds back to the *Noma*. Instead, one of the reporters following the story lent them his taxicab.

The newlyweds made their way back to the pier, where Colonel Astor took the helm of his awaiting motor launch. At anchor, the *Noma* looked spic and span from the efforts of her officers and crew to have the craft in sharp form, as called for by the occasion. Arriving on the *Noma*, John and Madeleine Astor were greeted by Captain Roberts and his officers as they came aboard. The honeymoon cabins were decorated with more American Beauty roses sent from Beechwood's greenhouses.

After the ceremony, in an attempt to defend himself and his wife and to put the entire matter behind them, Madeleine's father made the following statement: "In this marriage only the happiness of my daughter was considered. She and Colonel Astor are and have been very much in love. If they were not in love this marriage would not have occurred."

Before leaving Beechwood, the newly remarried Colonel Astor gave a statement of his own: "Now that we are happily married, I don't care how difficult divorce and remarriage laws are made. I sympathize heartily with the most straightlaced people in most of their ideas, but believe remarriage should be possible once, as marriage is the happiest condition for the individual and the community."

The *Noma* weighed anchor at 10:20 a.m. and headed westward, running at fast speed; reporters assumed it was going to Astor's country home, Rhinebeck on the Hudson in New York, or perhaps his residence in New York City. As the *Noma* sailed out of harbor and down the bay, her wireless operator was kept busy receiving and responding to numerous messages of congratulations flashed through the air by friends and family of the newlyweds.

* * *

The day before the wedding, Ava Astor's brother John received a letter from his sister in England, in which she protested violently against all the "noise" raised over the prospective second marriage of her ex-husband.

"I have absolutely no feeling in the matter, but I do wish he would get married if he is going to and drop out of the public prints. Every time his name appears somebody is sure to speak of me, and as I and Mr. Astor have nothing in common, I am sick and tired of it," wrote Ava Astor to her brother. "It seems a shame that Mr. Astor cannot be married without all this trouble. If he has found a woman willing to have him, I see no reason why he should not marry her."

Chapter 4

No Friendly Glance

The hostility of this dazzling company was evident. Mrs. Astor, scarce out of her teens, faced it with perfect composure. Neither her beauty nor her youth pleaded successfully for her. No friendly glance came their way.

—Astor trustee Joseph Choate on encountering the newlywed Astors at the Metropolitan Opera in the winter of 1911

Leaving Newport aboard the *Noma*, rumor had it that Colonel and Mrs. Astor were headed to Bermuda on a cruise for their honeymoon. Despite all efforts to track the *Noma*'s movements through stations along the East River, there was no record of her movement.

Instead, the *Noma* had anchored off the New York Yacht Club station at Twenty-Sixth Street. John and Madeleine Astor came ashore and entered an automobile that had been waiting for several hours. They were taken to the St. Regis, where a suite of rooms was always kept in readiness for Colonel Astor.

One of John and Madeleine's first acts as a married couple was to walk from the St. Regis down Fifth Avenue to the home of the Madeleine's parents on Thirty-Seventh Street, visiting for about an hour. The following morning, the couple was visited by Astor's secretary, William Dobbyn, who had with him scores of congratulatory telegrams from family and friends of Colonel Astor throughout the country and from

Europe. The newlyweds devoted some time to reading them. The *New York Sun* ran a story that day featuring the profile pose of "Women Well-Known in New York." The first of the seven pictures was Madeleine Astor.

The couple did spend time aboard the yacht while staying at the St. Regis, going for small cruises. There was speculation over where the actual honeymoon would be. Some thought Newport, some thought Ferncliff, and others said Europe aboard the *Noma*, which had recently been overhauled at a Brooklyn shipyard.

The Astors headed to Bermuda for the first part of their planned honeymoon. On the trip Madeleine became seasick and the yacht stopped at Norfolk, Virginia, where the couple abandoned the yacht for a railroad car home. They would return to the Astors' New York country estate, Ferncliff, paying several visits to the city for shopping, theater, and other social activities.

* * *

John and Madeleine Astor remained at Ferncliff through fall, avoiding the autumn season's social activities. Even though they remained in self-imposed semi-seclusion, the Astors continued to be criticized, now through the minister who had performed their wedding ceremony.

A week after uniting John Astor and Madeleine Force in marriage, Reverend Joseph Lambert was censured by the Congregational Ministers' Union of Chicago at its weekly meeting. The union decried the actions of Reverend Lambert as being an "affront to decency and the sanctity of the marriage relation." Shortly after the wedding, the Association of Congregational Ministers of Massachusetts denounced the marriage and urged uniform divorce laws for every state. In Philadelphia, Reverend Richmond of the St. John's Episcopal Church continued his attack on the Astor marriage: "One minister has at last been bought to do the nasty job. He was offered his price. Worse than Judas, he has taken his thirty pieces of silver and in a few weeks I hope instead of being driven by his own conscience of which he is lacking he will be driven from his sacred office and set to tending an Astor garage or cleaning out an Astor stable."

Ultimately, Reverend Lambert quit his position with the Elmwood Temple Church in Providence because of protests against his action. He was already due to leave on December 1 and go into private business, the nature of which he did not disclose.

"There have been a lot of unkind things said against me especially by ministers of this city. I did not feel that I could continue in the work as I could not put the same spirit into it as before," said Reverend Lambert, who had been serving at the church for a year. "The worst thing ministers can say against me is that I married a man who had been divorced for committing a statutory offence. It was simply his money which called attention to the marriage and if it had been a poor man nothing would have been said."

* * *

For a brief period, all that was talked about was Colonel John Jacob and Madeleine Astor. As fall proceeded into early winter, however, that talk appeared to die down. For a while the Astors seemed to drop off the map. Their strategy of lying low in upstate New York seemed to be helping, as was the lack of invitations to the fall social functions in the city. The damage had been done. Wrote the *Canton* (Ohio) *Commercial Advertiser*, "Now that he is married to the young woman of his choice, Col. John Jacob Astor, who occupied the centre of the stage for several months is being left severely alone by the sensational periodicals and newspapers, which made his life uneasy, following the announcement of his engagement. . . . The present silence of the venders of sensational society gossip emphasizes the old truism 'if you want to be left alone, get married.' No longer do photographers dog the footsteps of the couple, newspaper writers fill long columns on their trivial doings or ministers denounce them from the pulpit. Now they come and go like anybody else and excite no more interest than if they were the most ordinary of proletariats. To the Colonel and his bride it is a big relief and they are wondering now why they didn't save themselves much of the unpleasant notoriety heaped upon them, by getting married sooner. But for the daily commentary on their engagement and its propriety in which everybody who had nothing better to do took a hand, they probably would not have been married until this winter.

"What they are doing now, few know and fewer seem to care."

* * *

One matter that consumed Colonel Astor's time immediately after his marriage to Madeleine was his son's reckless behavior with automobiles. With all the negative headlines of the previous year, additional newspaper stories concerning Vincent's automobile accidents were unwelcome to the newly married couple.

There had been a problem with Vincent since his parents' divorce. In 1910, the first year after the divorce, as Colonel Astor was preparing to sail to Bar Harbor to avoid the presence of his ex-wife in Newport, Vincent had an accident involving the Bavarian royal family. On the morning of Saturday, August 20, Duke Franz Josef of Bavaria and a US congressman and his wife were all out for a summer morning's ride along Newport's Bailey's Beach. They had started to turn into the roadway leading to the residence of Mr. and Mrs. Nathaniel Thayer when along came Vincent Astor in his own automobile. Vincent did not see the duke's car until he was very close to it. Vincent tried to shut off the power to his automobile and applied the emergency brakes, which lessened the force of the impact. However, the Astor automobile struck the duke's car in the center, smashing the door and other parts and almost turning the car over.

The duke and his shaken guests huddled together beside the road after the accident. They were so frightened that their cries could be heard some distance away. Servants, passersby, and others rushed to their assistance. An "automobile ambulance" was called for, which took the badly damaged vehicle of the duke to a mechanic for repair. Vincent Astor apologized to Duke Josef and his party, offering every assistance possible. Efforts were made to keep the accident a secret, but the story quickly leaked to the press.

Immediately after the wedding, Colonel Astor and Madeleine, along with Vincent, stayed at Ferncliff in Rhinebeck, New York. Vincent was awaiting his return to Harvard. In late September 1911, just a few weeks after the wedding, Vincent was reported to police by a member of the summer colony of Newport for careless automobile driving. Vincent was summoned to police headquarters, where he was lectured on automobile laws and rules and was told what might happen if the careless driving did not cease. Vincent Astor departed the police station with a promise that he would give no further trouble on the road. "Today Mr. Astor was driving his racing machine very carefully," reported the *New York Times*.

Just a few weeks after making that promise, Vincent would be involved in another serious automobile accident. This time Vincent, though accompanied by his chauffeur, was driving a seven-passenger Oldsmobile, headed home from the Dutchess County Fair at Poughkeepsie. Charles E. Palmer, an inspector for the New York Telephone Company, was turning a corner on a motorcycle when he was hit by Vincent's automobile. Mr. Palmer was thrown from his motorcycle and suffered several bruises, broken ribs, and a broken leg. The motorcycle was destroyed. Vincent's car, after hitting the motorcycle, then bumped into a tree and was slightly damaged. Mr. Palmer said the accident was not Vincent's fault and that neither of them had time to turn and avoid the collision. Vincent paid for Mr. Palmer's carriage ride home, for his physician, for the loss of his motorcycle, and for his time.

* * *

Vincent was not the only member of the Astor family who was making headlines because of the new invention of the automobile. The *New York Times* noted on September 14, 1911, just a few days after Madeleine's wedding, that her mother was in an automobile that was pulled over for speeding, doing forty miles per hour along the Eastern Boulevard in the Bronx. Mrs. Force was described as being surprised when the automobile was pulled over by a police officer. She told the officer she was on her way to see her daughter at the Westchester Country Club and that the car belonged to Colonel Astor, but the name dropping did her no good. The officer told Mrs. Force that the law was the law and he was going to do his duty. He issued a summons to Mrs. Force's chauffeur, William Schappe, to appear in Westchester Court, where he was assessed a $10 fine.

* * *

With Colonel Astor and Madeleine lying low at Ferncliff, making fewer headlines since the wedding, the newspaper reporters were looking for stories about the family to fill the void. In October it was rumored that Vincent was engaged to a Miss Margaret Andrews, who reportedly had been in Vincent's company the previous year, but not more than any other girl.

"The child is only 16 years old, and you can't make the denial too strong," said the girl's father, Paul Andrews.

Vincent Astor talked that fall to reporters who had printed stories of his engagement to at least three young ladies during the summer season. He would deny rumors that he was engaged to Miss Ina Clair, a popular Broadway musical comedy star.

"Nothing to it," Vincent told reporters. "Miss Claire and myself are just good friends. I have met her several times, but as for any lingering attachment and that sort of mush, why, it is absolutely unfounded. I do hope the party writing such stories will stop, as there is absolutely no truth in these reports. Just at present I am thinking very much of entering Harvard."

* * *

As fall turned into early winter, the summer colonists of Bar Harbor and Newport returned to New York, where society would look forward to grand entertaining immediately before and after the holidays. After their period of autumn seclusion, John Jacob and Madeleine Astor signaled their intentions to resume their social presence in New York when they sent out invitations to the annual Astor ball, traditionally held shortly after the New Year holiday. The Four Hundred was about to be defined by Colonel Astor and his new eighteen-year-old bride.

Shortly after it had been announced, however, the Astor ball was canceled. Along with the announcement of the cancellation came the news that Colonel and Mrs. Astor would instead be sailing to Europe for a formal honeymoon.

The Astors had been snubbed since the time of the engagement announcement and through the fall after their wedding. Even with the legitimacy of marriage in their favor, they continued to be snubbed, now at the unofficial clubhouse of society, the Metropolitan Opera, after attending the 1911 season premiere on December 22. It had been the appearance there the previous season of Colonel Astor and Madeleine, with Madeleine sitting in his first wife's seat, that fed the rumors of their relationship. As a married couple in 1911, Colonel Astor and Madeleine would again attend the start of the winter season. With all the opera glasses in the grand auditorium trained again on the Astor box in the Golden Horseshoe, what people saw was a box that contained only Colonel Astor, Madeleine, and her sister, Katherine. No one stopped at the famed box seats to visit, as had been tradition when *The* Mrs. Astor ruled the Met.

Joseph H. Choate was an Astor lawyer and former ambassador to England. He had seen the Astors, along with Madeleine's sister, Katherine, at the opera that season. Colonel Astor invited him to the Astor private box.

"It was an open secret that New York had not looked favorably on the remarriage," said Choate. "The hostility of this dazzling company was evident. Mrs. Astor, scarce out of her teens, faced it with perfect composure. Neither her beauty nor her youth pleaded successfully for her. No friendly glance came their way. I talked with her for five interesting minutes and came away with an impression of intelligence, of charm also, and character."

Choate said that the Astors' appearance at the Met, along with the grand ball planned for the Astor mansion, was part of their planned return to society. "But New York declined to be conciliated by these good intentions," said Choate. "It became clear that time must pass before Col. Astor could expect to find himself surrounded by friends, as of old."

This change in the Astors' plans was fuel to the fire of the Astor–Force story. The news was intriguing back in Bar Harbor, where the story was discussed by the *Bar Harbor Record*.

"This question generally asked in the ultra society circles of New York yesterday elicited two answers, the first of which was that Mrs. Astor was tired out in maintaining her position as the bride of one of the foremost leaders of society, despite the fact that she is a splendid athlete, her diversion being tennis playing," wrote the *Bar Harbor Record*. "The second answer was that the charmed circle had not extended the warmest hand of greeting to her. The much talked of dance was planned by Col. Astor to launch his bride into the social season, and was one of the first events which the colonel had in mind for her entertaining during the winter. But now he has suddenly cancelled the affair. . . . While the season's round of social gaieties has been underway for several weeks, the Astors have taken but little part in them."

In making the announcement of the cancellation of the Astor ball, the Astors also said they would be sailing for Europe on January 24, just a few weeks later. Their plan, they said, was to spend a few days in London and Paris and then take a trip up the Nile, after which they would remain for several weeks on the continent of Europe, returning to the United States early in the spring. Colonel Astor reportedly was having a special steamship outfitted for him and Madeleine to travel up the Nile with a party of eleven.

John and Madeleine Astor would spend their last night before sailing as guests at the home of Colonel Astor's sister, Caroline Astor Wilson. The large dinner party was held at the Wilson residence, 3 East Sixty-Fourth Street, one of the largest residences in New York. The blue and gold dining room was simply decorated for the sixty invited dinner guests. Guests included John and Madeleine, along with Ruth Livingston Mills (the Astor cousin who had sponsored Madeleine in Newport) and Mr. and Mrs. Cornelius Vanderbilt (in-laws of Caroline Astor Wilson). A singer performed selections in the Wilson ballroom after dinner, before the Wilsons' guests traveled to a ball being held by a neighboring ambassador.

* * *

At the New York pier the following morning, preparing to embark on *Titanic*'s sister ship *Olympic*, John and Madeleine Astor braved chilly morning winds at the White Star dock. Mrs. Force was there to see them off, bidding her daughter "bon voyage." Another person to see the Astors off was Count Alfred Montgelas of Berlin, who made a habit of seeing people off at the pier, generally parties with young women in them. After Mrs. Force said goodbye to her daughter, Count Montgelas, with courtly ceremony, kissed Madeleine's gloved hand and then went ashore. Hardly had he arrived there than he remembered another word of parting. He darted back on the pier, said his words, kissed Madeleine's gloved hand one more time, and then again headed to shore.

Madeleine Astor was described by reporters as the picture of health as she embarked on the *Olympic*. A reporter was able to briefly interview Colonel Astor before he entered his suite, asking about his opinion of New York society after all he had been through to marry Madeleine.

"My boy, don't ask me what I think of New York society because it would pain me to tell you my exact feelings," reported the *Auburn Democrat-Argus*. "I am thoroughly disgusted with it. I am going to Egypt."

Soon the Astors were gone from the United States, and by February 11 Colonel Astor and Madeleine, along with their staff, had left Paris for Egypt, where they spent several weeks, including the Nile trip. On March 28, they arrived in Naples, Italy. Ten days later, the *New York Sun* would run a small piece about the plans for the Astors' return to the United States.

"Col. and Mrs. John Jacob Astor . . . will be passengers on the first trip of the *Titanic*, which sails from Southampton next Wednesday. Col. and Mrs. Astor will go to their country place in Rhinebeck, NY, soon after their arrival here and they will pass the greater part of the summer in Newport."

* * *

By the time of the announcement of their return travel plans, a rumor about Madeleine's pregnancy was already circulating.

"Astors Expect Stork," was the headline in the *Syracuse Herald* on February 22, 1912. "Due in July, According to Report Heard in NY."

"Society circles here have heard that the stork was expected to make a visit in July to Col. John Jacob Astor and his bride, who was Miss Madeleine Force of New York.

"Col and Mrs. Astor are in Egypt on a honeymoon tour, following their wedding September 10 of last year.

"The servants at the Astor place here have received orders to close up the big 'cottage' at this city [Newport] and go to New York to make the Fifth Avenue mansion ready for the return of their master and mistress, who will come home late in May."

* * *

Having faced harsh personal criticism and social rejection, and with the rumor that she was five months pregnant, Madeleine Force Astor arrived in Cherbourg, France, to board *Titanic*, to take her back to another year of personal attacks, splashy headlines, and large crowds watching her every move. Although the Astors may have hoped their wedding scandal had died down, Madeleine must have known her pregnancy would only inflame the story.

Madeleine Astor's arrival aboard the *Titanic* was described by first-class stewardess Violet Jessop: "We felt the thrill that the unknown always gives, when we screened that list and found world-famous names but, as yet to us, merely names. We speculated if their owners would tally with our conception of them. So it was not surprising when John Jacob Astor brought his bride of a year on board, about whom there had been so much publicity. Instead of the radiant woman of my imagination, one who had succeeded in overcoming much opposition and marrying the man she wanted, I saw a quiet, pale, sad-faced, in fact dull young woman arrive listlessly on the arm of her husband, apparently indifferent to everything about her. It struck me for the first time that all the money in the world did not make for inward contentment."

Chapter 5
Tragic Sights

One of the tragic sights to see was the beautiful Mrs. John Jacob Astor, whose marriage a short time ago was so widely discussed. Her first question when she came on the pier was "Have the others got in yet?" Her sister and Mrs. Astor's son, Vincent Astor, led her to the waiting limousine with murmured words of comfort. The courageous acts of her husband as reported in the press must be a solace in her days of anguish.

—Eva Shorey, Maine reporter sent to New York to cover *Carpathia*'s arrival

News of *Titanic*'s launching on her maiden voyage was the second story on the front page of the *New York Times* on April 10, 1912: "The Titanic Sails To-Day."

The movements of the Astors were also noted by the newspaper deeper in the same issue: "Col. and Mrs. John Jacob Astor are sailing to-day on the Titanic from Southampton, and will go to Rhinebeck upon their arrival there. They plan to spend the summer at Newport."

The following day, the launch of the *Titanic* was the lead story in the *Times*, including its near collision with another ship while leaving port in England: "TITANIC IN PERIL ON LEAVING PORT." The story told how the departure from port of *Titanic*, because of her large size, caused enough suction to break the lines of the *New York*, a steamship tied up at dock. The *New York* began drifting helplessly, stern first, toward the *Titanic*, and a collision looked imminent. Tugboats were able to get ropes on the *New York* and take control of her just before a crash could occur. With the *New York* again under control, the master of the port ordered the *Titanic* to take to the seas.

The near collision at *Titanic*'s launch brought back recent memories of an actual collision that *Titanic*'s captain had been in just seven months previously while master of *Titanic*'s sister ship *Olympic*. A smaller ship, the *Hawke*, had been passing the liner and was suddenly sucked into the *Olympic*. The theory was that the large size of the *Olympic* had drawn the *Hawke* into her by the undercurrent caused by the liner's powerful propellers. Blame was determined to be that of Captain Smith.

The accident with the *Olympic* had not diminished Captain Edward J. Smith's following among the famous first-class passengers who were now on *Titanic*. In a time when steamships were the only way to cross the ocean, Colonel Astor and many of his social colleagues would only travel aboard the ships of a specific captain. For many of *Titanic*'s passengers, including Colonel Astor, Edward Smith was that captain. This unofficial system afforded special favors for the passengers, who would spend their weeklong travel with a captain and crew who knew their likes and dislikes and who would cater to their every need.

There were 2,224 people aboard *Titanic* for her maiden voyage, 324 of whom were first-class passengers. Mr. and Mrs. Astor, along with his valet, Victor Robbins, and her maid, Rosalie Bidois, and her nurse, Caroline Louise Endres, joined *Titanic* at Cherbourg, France. On April 14, 1912, four days into the voyage, the *Titanic* struck an iceberg at 11:40 p.m. The ship was over six hundred miles away from New York City or any other land. Less than three hours later, at 2:20 a.m., *Titanic* sank and 1,500 people lost their lives in a most horrific manner.

From the time of the ship's collision until just before the sinking, the *Titanic*'s wireless had been sending messages of distress and calls for assistance. Though the range of wireless could be limited, some places (such as New York City) were hearing the calls as they were being made. By the time the *New York Times* put that day's edition together, only part of the story was known, and not the worst part.

"New Liner Titanic Hits an Iceberg; Sinking by the Bow at Midnight; Women Out Off in Lifeboats; Last Wireless at 12:27 a.m. Blurred," read the headline in Monday's *New York Times*.

With the assistance of hindsight, the headline seemed to tell the whole story. The *Titanic* hit the iceberg, it was sinking, women were being put off the ship, and there was no further news from *Titanic*—because the ship had sunk while in the process of unloading passengers. Though the sinking may have been suspected by reporters back in the United States, no one could say so with certainty.

Still, there were elements of the story that were reassuring and would bring heartbreaking false hope in the days following the sinking, the last comfort some of the survivors would ever know. According to newspaper headlines, several ships had responded to *Titanic*'s distress calls and were on their way to the scene of the collision, including the *Virginian*, the *Baltic*, and *Titanic*'s sister ship *Olympic*. The captain of the *Virginian* informed *Titanic* that he was 170 miles away and expected to reach her site at 10:00 a.m. on Monday morning, which ultimately would be eight hours too late.

As the distress call was heard (or heard about), many other ships in the North Atlantic changed course and headed to *Titanic*'s assistance. *Titanic*'s sister ship (and Captain Smith's former command) the *Olympic* had been in communication with *Titanic* and was making "all haste" toward her, but because of her distance from *Titanic*, she could not arrive until the following day. The steamship *Baltic* also reported herself being around two hundred miles east of the *Titanic* and making all possible steam toward her position. She would arrive around the same time as the *Virginian*. Like the *Virginian* and every ship other than *Carpathia*, those on the *Baltic* wired back to New York that they had arrived too late to be of any help.

The story in newspapers early Monday was that several ships were on their way to the injured ship. By the time the evening newspapers were out, the headlines were even more reassuring. "Titanic's Passengers Are All Safe/Steamship Being Towed to Halifax," read the Monday evening edition of the *Portland Evening Express*.

Those relying on newspaper coverage (which was most of the general public) went to bed Monday night with the sense that *Titanic*, though injured, was still afloat, with ships all around for assistance. For anyone following the story more personally, such as Vincent Astor, the news released by the White Star Line on Monday night kept them up all night.

* * *

Among the early visitors at the White Star Line offices in New York on Monday was Vincent Astor, accompanied by Astor estate trustee A. J. Biddle. With the early news that *Titanic* was being towed to Halifax, the White Star Line had arranged a special train with many passenger cars to leave New York and travel to Canada to pick up those passengers. Vincent Astor arranged to take passage on the train, hoping to meet his father and stepmother in Nova Scotia. He sent a cable to his father, which would never be delivered: "Shall be in Halifax with private car Wednesday morning at 8:55. Anxiously await word from you. With love, Vincent."

Stories conflict on whether Vincent Astor and A. J. Biddle actually embarked on the train, but as the news grew grimmer at the White Star Line offices in New York Monday evening, the train either had to be called back shortly after leaving New York or was canceled altogether.

Though White Star Line officials knew *Carpathia* had rescued 706 survivors, they held out hope that one of the other responding ships might have found additional survivors. Each ray of hope was diminished, one by one, as messages slowly trickled into the White Star Line offices throughout the day from the responding ships, each ship reporting that they had arrived too late. On Monday evening, hope for additional survivors was abandoned at the White Star Line offices as the last of the ships to arrive at the sinking site reported its negative findings back to New York.

By Monday evening, the White Star Line was forced to release the news of the horrible loss of life from the disaster. At 8:20 p.m., White Star Line president Philip A. S. Franklin admitted the truth to reporters and the public: *Titanic* had sunk, not all passengers had been removed before she went down, and only one of the reported rescue ships had made it to the scene in time to be of any help.

From that point on, the news bulletins being issued in front of the *New York Times* building changed in rapid succession until 10:00 p.m. and then at slightly longer intervals. There had been about one hundred people watching the flashing news on the Times Square marquee before the true story had been known. The crowd following the marquee grew from one hundred to four thousand within fifteen minutes. The streets became packed with stopped automobiles.

"People rushing along the street at 7:30 carried final editions of the evening papers declaring that all were saved, and that the Titanic was under tow en route to Halifax. Some of them stopped as if transfixed as they caught sight of the bulletin declaring the Titanic had gone down and all on board except the women and children had been lost," wrote the *New York Times*.

"Conversations, sometimes half hysterical, sometimes filled with sobbing, were heard on every side. Many women, when asked why they were crying, said they had no relatives aboard and no reason to sob except that the bulletins overcame them."

Now the halls of the White Star Line offices in New York were crowded with anxious families, some of them hysterical. By this time the list of survivors had started to come in from the *Carpathia*, slowly, inaccurately, but it was the only news available to an anxious public. The list was alphabetical and started with first class. There were no Astors on the list, which was well past the As by Monday evening.

With the change in news came more visits from Vincent Astor and A. J. Biddle, who were received in Mr. Franklin's private office. At midnight, after a fifteen-minute conference, Vincent emerged from the White Star Line building with tears in his eyes. He refused to answer questions from reporters as to what he had heard about his father.

Madeleine's father, William H. Force, accompanied by Colonel Astor's secretary, William Dobbyn, would also make a personal inquiry at the White Star Line offices for information about his daughter. The visit was made more difficult due to a broken leg Mr. Force had suffered. Friends and family of John and Madeleine Astor stayed up all Monday night, anxious for any news on their fate, as word quickly spread regarding the extent of the disaster. Vincent would stay up all night at the Fifth Avenue mansion, frequently telephoning the White Star Line offices for any available updates.

* * *

The next day's news was much different from that of the previous day. The headline ran across the entire front page.

"Titanic Sinks Four Hours after Hitting Iceberg; 866 Rescued by Carpathia, Probably 1250 Perish; Ismay Safe, Mrs. Astor Maybe, Noted Names Missing," read the *New York Times* April 16 edition.

"Col. John Jacob Astor, the American head of the Astor family, has held a prominent place in the life of this city for many years. Not alone has he been a conspicuous club member and leader of society, but he has engaged in vast business activities that gave him a place of rank apart from his immense fortune and social attainments," wrote the *New York Times*.

By now the survivor list had been compiled by *Carpathia*'s crew while in the middle of the Atlantic Ocean, and slowly this information was being transmitted by wireless to the mainland in the United States via the *Olympic*. There had been approximately one hundred survivors' names transmitted at the time. Because the list was well past the letter A in the names of first-class survivors, doubt was raised as to the Astors' survival. A reporter called on Madeleine's father in New York and asked whether the rumor about Mrs. Astor not being among the survivors was true.

"Oh, my God, don't tell me that! Where did you get that report from? It isn't true! It can't be true!"

Hope, however, had not been given up for Madeleine Astor. Because of the emergent nature of the situation, and because of the nature of wireless itself, the transmission of names to shore was slow, time consuming, and often inaccurate, as each letter of a word or name was tapped on a metal signaling device. Only one wireless message could be sent at a time. For those reasons, the wireless operators in America sometimes inaccurately transcribed the names being wired in from the stormy Atlantic.

Luckily for Madeleine Astor's family, the names were being wired in alphabetically. In the space where Mrs. Astor's name should have been, there was listed the name of "Mrs. Jacob P. and maid." The operator had missed the last name. As a result, the survivor's name was initially listed in the J section of the survivor list. After investigating the circumstances of the receipt of the name, White Star Line officials felt comfortable that the name listed was that of Madeleine Astor.

"This supposition is strengthened by the fact that, except for Mrs. H. J. Allison, Mrs. Astor is the only lady in the A column of the ship's passenger list attended by a maid," wrote the *New York Times*.

Though the assumption had been made that the name of Mrs. Jacob P. was that of Madeleine Astor, the White Star Line still wanted confirmation.

"We think your mother has surely been saved and we hope that your father is among the rescued. We will advise you of the first news," Vincent was told by White Star Line officials Tuesday morning.

Madeleine's father remained awake all night on Tuesday, April 16, in hopes of receiving definite news of his daughter and son-in-law. When he saw his daughter's name on the survivor list after the initial confusion, William Force was reported to be overcome with joy. He quickly communicated the news to his wife and daughter Katherine. He also requested that the White Star Line keep him updated the moment any definite news was received concerning his son-in-law.

* * *

Vincent Astor would reappear in the White Star Line offices on Tuesday at around 1:00 p.m. He was told there was no new list of survivors. He buried his face in his hands and sobbed. Vincent would stay up all night, hoping against hope for some reassuring word about his father. He went to the offices of the Associated Press to scan its latest reports, which would contain nothing of substance until *Carpathia* arrived with all survivors on Thursday evening, two agonizing days away.

"Almost hysterical from grief, Vincent cried out that he would give all the money that he could be asked for if the operator would only tell him that he had news of his father's safety," reported the *New York Times.* "The operator was unable to give this assurance."

On Wednesday, with still no definite news from *Carpathia* regarding John Jacob Astor's fate, a desperate Vincent Astor again visited the White Star Line offices. At 9:40 p.m., a specific inquiry was sent to *Carpathia* regarding the fate of Colonel John Jacob Astor: "Do all possible ascertain if Astor on Carpathia."

The rescue ship confirmed that while Mrs. Astor had survived, Vincent's father had not. Vincent would return to the Astor estate offices, where he collapsed. After a period of time, he recovered and was taken to his home.

The newspapers at the time described Vincent as having been a delicate child. They said he resembled his father, with his height, his dark, straight hair, and his dark-blue eyes. They noted how Vincent and his father had been almost constant companions since the Astor divorce until Vincent's entrance into Harvard.

"The young man was grief-stricken, for he was a chum as well as a son of John Jacob," wrote the *New York Times.* The headline to the story was "Vincent Astor's Grief Pitiable."

* * *

While reporting on Vincent Astor's grief on the front page, the *New York Times* was also reporting on him being the presumed future head of the Astor family in the event of Colonel Astor's death on another page. They immediately began speculating how Colonel Astor's money would be split between Vincent and Madeleine. "Would Probably Share $100 Million Estate with Stepmother in Event of His Father's Death," read the headline.

Another news story would speculate about the insurance payouts for the notable men aboard *Titanic.* "In the case of Col. John Jacob Astor, whose name has not appeared in the list of those reported rescued by the Carpathia, it is not believed that the accident insurance loss will be heavy, as men of his immense fortune seldom trouble themselves about providing such protection for their families," reported the *New York Times.*

Officials of the Astor estate would deny rumors that they held a secret meeting on the day of the sinking, before the true extent of the disaster was known to the public. Rumors were circulating in the real estate field that the meeting was held on Monday afternoon at 1:00 p.m. and lasted for several hours. The rumor was that the Astor estate had definite knowledge of the loss of the ship before anyone else. Charles Peabody, an Astor attorney who was said to be at the meeting, refuted the story, saying they did not know of the seriousness of the disaster until 7:00 p.m.

Colonel Astor's secretary, William Dobbyn, refused to comment on any matters regarding John Jacob Astor's will.

* * *

John and Madeleine Astor had embarked on *Titanic* at Cherbourg, France, along with their Airedale Terrier, Kitty, who reportedly never left the colonel's side. Their cabin was a set of suites reserved for the ship's managing director, J. Bruce Ismay, who was also aboard. It is believed that suite was given up by Mr. Ismay for the comfort and privacy of Mrs. Astor. By now Madeleine was five months pregnant and the rumor about her impending motherhood had been printed in the newspapers. John and Madeleine spent most of the voyage in their suite, inviting very small groups of people there instead of socializing at the larger gatherings in the public rooms.

During the voyage, Colonel Astor frequently consulted the ship's log and heard from Captain Smith and Mr. Ismay about how the ship was behaving. At one point, Colonel Astor sent a telegram to his secretary, William Dobbyn, making arrangements for Dobbyn to be at the pier when *Titanic* arrived in New York. This request was seen by some as a sign that Colonel Astor was anxious to have his will changed to include his unborn child.

Madeleine's self-imposed seclusion, along with sickness, prohibited her from going to the last grand affair to be held aboard *Titanic*, hosted by fellow Bar Harbor summer colonists George and Eleanor Widener.

* * *

Sunday, April 14, was *Titanic*'s last night afloat; it sank early the next morning. That evening, Eleanor Widener hosted a dinner party in Captain Smith's honor in the ship's first-class dining room. Mrs. Astor had declined the invitation due to her health, while Colonel Astor was in attendance.

George and Eleanor Widener, in their fifties, were also Bar Harbor summer colonists. George Widener was one of the leading financiers of the country and came from a prominent Philadelphia family that made its fortune in the tractor and tire industry. Ironically, George's father, Peter, was a partial owner of the White Star Line.

The Wideners' mode of travel to Bar Harbor every summer season was aboard the *Josephine*, a yacht just as familiar in Frenchman Bay as Colonel Astor's and just as welcome a sight to the name-conscious summer colony. "MILLIONAIRES' TOYS," read the headline of the *Portland Daily Press* on August 29, 1899, in a story about the yachts anchored off Bar Harbor and the "millions of dollars represented in fleet." The sub-headline read, "Handsomest of the Lot Was the Josephine."

The Wideners would rent a cottage in Bar Harbor each summer, bringing with them fourteen servants. The Widener name still lives on in Maine, for example, through their charitable contributions in building the Eleanor Widener Dixon Memorial Clinic in Gouldsboro, Maine, named after the Wideners' daughter, also named Eleanor.

Just two years before sailing on *Titanic*, the Wideners had made headlines when George Widener gave his wife a set of pearls worth $750,000, not adjusted for inflation. "Her Husband Gave Her the Costliest Christmas Present Any Woman Received," noted the *Bar Harbor Record*.

Colonel Astor had returned to the suite from the Widener dinner and already retired, as had Madeleine, when the *Titanic* hit the iceberg. John gently informed his wife that something was wrong and that he thought she had better get up and dress. After looking out a window and feeling the coldness of the night sea air, he added that her form of dress should be for warmth. He was dressed before she was, going out to find Captain Smith. Before he left the cabin, Colonel Astor assured Madeleine that the ship would not sink.

After consulting with the captain on deck, Colonel Astor returned to their cabin. Madeleine noted that his face was graver than it had been before he went on deck, but again Colonel Astor assured his wife that there was no danger. Later Madeleine would come to believe that her husband knew the truth about the danger the ship was in but said that he remained the calmest man on *Titanic*'s deck. In the open air of the top-most Boat Deck, with Madeleine at his side, Colonel Astor secured a deck chair for her while the crew uncovered and prepared the lifeboats for launching.

A group of fellow first-class passengers began to assemble around John and Madeleine Astor. Among the first on the boat deck was the Widener party. Soon they were joined by others, including Arthur Ryerson and his family.

The Ryersons were also prominent members of the Bar Harbor summer colony, sailing their yacht there season after season. Arthur Ryerson Sr. was one of the oldest members of the Mount Desert Reading Room (known also as the Oasis Club), Bar Harbor's first social club, formed in 1874 in a small house on the corner of School and Mount Desert Streets. Mr. Ryerson was one of the original rusticators, long before Bar Harbor's Golden Age.

Arthur and Emily Ryerson's oldest son, Arthur Ryerson Jr., a student at Harvard, had just been killed in an automobile accident, which was the reason for the Ryersons' sailing on *Titanic*. Three of the remaining Ryerson children were with them on the ship, and a fourth had stayed back in the United States. The party was accompanied by their maid, Miss Victorine Chaudanson, and their governess, Miss Grace Scott Bowen.

In mourning, Mrs. Ryerson had been avoiding people during *Titanic*'s voyage, sticking to her cabin during the day and walking on the decks after dark. On the last evening *Titanic* was afloat, Mrs. Marian Longstreth Thayer came to her cabin. The two went for a stroll.

The sky was pink. At approximately 6:00 p.m., the two women sat down in chairs by the companionway on A deck. Mr. Ryerson and Mr. Thayer were involved in a separate conversation. As the men's conversation came to an end, the ship's owner, Bruce Ismay, came along the deck. He showed the party a telegram, reporting, "We are among icebergs." Mrs. Ryerson said that Mr. Ismay reported the *Titanic* was to arrive in New York a day early. She asked whether the icebergs would slow the ship down.

"No, we will go faster," replied Mr. Ismay, slipping the telegram into his pocket.

After the *Titanic* hit the iceberg, Mrs. Ryerson quickly helped prepare her children and the rest of her party to go up from their cabins to the boat deck. She heard the tramping of feet on the deck above. She was very concerned about keeping her family together.

"Put on your life belts and come up on the boat deck," a passenger said to Mrs. Ryerson.

"Where did you get those orders?" she asked.

"From the captain."

Soon the entire party was waiting with the Astors and the Wideners, with the Thayers soon joining them.

"Everyone had on a life belt, and they all were very quiet and self-possessed," said Mrs. Ryerson.

* * *

Mrs. Ryerson's friend Marian Thayer was not part of the Bar Harbor summer colony in 1912, but her son, Jack, would marry into the very socially prominent Cassatt family of Bar Harbor just a few years after *Titanic*'s sinking and would establish a permanent presence there. His parents, John and Marian Longstreth Thayer, had also been guests at the Widener dinner party that evening. John Thayer was the second vice president of the Pennsylvania Railroad.

After *Titanic* hit the iceberg, Jack Thayer and his father, John, were soon on deck. Seventeen-year-old Jack was still in his pajamas, wanting to see "the fun." The fun turned serious when Jack and John Thayer talked briefly with Thomas Andrews (*Titanic*'s designer) and Bruce Ismay, both close acquaintances of John Thayer Sr. Mr. Andrews informed the Thayers that *Titanic* did not have much more than an hour to live.

The Thayers quickly returned to their staterooms to change into heavier clothing, covered by a life belt, covered by outer coats. Together, Mr. and Mrs. Thayer, along with Jack and Mrs. Thayer's maid, Margaret

Flemming, made their way to the boat deck. With the seriousness of *Titanic*'s situation now growing apparent to most people aboard, Jack Thayer was separated from his parents by a large wall of passengers who had suddenly emerged on deck also seeking lifeboats. Young Jack Thayer found himself alone. Ultimately, young Jack Thayer would be rescued while standing on the top of an overturned lifeboat along with twenty-two other survivors.

Soon the Thayers (minus son Jack) were with the Astors, the Wideners, and the Ryersons, waiting in a small group on the boat deck. According to passenger Helen Bishop, shortly after the crash, about thirty minutes, she witnessed Colonel Astor approach Captain Smith, who said something to Astor in an undertone. Colonel Astor left Captain Smith and returned to the small group. Colonel Astor told them they had better put on their life belts. Colonel Astor put on his own life jacket, which Madeleine tied for him. Later he would have a man retie the life jacket. Madeleine said he was perfectly cool and collected, and his only thought seemed to be for her comfort.

While preparations were being made to load the rest of the lifeboats from the boat deck, the forward-most portside lifeboat was lowered to A deck, one deck below. The Astors, along with the group of first-class passengers surrounding them, were escorted by a crew member down to A deck via a crew-only staircase near the bridge. These passengers should have been the first to leave *Titanic*. Ultimately, they would be the last.

Arriving on A deck, the Astors and the rest of the group found their exit from *Titanic*'s sloping decks blocked by a glass window, which separated the group from the safety of lifeboat 4, dangling just on the other side. *Titanic* was a sister ship to *Olympic*, which had been built a few years previously. *Titanic*'s designer, Thomas Andrews, made a point of sailing on the maiden voyage of the new White Star Line ships, taking notes on improvements that could be made on that ship and on the subsequent ships under construction. One problem noted with *Olympic* was that the large, square, glassless windows at the front of A deck allowed sea spray to come in and soak the first-class passengers, who spent considerable time during voyages walking along that deck. The fix for the *Titanic* was having glass installed on those first few A deck windows. Installed for comfort, the windows now prevented the quick and safe escape from *Titanic* of some of the richest, most noted names in society.

There was a specific instrument that could open this window, however, and members of the crew were dispatched to find it. But the *Titanic* was on her maiden voyage, and finding routine items took extra time. While the instrument was being sought, the ship's crew was pulled into the preparation and lowering of the subsequent lifeboats, making their way farther to the back of the sinking ship. The instrument to open the window did not arrive until 2:00 a.m., twenty minutes before *Titanic* sank.

During the Astor group's long wait for the special instrument, the crew ushered them back up to the top-most boat deck. They spent time on the deck and in the private rooms there, including the gymnasium. Colonel Astor sat on an exercise horse in the gymnasium next to his wife and her maid, Rosalie. With a pocketknife, he cut into a life belt to prove to his wife how sturdy it was, holding out the pieces in his hands. While they waited, the crew began firing distress rockets.

"They wouldn't send those rockets unless it was the last," Mrs. Ryerson said to her husband.

* * *

By 2:00 a.m., *Titanic*'s remaining crew was back to the millionaires' boat, with just twenty minutes left before the ship would sink. Lifeboat 4 would be the last lifeboat launched through regular means; the remaining few boats were being stored upside down on top of the boat deck. Astor's group would be led back down the crew-only stairs, now slanting severely, to their lifeboat on the A deck. Had lifeboat 4 been launched when it was intended, at the beginning of the sinking, the passengers aboard would have found a charmed experience in relation to the experiences of the later lifeboats. For a long period after hitting the iceberg, conditions were perfect for launching. By 2:00 a.m., however, the bow of the ship was entirely submerged, the decks were slanting, and *Titanic* was listing to port. Instruments had to be improvised to pull the dangling lifeboat closer to *Titanic*'s side. An attempt was made to use deck chairs as a bridge from the window of the deck to the side of the lifeboat. By the end, women and children were simply being thrown into the lifeboat by crewmen.

By now, the popular Captain Smith, the man to whom Colonel Astor and so many of the lifeboat's expected occupants had been loyal to throughout his career, was functionally no longer in charge. Now their fate fell to *Titanic*'s second officer, Charles Lightoller, who had been temporarily demoted for *Titanic*'s maiden voyage, from first officer to second officer, to accommodate Captain Smith's temporary assignment to *Titanic*, who in turn brought with him his following of the Astors and many of the famous society names on *Titanic*'s passenger list. The change had not sweetened the attitude of Mr. Lightoller, who managed to save himself while 1,500 others died. The politeness of society and the clout of the names of the first-class American passengers held no sway for the White Star Line officer at this particular moment.

The Ryersons had to argue for the admittance of their teenage son into the lifeboat. Their two daughters were admitted without question. Their son, John, attempted to enter the lifeboat, which still had ample room.

"That boy can't go," ordered Second Officer Lightoller.

"Of course that boy goes with his mother; he is only thirteen," insisted Mr. Ryerson.

Lightoller granted permission for the boy to enter the lifeboat.

"No more boys!" exclaimed Lightoller after young John Ryerson was safely aboard the lifeboat.

Mrs. Ryerson kissed her husband goodbye and then turned away, crossing the crude steps made from a *Titanic* deck chair into the lifeboat. Once seated, she looked back at her husband, who stood with Mr. Thayer and Mr. Widener. The trio of men stood together, all very quiet.

* * *

There are a few versions of the story about the Astors' actions during the loading of the last lifeboat. Many people said they witnessed the Astors' last moments together. Though John and Madeleine Astor were prominent and easily recognizable, many of these stories came from passengers who had already left the ship by the time lifeboat 4 was loaded. Several narratives were retellings of stories heard on the trip back to New York aboard *Carpathia*.

There is disagreement regarding whether Colonel Astor was ever in the lifeboat 4. One story circulating was that Colonel Astor was already in the boat but left when more women appeared on deck just before the lifeboat's lowering. Though this account gave Colonel Astor a certain bravery, the story was questionable.

According to Miss Margaret Hayes, Colonel Astor had his arms around his wife and assisted her into the boat. In Miss Hayes's account, there were then no women waiting to get into the boats and the ship's officers invited Mr. Astor to get into the boat with his wife. The colonel, after looking around and seeing no women, got into the boat, and his wife threw her arms around him. The boat was about to be lowered when more women came running out on deck. Raising his hand, Colonel Astor stopped the preparations to lower his boat and, stepping out, assisted the women into the boat. Mrs. Astor cried out and wanted to get out of the boat with her husband, but the colonel patted her on the back.

"The ladies will have to go first," Colonel Astor was reported to have said to his wife.

The problem with Miss Hayes's story is that she had left in one of the early lifeboats and was not close enough to the *Titanic* to witness the loading of lifeboat 4.

Colonel Archibald Gracie, a first-class passenger who became the unofficial historian of the *Titanic*, testified in front of the US Senate to what he had seen at the loading of lifeboat 4, with which he had assisted. Gracie said that Colonel Astor helped load Madeleine from the deck. Gracie heard Colonel Astor ask Second Officer Lightoller whether he would be allowed to go aboard to protect his wife, to which Lightoller responded, "No, sir, no man is allowed on this boat or any of the boats until the ladies are off." Mr. Astor then said, "Well, tell me what the number of this boat is, so I may find her afterward."

The answer came back: "No. 4."

"The conduct of Col. John Jacob Astor was deserving of the highest praise," Colonel Gracie told reporters. "The wealthy New Yorker devoted all his energy to saving his young bride."

* * *

Colonel Astor, Mr. Ryerson, and Mr. Widener were all seen from the lifeboat behind a rail on the boat deck, waving their arms to their families, throwing kisses, and calling farewell to their wives and children. Colonel Astor reportedly stepped back from the rail and lit a cigarette. He called to his wife and asked whether she was comfortable.

"Goodbye, dearie, I'll join you later. The sea is calm and everything will be all right. You are in good hands, and I will meet you in the morning," John Jacob Astor called to the young, pregnant Madeleine Force Astor.

* * *

Due to the hasty and difficult loading of the lifeboat, the members of the Bar Harbor summer colony found themselves scattered around the craft. Mrs. Ryerson sat at the bow of the lifeboat with her oldest daughter, while her son and the governess were placed in the stern and her second daughter in the middle with the family maid. *Titanic* would sink ten minutes after lifeboat 4 was launched.

There were only twenty feet to travel from the side of *Titanic* to the water. Normally the distance would have been seventy feet. The trip to the water was perilous itself, with the ropes sticking during the lowering, causing the lifeboat to be pitched at dangerous angles and threatening to throw out the occupants. On hitting the water, the lifeboat found that it was caught in a whirlpool. Deck chairs and barrels were being thrown overboard for the people already in the water. Though they were off *Titanic*, the passengers in the millionaires' boat were still in great danger and needed to quickly get away from the sinking ship.

The women of the boat took it on themselves to save their own lives. Mrs. Ryerson could see one of her daughters, along with Mrs. Astor and Mrs. Thayer, rowing. She said they all did the rowing clumsily, except for Mrs. Astor. Mrs. Ryerson said there was confusion regarding orders from *Titanic* given to the lifeboat, and for that reason they did not make much progress in getting away from the ship. Mrs. Ryerson said she heard an order about a gangway and that the boat started pulling for the ever-rising stern of the ship.

"No one seemed to know what to do," said Mrs. Ryerson.

Several of the women, badly frightened, were unable to give Mrs. Astor and the other women in the boat any assistance. Madeleine Astor was described by other lifeboat passengers as showing undiminished strength in her efforts to help save herself and the lifeboat's other occupants. On hitting the water, lifeboat 4 immediately started to take in water, until it was up to the knees of the passengers. Madeleine Astor and some of the other women started bailing out the water. Eventually the drainage plug was located, and the inflow of water stopped.

It was only then, looking back at the ship, that Mrs. Ryerson realized *Titanic* was sinking rapidly. The lights on the great ship went out, and the stern stood up for several minutes, black against the stars, and then plunged down.

"I was in the bow of the boat with my daughter and turned to see the great ship take a plunge toward the bow; the two forward funnels seemed to lean, and then she seemed to break in half as if cut with a knife," said Mrs. Ryerson. "And then began the cries for help of people drowning all around us, which seemed to go on forever. Someone called out, 'Pull for your lives, or you'll be sucked under,' and everyone that could rowed like mad."

* * *

Madeleine Astor was also credited for her lifeboat being one of the few that returned to help rescue passengers struggling in the water. After *Titanic* sank, amid the screams of the 1,500 people thrown into the icy water, Madeleine would stand up in lifeboat 4, claiming she could hear Colonel Astor calling to her. She would call out that she was coming back to help him. She urged the people in her boat to return to the mass of humanity, which could prove a threat to the security of the people in the small lifeboat. Other occupants of the boat made her sit down because she was threatening the safety of the precarious lifeboat. Some women in the boat grew hysterical at the idea and interfered with those rowing the oars and attempting to return.

Lifeboat 4 would return to the mass of dying humanity and pull six men out of the water. Mrs. Astor was noted as having played a conspicuous part in that rescue effort. Survivor Ernest Pierson said that he was holding onto a plank in the water. He heard Mrs. Astor say, "Please let them get in. They have as much right to live as we."

"A woman stood up and pleaded with the seamen. Then I was taken aboard it. I afterward learned this woman was Mrs. John Jacob Astor."

Two of the men pulled aboard the lifeboat would die before arriving at the *Carpathia*. The women of the boat did their best to help the rescued men, taking off their furs and placing them on the men to provide warmth. A member of *Titanic*'s crew, James Crimmins, said he was half naked when he was pulled into the millionaires' boat. He said Mrs. Astor ripped her big fur muff in half to help wrap him, which he said saved his life.

* * *

After spending at least two hours in an open boat on the Atlantic, at daybreak *Titanic*'s survivors watched as the *Carpathia* hove into view. Arthur Rostron, *Carpathia*'s captain, decided to stop the ship in one place and let the seventeen lifeboats come to her rather than trying to zigzag his large ship through all the lifeboats and all the icebergs that surrounded them.

Mrs. Astor and her fellow members of society in lifeboat 4 were described as having displayed the greatest courage and fortitude during their four hours in the cold darkness waiting for rescue. Though she had been strong in the lifeboat, Madeleine Astor reportedly had to be carried aboard *Carpathia*. She was escorted to the infirmary by the ship's senior hospital attendant. The doctor who tended to *Titanic*'s first-class survivors said he did not recognize the famous Mrs. Astor at first because of the condition of her hair, which obscured her face. When the doctor did realize who she was, she was put in the captain's stateroom. Mrs. Astor occupied the captain's berth and Mrs. Widener the lounge, with Mrs. Thayer and her son sleeping on the floor. The doctor said Madeleine did not come out of the cabin until the last evening of the trip, when she emerged at around 6:00 p.m., a few hours before *Carpathia* would dock in New York. Rumor had been circulating around *Carpathia* that Madeleine was very ill. She was reported to have experienced a nervous collapse after having been taken aboard *Carpathia*.

Mrs. Martha Stephenson of Haverford, Pennsylvania, said that she had seen Mrs. Astor several times walking about near the captain's cabin and that she had talked with Mrs. Astor. She described Madeleine as being in apparent delicate health, though she had borne up well under the terrible ordeal. Mrs. William T. Graham, wife of the president of the American Can Company, said she had seen Mrs. Astor aboard *Carpathia* and that she did not appear ill at all.

On April 18, Madeleine sent a cable from *Carpathia* to her mother in New York, stating simply, "Mrs. Astor safe."

Young Jack Thayer said the crew of the *Carpathia*, including Captain Rostron, who had given up his cabin, was good to the *Titanic* survivors, looking to their every need and comfort. He said the trip back to New York with 705 traumatized survivors on board was one of heartache and misery. He noted that the survivors on *Carpathia* were under the same misimpression as had been the people of the United States immediately after the sinking of *Titanic*. *Titanic*'s surviving wireless operator told the survivors aboard *Carpathia* the names of the ships that had responded to his distress call. Though people on the mainland knew within a day that the additional ships had been too late to help, the survivors on the *Carpathia* did not have that knowledge.

"All were hoping beyond hope, even for weeks afterwards, that some ship, somehow, had picked up their loved one, and that he would be eventually among the saved," wrote Jack Thayer after the disaster.

* * *

The *Carpathia* had been expected in New York on Friday morning, but throughout the day on Thursday the estimated time of arrival continued to change, until it became known that the sole rescue ship would be arriving earlier than expected, late Thursday night.

Vincent Astor's initial plan had been to take the *Noma* out to meet *Carpathia* in New York Harbor, where Madeleine, her maid, and her nurse would be transferred at sea onto the Astor yacht. The *Noma* had been at the Morse Yard in Brooklyn, and Captain Roberts had been hurriedly summoned a few days previously to begin the work of coaling her. The yacht was said to be shipshape by Wednesday and ready to head out as soon as *Carpathia* arrived. Vincent made plans to take along members of the Force family and William Dobbyn. This plan, mercifully, never materialized.

On Thursday night, in the light drizzle of a passing thunderstorm, tens of thousands of people awaited *Carpathia*'s arrival at the pier in New York City. The large crowd, the excitement, and the lack of knowledge of what was actually happening led to wild rumors being circulated among the waiting crowd. One rumor was that Madeleine Astor had died at 8:06 p.m., just as the *Carpathia* was approaching the pier. This rumor was proved untrue when Mrs. Astor emerged from the *Carpathia* unaided, but the rumor did make it to Madeleine's father, just up the street in the city.

The next rumor was that Colonel Astor, along with Isador Strauss and Major Archibald Butt (military aide to President Taft), had entered into a suicide pact aboard the *Titanic* just before it went down. The rumor was that Major Butt was to shoot the other two men and then himself just as the ship sank and that the pact had been carried out at the last minute. Later, multiple witnesses would publicly testify to the courage shown by these men in their final minutes.

* * *

One of the hundreds of reporters meeting the *Carpathia* was Eva Shorey, a well-respected staff writer for the *Portland Evening Express*. Eva Shorey had served as a secretary to notable Maine political figures and as a special agent of the Maine Bureau of Industrial and Labor Statistics, and in 1907 she prepared an influential report on working women in Portland. Among Eva Shorey's memorable stories was a three-part report on working conditions in Lewiston cotton mills.

Eva Shorey had been sent to New York City earlier in the week to await *Carpathia*'s arrival. The editors of the *Portland Evening Express* thought it best to send a female to interview the boat full of widows. When the *Titanic* docked, Eva Shorey had her story: "Strong Men Weep Aloud."

"Dramatic in the extreme was the arrival of the Cunard liner so eagerly awaited by the whole world. Like a funeral ship of state, the Carpathia, with the awful story of the shipwrecked Titanic, and bearing the pitiful remnant of the passengers and crew, crept out of the fog and silently came to her dock in New York tonight. A pall of rain added to the gloom. A sob went up all over the city where excitement in all quarters has been at fever pitch and the nervous tension at the breaking point.

"Thousands of men, women, and children choked the streets for blocks. Police regulations were unusually strict, and the line of motors and carriages was kept in place, as well as the throngs of surging humanity.

"When the survivors began to appear, strong men wept aloud, the hysterical cry of women was heard, and agonized faces looked in vain for the sight of loved ones they would not give up as lost. The reunions were tragic in the extreme, and the vast crowd were in one of those emotional states rarely witnessed. High and low, women of fashion and the immigrant met on a common ground. Joy and sorrow, happiness and agony and the sympathetic sob everywhere apparent.

"One of the tragic sights was to see the beautiful Mrs. John Jacob Astor, whose marriage a short time ago was so widely discussed. Her first question when she came on the pier was 'Have the others got in yet?' Her sister and Mrs. Astor's son, Vincent Astor, led her to the waiting limousine with murmured words of comfort. The courageous acts of her husband as reported in the press must be a solace in her days of anguish."

* * *

With the rumors of Madeleine's ill health, the Astors took no chances when it came to meeting Madeleine Astor at the pier. The awaiting party included her stepson, Vincent, and her sister, Katherine, along with two doctors, a trained nurse, and an ambulance.

Vincent Astor had received permission to board *Carpathia* when it arrived so that he could aid his pregnant stepmother off the ship. It would take Vincent several minutes to get through the disembarking passengers to find Madeleine. Mrs. Astor walked with Vincent down the gangplank, unassisted, wearing a white sweater. They used a freight elevator to avoid the crowd and quickly get to the street and the three awaiting automobiles, including Vincent's car at the head of the line.

Eva Shorey was discreet when reporting on Madeleine Astor's arrival, leaving out some of the distressing details. Madeleine had to be assisted off *Carpathia* by Vincent Astor and two of the ship's officers. Madeleine was hysterical and so plainly on the point of collapse that her sister, Katherine Force, was forced to support her to a seat inside the building. Mrs. Astor embraced her sister and asked her sobbingly, "Have you heard from anyone else?"

"No," replied Katherine.

Mrs. Astor broke out weeping again. In five minutes, she said she was able to go to the automobile that awaited her, and, on the arm of her sister and two friends, she was half carried to the machine.

"They embraced with tears, hurried to a limousine, and drove to the Astor town house," read the story in the *Bangor Daily News* compiled from New York wire dispatches.

Vincent cranked his car's motor himself and jumped into the driver's seat.

"How is Mrs. Astor?" he was asked by reporters as he attempted to drive off.

"She is well," he replied. "I am delighted to say that she is far better than I expected to find her."

"Are you taking Mrs. Astor home?"

"We are taking her there directly," Vincent replied.

"Have you any other good news to give?"

"No," he said. "I have not yet dared to ask Mrs. Astor any questions."

"No news of Colonel Astor?"

"No," he replied sadly.

Vincent said that Mrs. Astor was in the best condition possible in light of the circumstances, but she was in no condition to discuss the details of her ordeal.

Madeleine's first destination was the home of her parents, 18 East Thirty-Seventh Street. William Force now had difficulty with ambulation and could not meet his daughter at the pier. With the rumors that had been circulating, Mr. Force wanted to see his daughter for himself. When leaving her father's residence, reporters overheard Madeleine telling her family that she did not know what happened to her husband. She said she hoped he was alive somewhere. "Yes, I cannot think of anything else."

From the Force residence, Madeleine's mother accompanied her to the Astor mansion on Fifth Avenue. Madeleine's father made it clear to gathered reporters that no one was to apprise Mrs. Astor of the truth about her husband.

Chapter 6

The Girl Widow

The girl widow, now looking forward to an early motherhood, has not expressed any desire for the visit of old time friends.

—*New York Times*, 1912

Colonel Astor never did meet Madeleine in the morning as he had promised from the deck of the sinking *Titanic*. Instead, Madeleine Astor awoke in the safety of the Astor Fifth Avenue home. When Madeleine arrived home from *Carpathia*, she was greeted by friends at the Fifth Avenue mansion, who expressed concern about what they called her "nervous condition." The morning after her arrival, Dr. Ruel B. Kimball announced to awaiting reporters that Mrs. Astor had awakened after ten hours of sleep feeling refreshed and that her nervous condition had improved. He reported that she was out of danger but still bedridden and did not require any medication.

* * *

The first few days back in the United States, even in the safety of the Astor mansion, seemed somewhat chaotic. All attention was on Madeleine's Fifth Avenue home. People were waiting for her story—the public, reporters, and her own family, especially stepson Vincent.

Vincent spent much time with Madeleine in her first few days at the mansion, as did other members of her family and a few intimate friends. In addition to comforting his grieving stepmother, Vincent was looking for information about his father, whom he still believed to be alive. Vincent told a *New York Evening World* reporter that Mrs. Astor was in such a condition that she had not been able to tell even him and members of the Force family any details of *Titanic*'s sinking. Madeleine was described as being "utterly exhausted by her experiences" by Astor estate trustee and spokesman A. J. Biddle. Her physicians said that she was in no danger but gave out orders that neither Mrs. Astor nor her maid, who was saved with her, be permitted to talk about the disaster.

"Mrs. Astor Ill, But Not Critically," read the headline of the *New York Times*. "Alarming Reports as to Her Condition Formally Denied by Secretary. Suffering Now Only from Grief, Says Her Physician."

"Mrs. Astor is perfectly well, and suffering only from grief," Dr. Kimball told reporters. "She arrived in as good health as any one could be who had undergone such a strain. The reports that she has been seriously ill at any time during the last few days are incorrect."

Dr. Kimball reported that Madeleine kept recounting the events in the lifeboat over and over, including how she had to help bail out the lifeboat, which reads more as a hysterical repeating of words, not an accurate depiction of the actual events. Dr. Kimball described Mrs. Astor as being in a highly nervous condition, suffering from the shock of her experience: "Her nerves, however, are badly shattered, and in her waking hours she spends much of her time weeping with the recollection of the horror of the experiences she underwent." He blamed her exhaustion, her grief, and her "delicate condition." He continued to forbid anyone to ask her any questions about *Titanic*'s sinking.

Along with all that Madeleine Astor had to face, there was the extra burden of the news that she was being considered as a witness at the US Senate's investigation into *Titanic*'s sinking. She was never called.

"Mrs. Astor is very ill and under the care of a physician. It will be impossible for her to be interviewed or to give out any statement," said Dr. Kimball.

* * *

After Madeleine had spent a few days bedridden in her room, Dr. Kimball reported that the nervous condition that had caused her friends such concern on the night of her arrival had passed almost entirely, without any medicine. He reported that she was still not strong and remained confined to her bed but had sat up in bed for ten minutes for the first time since returning home. He said she continued to spend her time weeping with the recollection of the events on *Titanic.*

Madeleine was now being encouraged by her doctor to discuss her experiences on *Titanic*, believing that was the best way to relieve her feelings of nervousness. On April 22, with her maid Rosalie Bidois by her side, Madeleine was able to tell the family her story. Miss Bidois was described as playing an active part in lifeboat 4's work in its own survival.

Madeleine said she remembered that in the confusion of being put in the lifeboat, she thought her husband was standing at her side. She thought Colonel Astor had tried to follow her into the boat, to protect both her and the other women in the boat, but an officer stopped him. She was not sure what had become of her husband after the lifeboat was lowered. After that she had no clear recollection of the events until the boats were well clear of the sinking liner. Madeleine thought that all women who wished to be taken off the *Titanic* had been taken off. She said her lifeboat had room for at least fifteen more people. She said the men, for some reason she could not understand, did not seem at all anxious to leave the ship, that almost everyone seemed dazed.

"She was terribly frightened when she found herself alone, and the boat being lowered," wrote Colonel Astor's secretary, William Dobbyn, to a friend after having heard Madeleine's story. "I never saw a sadder face or one more beautiful, or anything braver or finer than the wonderful control she had of herself. You would be terribly sorry for her if you could see her and hear her tell of the awful tragedy."

* * *

April 22 seemed to have been an eventful day for Madeleine and Vincent Astor in the *Titanic* chapter of their lives. Besides Madeleine's telling of her *Titanic* experience, this would be the day that she and stepson Vincent gave up hope that Colonel Astor was still alive.

Until she finally was able to tell her story, Madeleine would share her stepson's belief that Colonel Astor might still be safe somewhere, on his way home to them. Madeleine and Vincent were not entirely wrong in this view. Though the world back home accepted that anyone not arriving on the *Carpathia* had perished in *Titanic*'s sinking, the *Titanic*'s survivors themselves had a different experience. When *Carpathia* left the scene of the wreck after picking up all the survivors, those survivors had seen many ships at the scene of the wreck, not knowing that all had arrived too late to help. The assumption that there might be more survivors than those on *Carpathia* was natural for the survivors, as was their reluctance to accept a painful fact. Fellow survivor Eleanor Widener, for one, who had shared a cabin with Madeleine Astor on *Carpathia*, for a long time after returning home to Philadelphia refused to believe her husband was dead, which her physicians thought best to allow while she recovered from a severe cold as a result of her *Titanic* experience.

Initially after *Carpathia*'s arrival in New York, Vincent Astor refused to discuss the foundering of the *Titanic* with reporters. Unable to get accurate information from his stepmother in those first few days, Vincent devoted much of that time to interviewing survivors before they left New York in the hope that he might obtain some further information about his father. He obtained little news that was comforting, however.

One of those Vincent interviewed was Robert Williams Daniel, a banker from Philadelphia who was staying at the Waldorf-Astoria before traveling home. Vincent went to the hotel on the afternoon after *Carpathia*'s arrival, accompanied by Mr. Dobbyn. Vincent told Mr. Daniel that he had heard Mr. Daniel had seen his father on the *Titanic* not long before the ship sank.

Robert Daniel told his story to Vincent. Mr. Daniel said he had not taken the time to dress before reaching the deck and that he wore only a bathrobe, under which he slipped a life preserver. On reaching the deck, said Mr. Daniel, he saw Colonel Astor and Walter M. Clark (who was also lost in the sinking) leaning against a rail of the ship, talking. By then, said Mr. Daniel, the boat containing Mrs. Astor had been safely launched. Mr. Daniel said he ran up to Colonel Astor and Mr. Clark and begged them to jump overboard in the hope of being picked up by one of the lifeboats.

"They refused to leave the ship," Mr. Daniel told Vincent. "[A]nd I left them standing there. What happened after that I hardly know myself."

Vincent was described as greatly agitated by the lack of details about his father's last moments aboard *Titanic*, and it was reported that he plainly showed the effects of sleepless nights and mental anguish.

People would try to take advantage of the Astors' desperate grief. Madeleine Astor would receive a cable shortly after the sinking saying a small board had been found in the water with a message scratched in the wood and signed by John J. Astor.

* * *

One reason the Astors started accepting the fate of Colonel Astor on April 22, a week after he died, may have been in part due to the recovery of the first *Titanic* bodies from the cold waters of the North Atlantic Ocean.

Even before *Carpathia* arrived in New York with *Titanic*'s survivors, a cable-laying ship named the *Mackay-Bennett* had been dispatched from Halifax, Nova Scotia, Canada, with the grim task of recovering whatever bodies could be found from the site of *Titanic*'s sinking. On April 22, the first of the bodies were recovered, the names of those identifiable being wired back to New York. Vincent Astor would admit to a *New York Evening World* reporter that he had given up hope that his father was alive that same day.

Along with that acceptance came a plan to recover his father's body. For Vincent Astor, money would be no object. The first idea, before believing Colonel Astor was dead, had been for the Astor yacht *Noma* to race to the scene of the wreck to search for Colonel Astor themselves. Unfortunately, the *Noma*'s wireless apparatus was out of order, and the plan was quickly ruled out. Vincent then said he was considering sending an expedition from Halifax to search for the body. At the office of the Astor estate, there was intense activity in making arrangements for the private recovery effort, on which the Astors were prepared to freely spend $1 million. The managers of the Astor estate had been in consultation with marine engineers, retaining several to go with the expedition. There was speculation over whether there might be a reward for the recovery of the colonel's body, and how large that reward might be, with some saying it might be $1 million, not adjusted for inflation. Eventually the idea was scrapped, with the Astor estate saying that the White Star Line seemed to be doing everything it could to recover the bodies. Captain Roberts, Colonel Astor's yacht captain, was sent to Halifax by train to await the arrival of the *Mackay-Bennett*.

* * *

Having told her *Titanic* story, Madeleine now spent her time, much like Vincent, awaiting news of the ongoing search for bodies in the North Atlantic. Vincent was visiting his stepmother constantly during those days with the updates he was receiving on the ongoing effort.

Steps were also being made to get Madeleine's life back to some sort of normalcy. On April 24, her pregnancy was formally announced.

"Mrs. Astor's New Ordeal," read the headline in the *New York Times*. "She Expects to Become a Mother before July—Her Health Improved."

"Mrs. Astor expects to become a mother some time before July, and her health is consequently the subject of much care and constant watchfulness. She was ill on the *Carpathia* after her hazardous experiences in the cold in the Titanic's open boat, but at no time then was her condition serious, and since she reached her home in this city her condition has daily improved."

Madeleine's health was pronounced by friends and family to have returned to as normal as could be expected under the circumstances. This was reported to be a great relief of the anxiety they had been feeling during the initial days.

"Mrs. Astor is by nature a strong young woman, and, considering the hardships she endured following the wreck of the Titanic, she is bearing up well physically," wrote the *New York Times*.

The *New York Evening World* the same day reported that doctors had given permission for Mrs. Astor to leave the house for short periods of time, though she would not leave for the first time for another four days. That announcement seems to have been made to fend off yet another rumor that her health had relapsed and she had turned critically ill while waiting for the results of the search for *Titanic* bodies. Family and friends emphatically denied the rumors, as did Dr. Kimball.

During this time, Madeleine would be visited by Bishop David H. Greer from the Cathedral of St. John the Divine in New York. She would also spend time picking out fabrics for new clothing to accommodate her progressing pregnancy.

* * *

The weeklong wait for the names of the identified bodies from the *Mackay-Bennett* was excruciating. When she left Halifax, the ship was loaded with a large number of coffins, along with undertakers and their embalming supplies and equipment. Bodies from the sinking had been spotted as far as sixty miles away from *Titanic*'s reported sinking coordinates. The *Mackay-Bennett* reached the vicinity at 8:00 p.m. on April 20. At daybreak the following day, their grim work began. Back in New York, the offices of the White Star Line stayed open all day, on a Sunday, in the hope that the *Mackay-Bennett* would report meeting with success on her sad mission. By the evening of April 22, a list of twenty-seven names of bodies picked up by the *Mackay-Bennett* was released by the White Star Line.

The world was anxious for news of the discovery of Colonel Astor's body. Final confirmation of his death was important not only personally, to his family, but also professionally. John Jacob Astor owned billions of dollars in New York real estate, and any lingering doubt over his death could cause legal nightmares both professionally and with the disposition of his estate among his family. This anxiety, along with a wireless system that was in its infancy, caused considerable excitement as the names started to come in. There was much activity in the White Star Line offices with the receipt of the name Necholas Rasher, which did not appear on *Titanic*'s passenger list. White Star Line officials thought this might be the name of John Jacob Astor, garbled in the relay of wireless.

At the time there were two types of wireless alphabet: Morse and Continental. In addition, the *Mackay-Bennett* was not wiring the names directly to shore; instead, the names were wired to the *Olympic* before that ship wired them into the White Star Line offices in New York City.

"Over Col. Astor's name there was much speculation in the White Star offices," reported the *New York Times*.

The following day, it was determined that the name Necholas Rasher was referring to another passenger, not John Jacob Astor. By now the *Mackay-Bennett* had recovered forty-two of its final total of 193 bodies. Colonel Astor was still among the missing. William Dobbyn was denying rumors that preliminary steps had been taken to file the Astor will. Mr. Dobbyn was indignant that there seemed to be "unseemly haste" in taking it for granted that Colonel Astor was dead. He said no effort would be made to legally declare Colonel Astor dead until all recovery efforts had been completed.

"Any statement in regard to Col. Astor's will is premature at this time, although it is felt by his family that he was lost with the Titanic," said a representative of Carter, Ledyard, and Milburn of Wall Street, Colonel Astor's legal representation.

* * *

The body of Colonel John Jacob Astor was found on April 26 floating in the near-freezing North Atlantic, clad in his clothing and a life jacket. In New York, the White Star Line delivered the news to Mr. Dobbyn at the Astor estate offices. Mr. Dobbyn relayed the news to the family. By the evening Vincent Astor and Mr. Biddle were in the Astor private rail car, the Oceanic, waiting to be attached to the 10:50 p.m. train leaving Grand Central Station for Halifax. Vincent had been anxious to go to Halifax since the launching of the *Mackay-Bennett* and was even more anxious to get there now, according to Mr. Biddle.

Before leaving New York, Mr. Biddle was asked about the filing of the Astor will for probate. Mr. Biddle responded that nothing would be done until it was definitively established that the body on board the *Mackay-Bennett* was that of Colonel Astor.

* * *

When the news was announced that Colonel Astor's body had been found, fresh rumors began circulating about the pregnant Madeleine Astor's deteriorating medical condition in response to that news.

Dr. Kimball quicky denied the rumors, saying that she was dressing herself and was now able to move about the Fifth Avenue mansion. He said that she still had permission to go out for a drive if the weather was favorable and "if there were no chance she might be disturbed by the curiosity of persons who might recognize her," wrote the *New York World*. She would leave the house for the first time the day after receiving news of the recovery of her husband's body, taking an automobile ride accompanied by members of her family. Dr. Kimball said that with Mrs. Astor's health steadily improving, she might leave shortly for the Astor country estate at Rhinebeck, in upstate New York.

* * *

Leaving Grand Central Station in New York close to midnight, the train carrying Vincent in his private car arrived at Union Station in Portland, Maine, at 8:30 the next morning. The Oceanic was held on a side track until the number 29 Boston-to-Halifax train arrived. Two other private cars were also attached to the train. The Oceanic arrived in Halifax on the morning train on April 27. Vincent did not go to the morgue or dockyard, instead staying very close to his railroad car, avoiding all forms of publicity. Rumors quickly circulated that special favors had been sought and granted to Vincent Astor, although they were denied by a city official. A special coffin would arrive in Halifax for Colonel Astor's body. Vincent also received word that a body had been recovered which might be that of Colonel Astor's valet, Victor Robbins. Vincent promised Mr. Robbins's family to return the body to his widow if the body was indeed that of the valet.

Vincent Astor would have two days to wait in Halifax for the arrival of the *Mackay-Bennett*. His stress would be compounded as the story of the body of fellow Bar Harbor summer colonist George Widener quickly circulated throughout Halifax and the train station where Vincent Astor waited.

The Astors and the Wideners had many shared *Titanic* experiences. Already acquainted through their summers spent in Bar Harbor, Madeleine Astor and Eleanor Widener shared the captain's cabin on the long voyage back to the safety of the United States, as well as an initial belief that their husbands might still be alive long after all hope of survival was gone. In Halifax, the Astors and the Wideners would share their final *Titanic* chapter together, with the sons of John Jacob Astor and George Widener Sr. sharing the fear of never finding their fathers' bodies.

Much like the Astors, the Wideners had suffered the anxiety over the confusion of names wired ashore by the *Mackay-Bennett*. For the Wideners, the name wired in for one identified body was "George Widen." After much confusion, the name was ultimately determined to be that of George Widener. George Widener Jr. had been in Halifax for almost a week when Vincent Astor arrived. By now, the captain of the *Mackay-Bennett* had wired in to shore that there were far more bodies than what his small ship had been equipped to handle. He announced that unidentifiable bodies would be recommitted to the sea. This announcement caused great concern among the families waiting in Halifax, who knew they might have some chance of finding an identifying mark or some other familiar means of identification that would be overlooked by a stranger. The *New York Times* described waiting relatives as being stunned by the news. The members of the *Mackay-Bennett* crew tried to reassure the public that they had at least made sure the unidentified bodies were those of crew members, as identified by uniforms worn or other means.

Three days before the *Mackay-Bennett* arrived back in Halifax, young George Widener received an unofficial wireless report that, although his father's body had been recovered as originally reported, it was one of those reburied at sea. George Widener took his concerns to the White Star Line officials in Halifax, who said they had no such information.

With all that Vincent Astor had gone through, and all that he was prepared to go through if necessary to retrieve his father's body, word of the recommittal of George Widener's body caused him even greater concern over the fate of his own father's mortal remains. If such a mistake could be made with the body of George Widener, whose father was a part owner of the White Star Line, the same could easily happen to the body of Colonel John Jacob Astor.

* * *

The *Mackay-Bennett* was expected on the evening of April 29, but it was delayed until the next day by bad weather. People had been assembling at the dock as early as daybreak on the chilly Canadian spring morning. Most were undertakers or reporters. The men would go between the dock and a tent that had been erected nearby to guard extra wires for the press, which would flash the news to a waiting world.

The dockyard was patrolled by twenty members of the crew and four petty officers from HMCS *Niobe* and by a squad of men from the local police force, who were instructed to keep out all without passes countersigned by the commandant. People there to try to identify and/or claim bodies of loved ones were urged not to come to the dock but, instead, to report to the curling ring, a chilled building up a hill just a few miles away.

The funeral ship, as it was being called, was spotted from shore a little after 9:30 a.m. The *Mackay-Bennett* had searched for several days amid miles and miles of wreckage, tables, chairs, doors, pillows, and other scattered fragments of the *Titanic*'s luxury. Sometimes the bodies were spread out, sometimes they were grouped together in the water, and "once they saw more than a hundred that looked to the wondering crew of the Mackay-Bennett like a flock of sea gulls in the fog, so strangely did the ends of the life belts rise and fall with the rise and fall of the waves," reported the *New York Times*.

The *Mackay-Bennett* was now returning to Halifax with a total of 193 bodies. Because she could not recover all the bodies, two other ships had to be dispatched to recover the rest.

On seeing the *Mackay-Bennet* coming into the harbor, the tolling of the bells in the city warned Halifax that the funeral ship was arriving. A hush fell on the waiting people. The gray clouds that had overcast the sky parted, and the sun shone brilliantly on the rippling water of the harbor as the funeral ship drew alongside her pier. In every part of the ship the dead lay. High on the poop deck coffins were piled and piled. Dead men in tarpaulins lined the flooring of the wells on deck that normally held the cable, both forward and aft, so that there was hardly room for a foot to be put down. In the forward hold, dead men were piled on one another, their eyes closed as in sleep.

The business of the moment was to discharge the bodies, and this task was done with all possible dispatch. The dead not in coffins were carried down in stretchers, placed in the rough wooden shells that were piled on the pier, and one by one driven up the sloping hill into town in a long line of hearses and black undertakers' wagons that had been gathered from every quarter. It was efficiently done, but quietly and without irreverent haste.

* * *

By now there was great confusion surrounding George Widener's body. With George Jr. having received an unofficial message that his father's identified body had been buried at sea, Captain Lardner still had a listing of George Widener's body being onboard the *Mackay-Bennett*. Young George Widener would meet with Captain Lardner and be taken to the crude wooden coffin that supposedly held his father's body. The lid was pried off and young George looked down at a body unidentifiable by the face but that clearly was not his father.

George Jr. quickly went through the personal effects that had been collected from the body. Inside a coat pocket was a letter addressed to Mr. Widener. Because of the letter, the body had been identified as that of George Widener.

Examining the coat itself, however, revealed to George Widener Jr. the true identity of the body that lay in the coffin in front of him. The coat was made of inferior quality and had the initial "E" inside it. The body was that of Edward Keeping, a butler to the Wideners. Another body had been identified as that of Edward Keeping by means of the contents of the coat that person was wearing. The body identified as Mr. Keeping had been buried at sea. The Wideners were left forever wondering whether the bodies had been switched and whether their father's recovered body had again been thrown into the Atlantic Ocean, this time not to be recovered, all based on the simple switching of coats between one of the giants of society and his butler.

With the Widener mix-up, an especially anxious Captain Richard Roberts was part of the waiting crowd allowed to get past the cordon that stretched all about the pier. After being admitted, he was taken to the wooden coffin that contained Colonel Astor's body. The lid of the coffin was opened so that Captain Roberts could identify the body himself. Unlike the bodies that were damaged or decomposed beyond recognition, Colonel Astor was entirely recognizable, not just by his face but also by his tall, slender build. Captain Roberts likewise inspected Colonel Astor's personal effects, which included a plain gold ring with two little deep-set diamonds, the gold belt buckle that he always wore, and a sum of money amounting to $3,000 (unadjusted for inflation). For Captain Roberts, there was no doubt that it was Colonel John Jacob Astor's body that had been recovered from the North Atlantic. Twenty minutes after boarding the ship, Captain Roberts was seen hurrying through the crowd to reach the nearest telephone so that he might call the anxious Vincent at the train station with the news.

Colonel Astor's body was taken off the *Mackay-Bennett* shortly before noon and brought with the others to the temporary morgue. At the curling rink, the necessary paperwork was completed and John Astor's body was the first to be claimed. After the signing of the papers and the formal claiming of the personal effects, Captain Roberts headed to the train station, where the body was transferred to the Oceanic.

Together, Vincent Astor and Mr. Biddle returned to the United States as quickly as possible, leaving on the evening train. Their destination was Rhinebeck, in upstate New York, where Colonel Astor's funeral and burial would be held. Captain Roberts would stay behind in Halifax to look for the body of Colonel Astor's valet.

There are no details of that long train ride from Halifax, Nova Scotia, to Rhinebeck, New York, via Portland, Maine. How very powerful that nearly one-thousand-mile train ride must have been for young Vincent Astor.

* * *

Even before his body had been found, tributes to and memorials for John Jacob Astor were being held around the country that he loved. In Newport, Rhode Island, flags were at half-mast throughout the summer resort, also in part for George Widener. Leaving Newport for Boston during that time, the United States cruiser *Salem* passed out of Newport's waters with her colors at half-mast in honor of the lost men, Colonel Astor being a veteran.

Many of the tributes seemed to be in atonement for the harsh words issued about Colonel Astor's marriage to Madeleine Force just a few months earlier. Regardless of whether the honeymoon in Europe would have changed people's minds about the Astors, Colonel Astor's brave death on *Titanic* had.

The Cathedral of St. John the Divine in New York, where Colonel Astor had contributed to the building fund only to resign during the marriage scandal, held a memorial service on the morning of April 21, two days after the arrival of *Carpathia*. Bishop Greer, who would visit with Madeleine Astor in her home three days later, presided.

The Church of the Ascension in New York also held a memorial service for the dead of *Titanic*. Reverend Perc Stickney Grant discussed many aspects of the disaster, including the loss of Colonel Astor. "Col. Astor, who lost his life on the Titanic, was last fall the target of a venomous attack," he said, "an attack which was at once hysterical and unwarranted. We should not judge a play until it is done, for the last act crowns a play. So it is with the lives and actions of men." As the church's orchestra began to play "Nearer, My God, to Thee," members of the congregation attempted to join in but broke down sobbing.

At a meeting of the Executive Committee of the American Boy Scouts, it was decided that in memory of Colonel Astor (who was the organization's vice president and one of the earliest and most active supporters of the American Boy Scout movement), Boy Scout troops would decorate their flags, pennants, and the side arms of officers with black crepe for thirty days as a sign of mourning and respect.

The National Committee for the Celebration of the One Hundredth Anniversary of Peace Among English-Speaking Peoples adopted a resolution of respect for Colonel Astor, who was a member. The resolution was signed by industrial giant Andrew Carnegie. "No epitaph needs to be written, no eulogy pronounced over them: For as long as the world endures, their epitaph and eulogy will be found in the women and children, and their descendants, for whom these men sacrificed their lives," wrote Mr. Carnegie, who would later become Madeleine Astor's Bar Harbor neighbor.

Owing to Colonel Astor's fascination with automobiles, he had been a member of the Motor Car Touring Society. The society's annual Spring Run was canceled on account of the disaster and the loss of Colonel Astor. The Board of Governors of the Aero Club of America passed resolutions of regret for Colonel Astor, who was a life member. The resolutions pointed out Colonel Astor's early interest in aeronautics and the continued attention he paid to the scientific and sporting features of aviation. The Board of Directors of the Niagara Falls Power Company thanked Colonel Astor for his support of the development of the novel discovery of electricity and the mission of their company. "His support of the novel undertaking of this company was constant and generous from its pioneer period until its complete demonstration of the extensive practicability of hydro-electric development and transmission of power. No one more surely than he foresaw the limitless possibilities of this new agency for the benefit of mankind; and no one was more ready to approve and to aid every reasonable measure for its development."

An example of Colonel Astor's more personal, quiet generous nature was attested to by Mr. C. W. McMurran, who rented an office in the Astor-owned Schermerhorn Building at 96 Broadway. Mr. McMurran had signed a lease with Colonel Astor, along with another man who rented the other half the office space. When that man died, Mr. McMurran was responsible for the entirety of the rent, which he could not afford alone. Mr. McMurran wrote to Colonel Astor for help.

In a short time, Mr. McMurran received a letter from Colonel Astor personally. Colonel Astor wrote that the Astor estate could not remit leases but that he would help Mr. McMurran personally. Mr. McMurran called at the offices of the Astor estate and met with Colonel Astor and two trustees. One trustee objected to any alteration in the lease. Colonel Astor went ahead with his offer.

"I want to help my young friend here, and, therefore, you can cancel the obligation," Colonel Astor told the trustee.

Mr. McMurran was subsequently told by a rent collector for the Astor estate that this was not the only case in which similar action had been taken by Colonel Astor.

Another story of his generosity was Colonel Astor being asked by a man whether he would donate $50 to a member of the New York Press Club who had recently lost his sight.

"If you would send him $50, I'm sure it would be a very gracious act," requested the man.

"I guess I'll send him $250, because if he is blind, he will need it," replied Colonel Astor.

Another story from the New York Press Club was of the club's formation itself. Colonel Astor purchased $2,500 in bonds in the club when it was opened. A few days later, the New York Press Club received a visit from Colonel Astor's secretary, who left an envelope. When the envelope was opened, it was found to contain the bonds, presented to the club as a gift with Colonel Astor's compliments.

One testimonial to Colonel Astor came from a member of the *Titanic* crew. Lookout Frederick Fleet, who had spotted the iceberg, was with other members of the crew detained until they testified before the US Senate about the sinking. A reporter came looking for Mr. Fleet, who was found drinking a cup of coffee. "You can take it from me," said Fleet, as he drained his cup, "that all of us as works below want to go on record for saying John Jacob Astor died like a man."

* * *

One of the smallest (yet genuinely touching) moments after the disaster was the immediate wiring of a cabled message of sympathy from Colonel Astor's first wife, Ava Astor, to the new Mrs. Astor. Madeleine Astor acknowledged the cable at once.

* * *

Subscriptions were being solicited aboard the *Carpathia* for needy *Titanic* survivors even before she landed in New York, as was being done across the country. Aboard the *Carpathia*, Mrs. Astor, Mrs. Widener, and Mrs. Ryerson promised to send a contribution as soon as they landed and had access to funds. The day after *Carpathia* arrived in New York, $77,000 had already been collected in that city alone. Vincent Astor contributed $10,000, delivered in the form of a check sent to the mayor's office by Mr. Dobbyn. The check was accompanied by a note: "Will you please accept the enclosed check as a contribution from me to the fund for the needy survivors of the Titanic disaster?"

Mayor Gaynor replied with the following letter:

"Dear Mr. Astor: Your generous contribution to the fund for the relief of the survivors of the Titanic disease and of the dependents of those who lost their lives is at hand.

"Permit me to express to Mrs. Astor and to the whole family through you my sympathy with you all in the great loss which you have sustained. My acquaintance with your father was a most agreeable one, and the oftener I met him the more his generous, superior and democratic qualities grew on me. He was a man among men. The heroic way in which he met his death, disregarding himself and looking to the safety of others, is exactly what every one well acquainted with him knew to be the case even before authentic accounts were received. Sincerely yours, W. J. Gaynor, Mayor."

* * *

Flags on public office buildings were at half-mast in New York City during the entire week after *Carpathia*'s arrival. Even before Vincent Astor left for Halifax to retrieve his father's body, he had attended a memorial in the chapel of St. Luke's Hospital in New York, where special services were held for *Titanic*'s dead, many of them New Yorkers. The chapel of the hospital was filled to capacity. In attendance also was Anne Morgan, daughter of fellow Bar Harbor summer colonist J. P. Morgan, another of *Titanic*'s owners.

Before the announcement that Colonel Astor's body had been recovered, the members of his family had already planned a memorial service. Once word was received from the *Mackay-Bennett* that Colonel Astor's body had been found, however, those plans were changed, and it was announced that the funeral would be held at Rhinebeck. The exact date of the funeral would not be announced, said a representative of the Astor family, until the *Mackay-Bennett* arrived with the bodies.

All the flags in Rhinebeck, New York, were at half-mast when Colonel John Jacob Astor's body returned home on the afternoon of Thursday, May 2, accompanied by his son. The train from Halifax made a special stop at Ferncliff, a mile below Rhinebeck Station, to allow the coffin to be taken from the train to the Astor country mansion.

The funeral was two days later at the Church of the Messiah in Rhinebeck. The first party from New York City to reach Rhinebeck arrived at 11:07 a.m. A special train arrived at 11:34 a.m. and was met by twenty automobiles, in which the arriving party was carried to the church. Colonel Astor's body was escorted from Ferncliff to the church by Madeleine, Vincent, and the Force family. The funeral was held at noon.

Every seat in the church was occupied, and the adjoining chapel was filled with employees of the Astor estate and the Poughkeepsie Hudson–Fulton Celebration Committee, of which Colonel Astor was a member. Many of the floral offerings that had been sent to Ferncliff were taken to the church, where the altar and the choir were almost hidden behind them. The area outside the church was patrolled by police so that only invited family and friends were admitted to the funeral.

Colonel Astor's body was taken out of the chapel after the service, and the procession for the train station—and ultimately the Trinity Cemetery—began, with two carriages and four automobiles. The funeral party included Madeleine Astor and her mother and sister, as well as Vincent and Muriel Astor, along with Muriel's governess. Also included was Colonel Astor's sister Caroline. Mrs. Astor's maid, who had survived the sinking, was another member of the funeral party, as was Colonel Astor's Bar Harbor cousin, John Innes Kane. Ava Astor, back in America to deliver her daughter for the service, did not attend.

Vincent Astor assisted Madeleine into the first carriage, together with his sister, Muriel, and Mr. Dobbyn, Colonel Astor's secretary. Four Astor employees marched behind the hearse carrying Colonel Astor's body from the train station to the cemetery. Floral tributes from Colonel

Astor's friends and relatives filled to overflowing three large delivery wagons.

Though the funeral was private, onlookers had started assembling at the cemetery early, and by the time of the burial there was a crowd of an estimated five thousand people. Only the very few who possessed cards of admission were allowed to enter the cemetery, with the rest drawing themselves close around the cemetery walls and fence on either side of Broadway and 155th Street, while others sought the roofs of adjoining apartment houses and the viaduct along the river overlooking the burial ground for viewing vantage points. A squad of twelve policemen was detailed as a funeral escort from the train to the cemetery, while another detail held back the crowds at the 155th Street entrance of the cemetery.

The approach of the funeral procession was announced by the tolling of a bell. The choir of the Trinity Chapel began singing. The coffin was completely covered with lavender orchids. After a prayer was offered and the Episcopal burial service performed, Colonel Astor's coffin was placed in the Astor family vault, above that of his father, William Backhouse Astor, near the remains of his mother and those of the original John Jacob Astor.

* * *

Since the time of *Titanic*'s sinking, there had been much public discussion of Colonel Astor's will, which was especially heightened by the fact that Mrs. Astor was pregnant with a baby who was conceived after the will had been drawn up. The Astor estate offices did their best to quell this talk until after Colonel Astor's funeral.

According to a story that began circulating immediately after *Titanic*'s sinking and was attributed to those "in the confidence of Vincent Astor and from the managers of the estate," Colonel Astor had chosen to sail aboard *Titanic* because of a desire to return home earlier than planned, so that he could make a change in his will. Colonel Astor's estate was estimated to be at $100 million, or approximately $2 billion when adjusted for inflation. As was Astor family tradition, it was expected the bulk of the estate would go to a single male heir. Because the will was written before Madeleine's unborn child had been conceived, Vincent was presumed to be that heir.

After the sinking, there was much speculation as to what percentage of Colonel Astor's estate Vincent would receive as opposed to his stepmother and half-sibling. There was also discussion about the ages of some of the heirs, particularly Madeleine. She was only nineteen years old, technically a minor in the eyes of the law (until the age of twenty-one). Some speculated on what rights that would give her father over anything that she inherited and whether he had the legal right to sign away her rights to everything to anyone he wanted.

Colonel Astor had signed his will in New York on September 18, 1911, eight days after he married Madeleine. One of the witnesses was his Bar Harbor cousin John Innes Kane. James Roosevelt (husband of Colonel Astor's late sister Helen) and Mr. Biddle were among the executors. According to the Astor estate, after Colonel Astor's internment there was no formal gathering of the Astors to hear a formal reading of the will, but its contents had been communicated to all those interested as soon as the report of this death was confirmed. There was a group of thirty reporters at the filing of the will in court. The Astor estate ultimately released an abstract of the will to avoid a crush of reporters at the office.

"Astor Fortune Goes to Vincent," read the headline of the May 7, 1912, edition of the *New York Times*.

Madeleine was made the beneficiary of a $3 million trust fund, receiving the interest for life or until remarriage but never receiving the principal, as well as use of the Fifth Avenue Astor mansion in New York City. In the event of her death or remarriage, Madeleine would forfeit everything; the trust fund and the use of the Fifth Avenue mansion would revert back to Vincent, who still retained the mansion's ownership in any event. Madeleine's stepdaughter, Muriel, would do better than her stepmother with a larger trust fund, at $5 million, and control over the principal when she reached the age of twenty-one. The rest of the considerable Astor estate went to Vincent, as expected.

The terms of Colonel Astor's will, which was drawn up before Madeleine had become pregnant, allowed only a $3 million trust for any unborn issue. This was only 2 percent of his father's fortune, while Vincent inherited 98 percent. This uneven distribution of Colonel Astor's wealth would cause friction between the two brothers as long as they both lived.

Vincent Astor would inherit everything else: Beechwood at Newport, Ferncliff at Rhinebeck, and ownership (but not possession) of the Fifth Avenue mansion, the yacht, and all personal effects, including jewelry and clothing.

"Vincent Astor in Full Control," reported the *New York Times*. Yet he technically was not, being under the age of majority, which was twenty-one years. Vincent would need to have a surrogate appointed by the court, as would Mrs. Astor and her unborn child. Though Vincent Astor owned the Astor estate, he could not legally collect the rent.

There was criticism of the terms of Colonel Astor's will that required Madeleine's forfeiture of her inheritance if she remarried. The *New York Times* ran an editorial titled "Making It Costly to Remarry," saying that the need to use a will to ensure fidelity to the "departed shows little confidence in the ability of that memory to survive unless helped by the threat of a money penalty in case of forgetfulness."

* * *

By May, Madeleine was spending part of each day with her mother or sister, receiving no other callers. By the end of May, Madeleine Astor was taking a daily drive and/or walk through Central Park. She would be accompanied by police officers to protect her privacy from the crowd of onlookers and reporters that would appear when she left the Fifth Avenue mansion. Her father was looking after her financial interests with the aid of counsel.

On May 31, less than two months after *Titanic* sank, Mrs. Astor would welcome Captain Rostron, master of her rescue ship, *Carpathia*, as the guest of honor at a small luncheon in her Fifth Avenue home. The trip from the Cunard dock to the Astor mansion would prove to be an adventure for Captain Rostron and Dr. William McGee when the taxicab in which they were riding threw a wheel. The cab skidded onto the sidewalk and almost turned upside down, but no one was injured.

Arriving on Fifth Avenue at the Astor mansion, Mrs. Astor's two guests had to make their way through a cordon of photographers, moving picture operators, and onlookers to get to the front door. Because Mrs. Astor was in deep mourning, the luncheon was very small, including only two other guests: Mrs. John B. Thayer of Haverford, Pennsylvania, and Mrs. John Bradley Cumings of New York. Both women were dressed in deep black. Mrs. Eleanor Widener, who had been the third occupant of Captain Rostron's surrendered cabin along with Mrs. Astor and Mrs. Thayer, had planned to accompany Mrs. Thayer from Pennsylvania for the luncheon but had to cancel at the last minute due to the extreme cold she was suffering from her time on the open water.

In comparison to the mourning black of the women at the luncheon, the Astor dining room presented more color, decorated with pink roses and wildflowers. The menu, arranged personally by Madeleine, was described as simple. Mrs. Astor would present Captain Rostron with a gold watch for her appreciation of what he and the crew of the *Carpathia* had done for her comfort and for all the survivors of the *Titanic.*

* * *

Madeleine Astor's every movement was being watched by the people of Maine, the country, and the world, all wanting to hear the good news that the Astor baby had been born. Conceived and carried through such trying times, curious people wanted to see that the baby had not been affected by such a trying prenatal life. They also looked for a ray of hope from the overwhelming tragedy that had so strongly been a part of their world for the past few months. Just as Madeleine was a symbol of a vastly changing society, her son was a symbol of *Titanic.*

The due date of the Astor heir had been publicly announced as July, and at the first of that month all eyes turned (or stayed) on the Astors' Fifth Avenue mansion. "Awaiting an Astor Heir," was the headline in the *New York Sun*'s July 4 edition.

By that time, Madeleine was seven and a half months pregnant, and she seemed to want to get out of the Fifth Avenue mansion, along with its waiting reporters and curious crowds. At first, she favored going to the country estate of Rhinebeck to get away from New York City's summer heat, but she ended up in Bernardsville, New Jersey. Her father, who was ill, had taken a cottage there for the season, and Madeleine visited with her parents and her sister before Vincent persuaded her to return to the Fifth Avenue mansion for his brother's birth. Mrs. Force accompanied her daughter on the trip back to New York and stayed until the baby was born.

As July turned into August, the curiosity of the public grew. Madeleine was past her due date. Had her trauma aboard *Titanic* had an effect on the unborn Astor heir? More and more, Mrs. Astor was inconvenienced by the growing curious crowd. Since recovering from the *Titanic* ordeal, she had started a habit of taking a daily drive, along with her nurse, in an automobile through Central Park. On August 6, the crowd grew so large that Madeleine Astor was "forced to considerable inconvenience" when taking her afternoon drive.

The sight of the automobile in front of the house that day to pick up Mrs. Astor and her nurse for the ride caused a larger-than-normal crowd to collect in front of the mansion. The chauffeur was forced to leave the front entrance and try to drive to the back entrance unnoticed. He was successful, and Mrs. Astor and her nurse were able to escape the crowd and take their ride through Central Park.

By now, Dr. Edward B. Cragin had also temporarily moved into the Fifth Avenue mansion. He would stay through the delivery. Dr. Kimball, who had helped Madeleine through her recovery after returning from *Titanic*, continued to call frequently at the Astor home. Dr. Cragin's arrival caused rumors and a growth in the already large crowd outside the mansion, with everyone expecting the delivery at any moment. That day, a small crowd (mostly women) stood during the evening for a time on the opposite side of Fifth Avenue, discussing the upcoming event. The Astor watchman who patrolled the corner of Fifth and Sixty-Fifth Streets was besieged with inquiries about the status of the upcoming birth. At one point in the evening, a group of children were playing in front of the house, and one little girl about three years old sat down for a while on the doorstep. The old watchman was about to order the child and her companions away, but several women persuaded him to allow them to remain, as they declared the child being there was a good omen for the baby's delivery.

Soon the Astor doctors were calling for quiet for Mrs. Astor. As a courtesy, the workmen who had been laying electric wires for more than a week on the other side of the street from the Astor home began to put in fourteen hours' labor to have the work finished by the first of the following week so as not to disturb Mrs. Astor during the delivery.

Though everyone seemed to be working toward peace and quiet for the expectant Madeleine Astor, she would find that she had inherited the Astor misfortune. The night after Dr. Cragin arrived, a bus ran into the Astors' Fifth Avenue home, hitting just below Madeleine's second-floor bedroom window.

At approximately 7:00 p.m. that evening, the Fifth Avenue bus was running northward and became entangled with a department store delivery car at the corner of Sixty-Fifth Street. In crashing with the delivery car, the driver of the bus was knocked unconscious, allowing the bus to hit the Astor mansion, passing through the outside heavy, imported-stone balustrade and iron railing, where it hung in the archway, against the building itself, directly under the bedroom of Mrs. Astor.

The faces of the Astor mansion's occupants instantly appeared in the windows, drawn by the crash and by the cries of the passengers. With the crowd that was already outside the mansion, combined with the crowd drawn by the crash, there were now more than one thousand people outside Madeleine's bedroom window. Traffic was blocked all around the block.

There were only six people on the bus at the time, thrown around the floor of the vehicle. The Astor servants quickly rushed from the mansion to help free the passengers from the wreck. Madeleine Astor watched the rescue work from her bedroom window, giving orders that the injured be brought into her home and cared for there. The victims entered the Astor mansion through the servants' entrance on Sixty-Fifth Street. They were given everything necessary for their comfort. They all refused an ambulance. Madeleine's doctor sent word that he would not leave the side of Mrs. Astor unless someone had been seriously injured, which they had not.

The accident caused a backup of traffic along the busy Fifth Avenue, which led in turn to a clog of vehicles waiting to move again, with horns blowing and men shouting to clear the road. Dr. Cragin was soon on the phone with the New York police. Six officers were sent from the Sixty-Seventh Street Station to keep order in front of the mansion. Within half an hour, the crowd was cleared away and all that remained was a score or so of the curious, as well as the big bus hanging over the archway, with a little broken stone and bent iron lying about.

Dr. Cragin later issued a report that the shock had not had a lasting effect on Mrs. Astor.

* * *

On August 13, the *New York Tribune* reported that lights were showing at many windows of the Astor mansion early in the morning and that there appeared to be quite a stir within the house. Dr. Cragin sent word through the Astor butler that he would issue a bulletin when the child had been born.

On the morning of August 14, the same day as the opening of the Astor Cup yacht race in Newport, Madeleine gave birth to her first son, John Jacob Astor VI. He weighed seven pounds and three-quarters of an ounce. Young John Astor was said to bear a striking resemblance to his father. Mother and son were reported to be doing splendidly. Two nurses had been in attendance during the birth, assisting the doctor. The first news to the public came from a bulletin issued by Dr. Cragin, which read, "Mrs. Astor has a son, born at 8:13 o'clock. His name is John Jacob Astor. Mother and son are in good condition."

The statement was given to newspaper reporters who were waiting outside the house by members of the household staff. The Astor servants were made part of the celebration of the victory of life, reportedly wearing broad smiles as they gave out Dr. Cragin's bulletin. Those who had been with the Astor family for years were allowed to have a look at the baby immediately after he was born.

"Naturally there was some little excitement both within and outside the house when it became known that the baby had been born and that it was a boy," reported the *New York Times*.

The public interest that centered around the posthumous birth of the child of the late Colonel John Jacob Astor was responsible for a new institution, one that continues today with England's royal family—what the newspapers call the birth watch.

Mrs. Force had been with Madeleine continually since her return from New Jersey, and Madeleine's sister Katherine had also come to the Fifth Avenue mansion for the delivery. Mr. Force would visit his daughter and first grandchild afterward. Madeleine received many messages of congratulations from friends and relatives, among them being a cablegram from Vincent Astor, who was on a motor trip with his mother on the European continent. Shortly after the arrival of the cablegram, Vincent sent an immense box of American Beauty roses.

News of the birth spread quickly in Newport, and as people began to assemble at the Casino for the evening, the birth was the general topic of conversation there. "There were many expressions of pleasure and good will," reported the *New York Sun*.

Eleanor Widener, who by now was spending the summer in her Newport summer home, sent a congratulatory telegram to Mrs. Astor, as did Margaret "the unsinkable Molly" Brown, also spending her summer in Newport. Mrs. Brown would sponsor a fundraiser for a new maternity ward at the hospital in Newport, Rhode Island, for the occasion, with one hundred Newport women pledging their sponsorship for the project.

* * *

Two months later, Vincent Astor would turn twenty-one and legally inherit the Astor fortune and control of the business. By now Vincent was living at 1025 Fifth Avenue in a four-story marble home that he had leased for the winter from the US ambassador to Holland. He was not too far from Madeleine and his brother. Vincent Astor spent his birthday working at the Astor estate offices, where a small crowd of curious persons had gathered out front to witness the 10:00 a.m. arrival of the slim, serious-faced young man on his first day at work. At the office, Vincent was met by Mr. Dobbyn and Mr. Biddle, who turned over possession of Colonel Astor's private office, where Vincent worked at the desk formally used by his father. Vincent worked several hours that day in order to familiarize himself with the many details that entered into the management of an estate made up so largely of diverse parcels of New York property, as well as answering a large pile of letters on his desk that required attention. In his office were also birthday reminders in the form of several registered packages containing gifts. There were two large bouquets of magnificent roses, one bearing the congratulations of Mrs. Madeleine Force Astor and the other containing the card of his baby brother, John Jacob Astor VI. Vincent had his father's famous fortune, and John had his father's famous name.

When leaving the office for luncheon, Vincent was greeted again by the crowd that had been waiting outside the Astor estate offices that morning. He accepted the congratulations of the curious strangers with a quiet nod, but without a smile. After leaving work for the day, he traveled to Rhinebeck, where he spent a simple family birthday dinner with his mother and sister.

In the end, with one more year left before graduation from Harvard, Vincent chose to withdraw from the university so that he could focus on the Astor business. A reporter who covered Vincent's announcement regarding the Harvard decision asked the new head of the Astor estate whether Vincent was considering an increase in the settlement received by his half brother.

"Young Mr. Astor was considerably fussed when asked," reported the *New York Sun*. Vincent replied that it was a matter that he would never discuss.

* * *

As the *Carpathia* was arriving in New York with Colonel Astor's second wife, his first wife, Ava, was announcing her hasty return to the United States to be with her grieving son. Soon she and her daughter, Muriel, were sailing aboard the *Kaiser Wilhelm der Grosse*, traveling under assumed names. Ava Astor occupied a cabin on the promenade deck of the liner, where she had the meals served. She did not mix with her fellow passengers. "Her aim appeared to be to avoid notice and to conceal her presence on board the ship as much as possible," reported the *New York Times*.

Before she disembarked, Ava Astor was sent a note by reporters requesting an interview. She wrote on the back of the paper, "Mrs. John Astor regrets that it is impossible for her to give any interview. She has nothing to say." Though this seemed to be a nonresponse, the name she signed let New York society subtly know that she considered herself *the* Mrs. Astor, even after Colonel Astor's death.

Ava Astor would arrive in New York on May 1, the day before Colonel Astor's funeral, so that their daughter, Muriel, could be in attendance, accompanied by her governess. Arriving back in the United States, Ava Astor was clad in mourning clothing in a long, loose, black satin coat, with skirt and waist, straw hat, and bow of same somber hue, black pumps with silver buckles, and a half mourning veil that completely screened her face. The only jewelry she wore was a diamond brooch and a thin diamond chain attached to a gold watch.

Ava and Muriel were met at the pier in Hoboken, New Jersey, by Ava's brother, William, and her lawyer from Philadelphia. They traveled in an automobile to the Ritz-Carlton Hotel, where apartments had been reserved for Ava and her party. When asked by the reporters whether she had anything to say as to her plans for a stay in this country, Mrs. Astor replied in a subdued tone that she was not accustomed to giving interviews at any time and particularly not under the present circumstances. "I have come over to be with my son and I cannot tell what my plans are or how long I shall remain on this side of the water. All that will be settled when I have consulted with my family and my friends."

The *Chicago Examiner*, which had taken shots at Madeleine Force's mother after the announcement of her engagement to Colonel Astor, now questioned Ava Astor's motherly motivations: "Mother Love or Ambition?"

"Has Mrs. Astor No. 1 Returned to America to File Her Claim on Social Leadership as the 'Real Widow' of Col. Astor—or Just to Keep Vincent from Some Ill-advised Marriage?

"Fashionable society imagines Mrs. John Jacob Astor No. 1 standing at the beginning of two widely different roads. Has she chosen the one that leads to social supremacy and will enable her to extinguish all the social claims of Mrs. Astor No. 2? Or has she chosen the one that leads to a happy home for her son Vincent?

"If she succeeds in breaking off all communication between Vincent Astor and his stepmother there is no manner of doubt that society will continue its present policy of neglecting the young widow. Many of Mrs. Astor's friends say that this is her sole reason for returning to New York. One prominent matron says that Mrs. Astor does not intend to let the young widow and her family carry things with a high hand; that Vincent is not to be allowed to be on friendly terms with the new connections brought into the family by his father's second marriage, that he is to be a stranger to his baby stepbrother.

"Her active preparations for the coming social season have added complications to an already extremely complicated social situation. Mrs. Astor's determination to take part again in American fashionable activity was quite unexpected.

"She can no longer reign in the three-million-dollar mansion fronting Central Park where her former triumphs occurred. But the women who will flock to her in her new home further down the avenue will never call on the second Mrs. Astor."

The *Chicago Examiner* also painted a bleak picture of Madeleine Astor's current situation, as well as her seeming lack of interest in reentering the society that she should, by rights, be leader of: "From the day of the marriage a great part of New York and Newport society has ignored the new Mrs. Astor. She is today hardly more than a very rich young woman, living in the magnificent mansion on Fifth Avenue built by the late Mrs. William Astor and her son for their joint use. This will be her home until she marries again. Not even her tragic widowhood won her the friendship of society. She is as much apart from the fashionable world as though she had not married one of its most important men. She lives alone in her superb home, unsought by society—and not seeking it.

"Was there ever a more peculiar state of affairs? The divorced wife wearing mourning, refusing all social engagements, and insisting on her right to be 'Mrs. Astor.' The second wife, wearing deeper mourning, living quietly and with dignity in her husband's home, caring for her baby . . . what will happen when her period of mourning is over? Will she then make an effort to conquer society for the sake of her small son? Or will she marry one of the friends of her early life, giving up the five million?"

* * *

John Astor VI had his first picture taken a month after his birth at the Fifth Avenue mansion. Madeleine had only four copies printed. The first copy went to the friend who took the picture, one went to Madeleine's parents, and one went to Vincent; Madeleine kept the fourth. Afterward, Madeleine took her son on his first trip away from home, leaving one afternoon for a week's visit to the country home of her parents at Bernardsville, New Jersey.

As the time passed, attention turned to Madeleine Astor's social plans. Society had unofficial rules of ascension, with the wife of the current head of the Astor family being the leader of society. The Astor divorce had happened just as that change was to take place, throwing the unofficial rules of ascension into chaos. Ever since the Astor divorce, Ava Astor had been using the name Mrs. John Astor. Who truly was the head of society? Or had the Astors ruined their claim to that position due to their scandals of the past few years?

Slowly Madeleine started making her way back into society. Until the sinking of *Titanic*, she was called Mrs. Madeleine Force-Astor. She now announced that she would like to be known as Mrs. John Jacob Astor. Madeleine Astor would break with generations of social tradition and wear white for her mourning clothing instead of the traditional black.

"Mrs. Astor to Wear White," read the headlines. The *Portland Evening Express* was among those applauding Madeleine's bold decision, looking forward to the effect Mrs. Astor's decision would have on society: "If the usage of black can be changed, it will be a boon to humanity. Death is sad enough without making it more impressive and gloomy by the trapping and habiliments of woe. Less and less do we thrust our private troubles into public notice. All of us have troubles and griefs which we cannot betoken. Why should one particular sorrow be singled out for exhibition?"

There was soon speculation about Mrs. Astor's summer plans. With her name and position as Mrs. Astor, this information was incredibly important to society. The people of Bar Harbor were encouraged when the *New England Resorter*, a magazine devoted to news of the summer colonies of New England, announced that Mrs. Astor would spend the summer there.

A return to Bar Harbor would be a natural choice for Madeleine Astor. Newport, though thought of as more fashionable, had not been Madeleine's territory. She and Colonel Astor had been received there after the engagement announcement, but after a week of large-scale engagements, the couple had to retreat. That was the extent of her socialization at Newport, Rhode Island. Though she could afford to rent a summer cottage there, she had lost the use of Beechwood through Vincent's inheritance and his use of the cottage himself.

Besides, Madeleine had already made Bar Harbor, Maine, her own territory by way of her play on the tennis courts of the Bar Harbor Swimming Club. While Bar Harbor in the early 1900s was about society, it was also about free thinking. The original summer colonists had been artists. Society was important there, but it was not the only item of importance.

Ultimately, Madeleine Astor would not return to Bar Harbor that summer. Instead, she chose to stay in the Fifth Avenue mansion after Vincent Astor persuaded her that an Astor heir should be born there, as he had been. Vincent said the medical care was vastly better in New York City than at any summer resort.

* * *

Despite whatever rifts that might be forming in the Astor family, whether real or imagined by the newspapers, the family came together for young John Astor's christening.

John Jacob Astor VI was almost four months old when he was christened on December 2, 1912. The ceremony was performed in the library of the Fifth Avenue mansion, which had been decorated with pink and white roses for the occasion. The godmother was Colonel Astor's sister Caroline Astor Wilson, and the godfathers were Madeleine's cousin Lyndon Dodge and M. Orme Wilson Jr., Caroline's son. In attendance, besides the godparents, were Vincent, as well as relatives from the Kane family and Madeleine's family. Everybody said afterward that the baby "behaved splendidly" throughout the ceremony. Those who took part in the ceremony received dainty little boxes done in white and pink and filled with bonbons. The cover of each box was ornamented with a baby's head surrounded by cherubs, the initials "J. J. A." in gold in one corner, and the date, "Dec. 2, 1912," delicately traced in gold on the opposite corner of the box.

CHAPTER 7
Plain Madeleine

Her marriage to Colonel Astor, whom she won solely by her beauty and charm, at once placed her in a position to dictate to the resort here and families who would have gladly snubbed her as plain Madeleine Force were forced to recognize her unquestioned social leadership as Mrs. John Jacob Astor, and mother of the heir to the Astor millions.

—*BAR HARBOR TIMES*

THE NEW YEAR OF 1913 WOULD START OFF WITH ANOTHER INVASION into Madeleine Astor's privacy at her Fifth Avenue home. Though the young widow, with her five-month-old child, was living quietly in the Astor mansion and had not involved herself in politics, attempts would be made to pull her into different political causes. Just a week after the New Year's holiday, the Astor mansion, along with other mansions along the fashionable Fifth Avenue, was the target of a protest held by the city's suffragettes.

"Suffragists Storm Upper 5th Avenue. Battle of the Butlers," read the headline in the *New York Sun*.

At 8:00 p.m. on January 6, 1913, a large group of suffragettes gathered on Fifth Avenue. The group broke into smaller groups of two, and down the avenue they walked, knocking on doors all the way.

Miss Martha Klatschken had drawn the address of Mrs. Astor. A reporter described Miss Klatschken as approaching the imposing mansion "quite unabashed by the fact that it seemed to be entirely dark."

Another young woman rang the bell, receiving the flash of outside lights as a response. The Astor butler opened the door a crack and surveyed the two women outside. Most butlers along Fifth Avenue had replied that the occupants of the household were not at home. The Astor butler said that Mrs. Astor had already retired for the evening. Miss Klatschken handed the butler a card.

"I said to him that if Mrs. Astor would let me know, I would come over any day and tell her about votes for women," Martha Klatschken told a reporter. "The Astor butler was not a citizen, so of course there was no use spending time on him."

Miss Klatschken went on to complain about the expense of a wasted calling card. "They cost me thirty-nine cents a hundred and naturally were not engraved," she was heard telling her friends as she walked away from Madeleine Astor's home.

* * *

In Bar Harbor, having missed the visit of Madeleine Astor the season before, the people of the summer resort again spent the spring awaiting news of whether Mrs. Astor would spend her summer season there or go elsewhere. With her name and her resources, she could summer anywhere she desired.

Bar Harbor had already lost one member of the Astor family from the summer colony that year with the death of summer colonist and Astor cousin John Innes Kane. Though the Kanes had been visiting Bar Harbor for years, John was able to enjoy his cottage, Breakwater, for fewer than ten of them.

"Bar Harbor Sincerely Sorry," wrote the *Bar Harbor Record* in the February 5, 1913, edition.

Mr. Kane had taken ill while summering in Bar Harbor the previous year. He died after an operation in New York for intestinal trouble. The newspaper reflected the "universal" feelings of sorrow felt by Bar Harbor, which was a small community where the lives of the summer colonists and the year-round residents interwove and depended on one another. There was a real sense of familiarity. "Mr. Kane was thoroughly respected," wrote the *Record.*

Having no children, John Innes Kane would leave Breakwater to his widow, Annie, who would continue her annual summer season visits to Bar Harbor.

* * *

On June 4, the *Bar Harbor Record* was able to report the headline it had waited a year to announce: "Mrs. Astor's Summer Home."

"The New York HERALD Says Mrs. John Jacob Astor will spend the summer at Bar Harbor, where she has taken a cottage, and will go there next week with her little son, John Jacob Astor, who is developing into a vigorous boy. Mrs. Astor's sister, Miss Katherine Force, has arranged to spend most of the summer with her. Later in the spring or in the early summer, Mrs. William H. Force will join them, to remain until the autumn.

"Because of her mourning, Mrs. Astor will not take any part in the social activities at Bar Harbor, and another year may elapse before she will appear in society."

The 1913 summer season started off chilly in Bar Harbor, with the month of June being cooler than normal. Madeleine arrived that month, along with her sister, taking the Eden Street cottage La Selva.

The eleven-year-old La Selva had been built by a Pennsylvania coal operator who had recently died, making the cottage available for lease for the summer. The Bar Harbor Swimming Club lay in the center of Bar Harbor, and to its left ran West Street with its historic cottages. Beyond West Street ran Eden Street with its new cottages built along the water.

La Selva was a grand three-story cottage that sat on 2.11 acres with 360 feet of shore frontage and a high stone wall along Eden Street that would help shield the cottage's grand entrance from the curious crowds that inevitably formed and lingered anywhere Madeleine Astor went. The water side of the cottage featured a patio of flat stone with a commanding view of Frenchman Bay, the private stairs to which lay just feet way, across from a well-manicured lawn. The cottage was designed by architects Andrews, Jacques, and Rantoul, who had designed many of Bar Harbor's elaborate summer cottages, including La Rochelle, originally the Bowdoin cottage and now the home of the Bar Harbor Historical Society, as well as the Bar Harbor Swimming Club.

La Selva was described as slightly smaller and more intimate than the neighboring cottages. The outside patio was surrounded by a granite railing with ornate decorations at the top of the stairs to the water. The interior of the hundred-foot-wide La Selva featured more than twenty rooms, with the main first-floor rooms opening to the scenic patio. Five master bedrooms on the second floor opened to balconies overlooking the water. The third floor was an attic with master bedrooms and five maids' rooms.

Despite La Selva's close proximity to the Bar Harbor Swimming Club, Madeleine spent a very quiet summer in the cottage, reportedly taking an active role in the mothering of her baby, John, often seen walking him in the "perambulator," accompanied by Madeleine's nurse. Along with her mourning, part of Madeleine's self-imposed seclusion may have been a need for privacy. Ever since her name had been linked with Colonel Astor two years previously, crowds of curious people did what they could just to get a look at her. Now she also had her newborn son to protect. John Jacob Astor VI was the "*Titanic* Baby." His father had been famous, his mother was now the most famous person in the country, and people wanted to get a glimpse of the Astor heir. They wanted to see the baby who symbolized so much tragedy and hope—or at least see a picture. They wanted to see whether he physically bore the effects of the trauma he had endured in the womb. They just wanted to see.

"The local newspapermen have been besieged with demands for the securing of such a photograph, and a news photographer for one of the largest cities has been here for a week in a vain attempt to secure a snapshot of the features of the heir of the late John Jacob Astor," wrote the Bar Harbor correspondent of the *Bangor Daily News* that summer.

Though Madeleine Astor's name would not be noted in the newspapers much that season, her sister Katherine did receive headlines during her stay that summer after rumors were confirmed from La Selva regarding her engagement.

The name Henri C. Harnickell did not command the attention of society as did the name John Jacob Astor. Mr. Harnickell was a stockbroker who lived in an old-fashioned brownstone in Brooklyn with his sister, his mother having died two years previously. Mr. Harnickell was a director of the Christopher and Tenth Street Railroad Company, among whose ten largest stockholders was the very wealthy and influential Rockefeller family of New York and Mount Desert Island. Mr. Harnickell did not appear to be well known in society circles.

For the past year it had been rumored that Mr. Harnickell was paying attention to Katherine Force. In 1912, they were seen often together at Katherine's parents summer home in Bernardsville, New Jersey, while widowed sister Madeleine was in the midst of preparing for single motherhood. Floral arrangements frequently arrived for Katherine from her suitor. Stories of an engagement spread, and an informal, private announcement was made, but no formal announcement was issued because the Force family was still in mourning for Colonel Astor, it being within the first year of his death.

Mr. Harnickell would arrive in Bar Harbor from New York in 1913 shortly after the engagement rumor had been printed in the newspapers. The couple was seen often, having attended the opening ball of the Bar Harbor Swimming Club for the season and playing tennis there the following day. At La Selva in July, the Force family confirmed the engagement rumor. They would have preferred to have made a formal announcement, they said. Though no official date had been set and no wedding plans had been made, it was understood that the ceremony would take place in Bar Harbor.

"The announcement has created widespread interest," wrote the *Bar Harbor Record*.

* * *

On August 14, 1913, John Jacob Astor VI reached his first birthday. The occasion was spent in Bar Harbor, though the day was marked with privacy. Madeleine would spend that season teaching her young son the ways of Astor philanthropy. Mrs. Astor would announce that she had donated $100 in her son's name to a national organization called Diet Kitchen, which strove to reduce infant mortality. The group provided meals to children during the summer months, "when the heat saps the vitality of babies." The dues were $1. The aim of the group was to "have babies of the rich help the babies of the poor."

Though Madeleine did not socialize much, she stayed in Bar Harbor until the end of October, a while after most cottagers had returned to their homes.

"Mrs. John Jacob Astor of New York and Bar Harbor, and her sister Miss Katherine Force, also the famous Astor baby, and servants were in Bangor for almost an hour last Friday, on their way to New York," reported the October 29, 1913, edition of the *Bar Harbor Record*. "They arrived in a Pullman car at 1:05 o'clock from Bar Harbor and left with the 1:50 train. The party carried a large amount of baggage.

"Mrs. John Jacob Astor still refuses to indulge in even the mildest social activities and wears heavy mourning clothes."

* * *

A week before leaving Bar Harbor, it was announced that Colonel Astor's first wife, Ava, would not be returning to London for at least a year. It was said that she wanted to help guide her son in his social and matrimonial destinies.

"Newport welcomed her back with open arms," wrote the *Bar Harbor Record* of Ava Astor.

* * *

Madeleine Astor's name would continue to appear occasionally in the newspaper headlines between leaving Maine in October and her return the following season. With her father taking care of her financial interests, Madeleine Astor would fight the tax valuation on the $3 million trust fund left by her late husband. She said that some of the properties included in the fund had been promised to her tax free.

Christmas 1913 must have been bittersweet for Madeleine, now twenty years old. With Colonel Astor gone two years, she now had one more Christmas without him than she did with him. Four days before Christmas, Madeleine would travel to the church in Rhinebeck, New York, where she had said goodbye to her late husband at his funeral the previous year. She had donated a stained glass window to be placed in the church in memory of her husband. The memorial window had three panels, with the central panel representing Jesus Christ walking on water and each of the two side panels showing a standing female figure. The words "Be Not Afraid" were near the top.

"In loving memory of John Jacob Astor, born July 13, 1864, died April 15, 1912," read the inscription.

Madeleine was met at the church by the church's rector and members of the vestry. The window had been placed, and together the group made plans for the official dedication, to be held a week later, on December 27, two days after Christmas.

"Mrs. Astor was much pleased with the appearance of the window," reported the *New York Sun*. "At her request it will remain veiled until Saturday."

* * *

The first photograph of John Jacob Astor VI was released to the public by his mother the following month. The picture had been taken in the nursery of the Fifth Avenue mansion in New York. The *Bar Harbor Record* at the time described John Astor as being rather delicate at birth but having grown into a "lusty youngster, and is now one of the healthiest and most rugged of all babies in New York." He was described as having blue eyes and a pink complexion, with the "happiest disposition imaginable." Before the official photograph was released, John had been carefully shielded from eager photographers, of which there were many, during their daily walks in Central Park.

Madeleine did not spend all her time away from Bar Harbor in New York. She would travel to Bernardsville, New Jersey, to spend time with her ailing father, who had only three years of life left. In the spring of 1914, she would travel with her son and sister to visit White Sulphur Springs, West Virginia, staying for five weeks for the health of the baby. At one point the sisters, the baby, and Mr. Harnickell drove to Elmhurst Farm, a popular large brick tavern on the Greenbrier River, for a "Virginia luncheon." During the visit Katherine participated in an indoor lawn tennis championship tournament but was eliminated in the second round.

"The national indoor champion, who drew a default in the first round, proved to be too good for Miss Force, whose lack of tournament experience operated against her. Although she put up a plucky game, Miss Force was no match for Miss Wagner," wrote the *New York Times*.

The Force sisters returned to New York in early May. Mrs. Astor was reportedly delighted with the improvement in her son's health after their stay in the south.

* * *

The Bar Harbor summer season to which Madeleine Astor arrived in 1914 was overshadowed by concerns over a European conflict that would later become World War I. In July of that year, Germany would declare war against much of Europe, with the United States joining in the conflict three years later. There was talk of a submarine force being headquartered at the strategic Bar Harbor, one of five locations in the United States being considered. Some expressed concern that Bar Harbor might be attacked by the Germans because of its geographically strategic importance.

With war about to break out, more socialites were choosing to spend their summers in the United States rather than risking a trip abroad. The *Bar Harbor Record* reported that more cottages were open that season than the previous one. The Brewer Ice Company reported that it was furnishing 147 cottages with ice that summer, with 128 cottages having been supplied the previous season.

The effects of the war were brought to the doorsteps of the cottagers of Bar Harbor immediately after it was declared in July. The *Kronprinzessin Cecilie*, a German passenger ship headed from the United States to Europe loaded with passengers, gold, and silver, was instructed to find safe harbor immediately after Germany declared war. In the darkness, the ship made its way into Frenchman Bay, with the elite of society waking up the next morning and looking out the windows of their glamorous cottages to enjoy their million-dollar views only to see a large German ship at anchor. Before noon that day, the public Shore Path, which ran along the front of some of Bar Harbor's largest mansions, was filled with people. Small boats took groups of the curious out to take a look at the spectacle. The ship's 1,400 passengers soon would be unloaded and transported back to their homes on trains, and the gold and silver were unloaded onto an American warship that promptly arrived from Newport. The *Kronprinzessin Cecilie* and her crew, however, stayed in Bar Harbor until almost the Christmas holiday while officials decided what to do with them. Through the end of the 1914 summer season and beyond, the members of the Bar Harbor summer colony watched with amusement as the members of the crew were seen walking through town with supplies obtained at local farms slung over their shoulders or going fishing here and there.

* * *

There was already talk late in the spring about whether Mrs. Astor would again take the cottage La Selva, as she reportedly desired a cottage closer to the post office and the center of the village. In the June 10 edition of the *Bar Harbor Record*, Madeleine Astor was reported as "Expected Daily." By June 17, Mrs. Astor's domestics had arrived at La Selva to prepare for her arrival. By the end of the month, Madeleine's mother and sister had arrived for the summer, as had Henri Harnickell, who was there for a visit. Another guest was Miss Helen Dodge of New York, a cousin to the Force family through Madeleine's mother. Mr. Force would join them later in the season.

Before the *Titanic* disaster, Katherine Force had been overshadowed by her famous younger sister. By now she had caught the attention of society in her own right, with her announced engagement drawing more newspaper attention to her. Though Madeleine Astor's name would always make headlines, the sensation of those headlines was not what it had been the past few years. Madeleine seemed to have no interest in dating, which was the next headline for which the newspaper reporters were looking. The newspapers turned more and more to Katherine Force for their stories.

Katherine's picture, along with Madeleine's and those of twenty-five other society women, was featured in the July 1914 edition of the popular weekly magazine *Harper's Bazaar*.

"The stranger is not welcomed within the gates at Bar Harbor," wrote *Harper's*. "This garden spot tucked away on Mt. Desert Island has not been invaded by the forces of progress during the last decade, because the ruling powers have decreed that it shall be kept as nearly as possible like the resort their forebearers discovered. Until a year ago an automobile was not allowed on the Island. The hotels are in reality big boarding houses where the guests are the children and the grandchildren of the original summer visitors. A proposition to build an up-to-date hotel is being met with strenuous opposition from the owners of the cottages. The majority of these owners are the socially select from Boston and Philadelphia and the atmosphere of exclusiveness which envelops them in their home cities is not lifted in the Maine resort. Truly the pathway of the social-climber in Bar Harbor is as rocky as the coastline of the resort."

Unlike the previous year, Madeleine now accompanied her older sister and mother on social visits, many of them athletically centered. Madeleine, and Katherine as her guest, enrolled in the golf tournament at the Kebo Golf Club in the middle of July along with twenty-six other players. A week later, they were playing in the tennis tournament at the Bar Harbor Swimming Club.

"The Swimming Club still is the life of Bar Harbor, with its daily half hour of dancing, its symphony concerts, afternoon teas, tennis courts and its swimming pool, which at the noon hour attracts large numbers," wrote the *Bar Harbor Record*.

On July 27, Katherine won her tennis match against socialite Miss Augusta McCagg, while Madeleine won against Miss Helen Draper, who would marry the nephew of President William Taft three years later. The following week, Madeleine was playing mixed doubles, teamed with Mr. Edgar Scott.

* * *

August 1914 would find the Astors celebrating John's second birthday with a party at La Selva. Among those at the party were Katherine and both of Madeleine's parents, her father having traveled there especially for the celebration.

"Rather delicate at his birth, the baby has grown into a healthy youngster and is one of the most rugged babies seen at Bar Harbor this summer," wrote the *New York Times*. "The child closely resembles his mother. He has a wealth of light golden hair, the clearest of blue eyes and a pink and white complexion. In the baby appears no trace of the grim tragedy in which his father bravely lost his life."

Vincent Astor was also in Bar Harbor at the same time, though whether he visited his brother and stepmother was not reported. Vincent was traveling with his new bride, Miss Helen Dinsmore Huntington. The couple had sailed into Frenchman Bay aboard the *Noma* to view the *Kronprinzessin Cecilie* and interview her captain. After leaving there, the couple would sail up the Kennebec River and down Back Bay to Boothbay Harbor. Ultimately, they would travel to Montreal and then head to Europe later in the year.

Vincent and Helen Astor were married at the bride's father's estate in Rhinebeck, New York, four months before the August visit. Miss Huntington was described by newspapers as scarcely more than a schoolgirl, and Vincent was twenty-two. In Vincent's wedding party was George C. Douglas of Minneapolis, Minnesota, who served as an usher. His father, Walter E. Douglas, had perished on *Titanic*. The two young men met and became fast friends during the sad wait at the train station in Halifax for the arrival of their fathers' bodies. Vincent's mother and sister were also in attendance at the wedding. Because Vincent had become seriously ill a few days before the wedding date, a simple ceremony was held, with Mrs. Vincent Astor doing most of the handshaking in the reception line. The two honeymooned at Ferncliff.

By now Vincent's mother, whom many thought would try to claim the role of leader of New York society, was spending less time in the United States and more time in her town house in England. She would remarry in that country in 1919, becoming Lady Ribblesdale.

* * *

The Madeleine Astor who spent the summer season in Bar Harbor in 1914 was not the same Madeleine Force who had arrived on its rocky shores six years previously. She was taking notice of her world and her responsibilities in it, especially with her famous name and the influential position she held. This change in young Madeleine would cause controversy.

While in Bar Harbor that season, with the war only a few weeks old, Mrs. Astor was offered membership on a committee planning a peace parade in New York City. Though it would be another three years before the United States joined the war, peace protests were soon springing up across the country. Feminists began to mobilize against the war, forming a Women's Peace Parade Committee to plan a silent protest march against the war. The committee was composed of women from trade unions, feminist organizations, and social reform organizations. Madeleine Astor and her cousin Helen Dodge, who had been visiting Madeleine in Bar Harbor that summer, were both invited to join the Peace Parade Committee. Mrs. Astor telegraphed her acceptance on the committee from Bar Harbor, while Helen Dodge wanted to know what groups were behind the demonstration before joining.

"Mrs. Astor Works for Peace Parade Committee," read the headline in the August 14 edition of the *Bar Harbor Record.*

On August 29, 1914, the parade was held, with 1,500 women marching down Fifth Avenue in protest of the war. It would appear that Madeleine Astor was not at the protest but instead continued her first summer socializing in Bar Harbor. At the same time as the protest, the Astor and Force families had a table at the Cabaret Show in Bar Harbor, held to benefit the Mount Desert Island Hospital. Less than a week later, Madeleine would attend the Red Cross Ball, held in the Grand Hall of the Bar Harbor Swimming Club for the benefit of the International Red Cross Society. Almost all of Bar Harbor's summer society was in attendance.

"It was one of the largest and most successful events ever given in Bar Harbor and almost the whole of the summer residents joined in making it a notable affair," wrote the *Bar Harbor Record.* "Mrs. John Jacob Astor was a patroness, along with most of the Bar Harbor Summer Colony."

* * *

The change in Madeleine was observable in not just the political events in which she was involved but also her intellectual pursuits. She had spent the previous winter in New York taking classes at the New York Training School for Deaconesses. She was one of six nonresident special students, along with her Bar Harbor Astor cousin Miss Sybil K. Kane. All the special students were unmarried women.

The school, which had been in existence for twenty-three years, provided two-year nonresidential courses for women interested in becoming deaconesses, serving as missionaries, or working in Christian education. Courses included Old Testament, New Testament, church history, and theology, all taught by local priests. For the residential students, there were practical courses in household management, embroidery, and the cutting and making of clothing. The Astor family, along with other prominent New York society families such as the Vanderbilts, were supporters of the program.

"Often she has been heard to remark 'As [Thomas] a Kempis says in his "The Imitation of Christ"' . . . or 'Speaking of socialism, if you will read [James] Keir Hardie's "*From Serfdom to socialism*," you will see it in entirely a new light. I am sure I did,'" reported the *Bar Harbor Times*.

People who socialized with her that summer were struck by the wisdom that fell easily from Madeleine's young mouth. They found her quite able to carry on her end of a conversation on such subjects as ethics, biblical history, and even socialism.

* * *

Before Madeleine Astor's first summer out of mourning was over, she had regained her title of tennis champion on the Bar Harbor Swimming Club courts. Playing with her sister as her teammate in the doubles tournament at the end of August against Mrs. Edgar Howard and Miss Dorothy Sturges, Madeleine won both sets "easily" with a score of 6–4, 6–3.

It was almost November before Madeleine Astor left Bar Harbor in 1914.

* * *

The effects of the war seemed to help Bar Harbor's 1915 season. By now overseas travel was forbidden, making resorts such as Bar Harbor more attractive to the country's wealthy. The *Bar Harbor Record* reported that the number of cottagers that season had more than doubled. Among the visitors that season were Miss Margaret Wilson, daughter of the president, and the grandson of former president Taft. The prominent DuPont family would also take a cottage for the season.

Bar Harbor continued to grow and evolve despite the war. What is now known as the Jackson Laboratory was established in 1915, the same year the federal government was discussing the possibility of establishing a national park on Mount Desert Island, now known as Acadia.

* * *

That spring the anniversary of the sinking of *Titanic* was noted in the April 21, 1915, edition of the *Bar Harbor Record.*

"*TITANIC* SUNK THREE YEARS AGO," read the headline. "Bar Harbor's summer colony was particularly interested."

* * *

The year 1915 started off with Madeleine Astor's picture on the front page of newspapers across the world. On January 4, along with other New York debutantes and matrons, Madeleine helped pack five thousand comfort kits for the people of war-torn France.

Madeleine would make headlines later that spring when she filed a required accounting of her expenditures from the allowance from her son's trust fund. When the relatively exorbitant amounts spent on John Jacob Astor VI's toys were revealed to the public, newspapers had fun with the story.

The claims in Mrs. Astor's court action caught the attention of the people of Maine, including the *Waterville Sentinel.* They were not as concerned about the way the money was spent, focusing on the loss of the spirit of fun that normally accompanies childhood: "Last year his toys cost $5,000 and everybody knows that as a boy gets bigger, the toys cost more. When the boy gets to be six years old, what a hardship it would be if half his income were required to keep him in playthings.

"The case of Baby Astor has been attracting much attention. There are many people who are indignant at the thought that his toys should cost so much. These good people have a great deal to say about the things which $5,000 would buy for the children of the poor. But perhaps, the saddest figure in the story is that of the little one whose playthings cost thousands of dollars annually. He will never know a lot of fun that comes to other boys.

"For with a $5,000 allowance for toys go a lot of other things. There are nurses and guardians who watch the little fellow every hour of the day. He never gets a chance to steal away and go in swimming with the other fellows. He will be taught to swim, of course, be he will never know the fun of cutting across a lot to dive into the big pool under the willows.

"When the circus comes to town, he will go and sit in a box. But he won't have the exquisite delight of getting up in the early morning to see the trains come in and follow the wagons to the lot with, perhaps, the chance of actually carrying water for the elephants. And he will never know the pleasure of getting out with the other fellows and rollicking around until there are rents in his clothes and his face is plastered with the mud of Mother Earth."

Madeleine's court action would bring the occasional small jabs aimed at her son.

"They are making much over the John Jacob Astor baby in New York. He is two and a half years old. There are several babies in Newberry who can excel the Astor baby in everything but one. John Jacob is paraded because of his money," wrote the *Herald and News* of Newberry, South Carolina.

* * *

A month later, Madeleine hired a sculptor to make a small statuette of her son. Sculpted by a new artist in New York City, the statuette depicted the baby in the nude, "as if he were enjoying his freedom from clothes," wrote the *Bar Harbor Record*. "It is easy for a sculptor to model a baby sleeping. . . . But to catch one in this position is to do a spontaneous work, the most difficult feat for an artist. This difficulty was increased by the bounding vivacity of the subject. Not only is the portrait full of beauty and grace as a piece of modeling but it is also, members of the Astor family say, a remarkably good portrait."

* * *

Shortly before arriving in Bar Harbor that season, Mrs. Astor's name was again in the headlines, this time with a story about a planned second marriage, which never happened.

"Madeleine Astor to Wed!" was the headline in the May 12, 1915, edition of the *Bar Harbor Record*.

The story was that Madeleine Astor was engaged to fellow Bar Harbor summer colonist Clarence H. Mackay. Madeleine remained silent on the rumor. In Boston, Vincent Astor was asked by a reporter about the story. Vincent reported that he did not know whether his stepmother was engaged to Mr. Mackay.

"I haven't seen Mrs. Madeline Force Astor for several weeks, so I cannot comment on this report. I do not know whether she is engaged to Mr. Mackay or not, nor do I know whether anything of that sort is probable," replied Vincent. "So far as I know they are merely friends."

* * *

A rumor would spread around the island that Vincent Astor, who had spent some time off Mount Desert Island's Seal Harbor aboard the *Noma* with his wife the previous year, had purchased the E. B. Dane Estate there, described as "one of the finest estates in that resort and is right on the water front," according to the *Bar Harbor Record*. "The house is a palatial summer home built of red granite and has all the conveniences, including a boat house and slip, gardener's house, and everything that can be desired in a country home."

The rumor would prove not to be true. Mr. and Mrs. Vincent Astor would spend time in Maine during the 1915 season, however, in keeping his father's tradition. At the end of August, they were entertained at a Saturday night dinner party at the Malvern given by Mrs. James G. K. Lawrence of New York. From there they traveled to Seal Harbor for a short visit.

* * *

The announcement of Madeleine and John Astor's seasonal visit first appeared in the May 19, 1915, edition of the *Bar Harbor Record.*

"The two summers of his life he has passed in Bar Harbor with his mother, and Mrs. Astor expects to take him there again for the coming summer, the atmosphere agreeing well with his babyship," reported the *Bar Harbor Times.*

Madeleine and John would arrive on Friday, June 4. Mrs. Force would arrive two weeks later, and Katherine would not arrive until July 4. John Astor was described by the newspaper as gaining weight rapidly.

This season the Cottage Directory would list Mrs. Astor as staying at the cottage named Islecote, which she had rented for the season. The change in Madeleine's summer location from Eden Street afforded her more privacy. Islecote was one of the Vanderbilt cottages located just outside of town, though still close enough for easy accessibility to Bar Harbor's summer social institutions. The cottage was located on the water at the end of a long, wooded road.

"Mrs. Astor apparently will take a very prominent part in society this summer," wrote the *Bar Harbor Record* at the beginning of 1915.

Madeleine's neighbor in another cottage at the secluded Pointe d'Acadie, famous Pittsburgh steel tycoon Andrew Carnegie, was a new and welcome addition to the Bar Harbor summer colony.

"Carnegies Coming Here for the Summer, Good Season Promised," reported the *Bar Harbor Record* in February.

"Mr. and Mrs. Andrew Carnegie will pass the summer in Bar Harbor. It is with pleasure that Bar Harbor people learn that they will join the summer colony here instead of following out their custom of spending the summer months in Skibo Castle in Scotland. Many other rentals are giving promise that Bar Harbor will have a big season next summer."

By the end of the season, Mr. and Mrs. Carnegie and their daughter, Miss Margaret Carnegie, had fallen in love with the climate in Bar Harbor. Margaret was four years younger than Madeleine and an only child. The Carnegies stayed until November.

"This is good news for Bar Harbor, which is fast becoming something of a fall resort," reported the *Bar Harbor Record.* "The Malvern is due to remain open until the first of October this summer, and this is possibly the first time in the hotel life of the place that one of the big summer hotels have remained open so long."

Madeleine Astor's summer home that season was described by reporters as the center of Bar Harbor entertainment. She gave luncheons for small groups of friends. She attended dances at night, many at the Bar Harbor Swimming Club. One evening she was at one of Bar Harbor's cottages at a small dinner hosted by a trustee of the Rhode Island School of Design. In early June, she was a guest at a dinner at the Pinchot Cottage. Another guest there was Mr. William Dick, a childhood friend of Madeleine's from Brooklyn. William's younger sister, Julia, had been in the same circle of "Winter's Buds" to come out in the 1910 winter season as Madeleine, attending many of the same debutante events.

Madeleine Astor would also be a guest at a dinner held at the Kebo Valley Club hosted by A. E. Gallatin, the Astor family friend who had been on Madeleine's first date with Colonel Astor. The dinner was the first at the club for the season. At this point Mr. Gallatin had donated fourteen handsome original prints and etchings to the Jesup Library, including those of Rembrandt, Whistler, and Dürer. Along with a number of books on etchings, prints, and other art subjects, the library arranged a special exhibition based on Mr. Gallatin's donations.

Madeleine Astor would receive a prominent invitation to appear in the Building of Arts tableau that year, as she had the first year that she won the tennis championship. She, along with other members of the summer colony, portrayed living statues of historical figures. The event was followed by a costume ball. Mrs. Astor would portray English painter Joshua Reynolds. Her portrait was the first listed in the newspaper story covering the event. Mr. Gallatin was also in attendance.

A week later, Mrs. Astor would be a patroness for the Fashion Fête, an event held at the Bar Harbor Swimming Club to benefit the American Ambulance Corps. Fellow patronesses would include Mrs. Pulitzer and Mrs. Vanderbilt, among other prominent names.

Madeleine's name was seen weekly in the *Bar Harbor Times* during the 1915 season, usually several times per issue. At the beginning of July, she was a guest at a dinner at the cottage of General Horace Porter. The fourteen guests enjoyed General Porter's water fountain, which was a special feature of attraction. Yellow roses were used for table decorations. Mr. Gallatin was among the guests.

The following week, Mrs. Astor entertained a few friends at a Sunday luncheon at her cottage. A few evenings later, she hosted a dinner for twenty guests, with the decorations of pink roses and orchids provided by local florist Edward Kirk. After the dinner, she attended the ball at the Bar Harbor Swimming Club along with a number of her dinner guests, including her mother and sister.

Toward the end of the month, Madeleine, Katherine, and Mrs. Force attended a dance at the Malvern, described as the best of that hotel's dances so far that season. There were about 250 people in attendance. Madeleine and her family were listed first in the story, as was common.

* * *

A sign of Madeleine Astor's strength might be seen in her return to Bar Harbor after the *Titanic* disaster. The area was full of memories of her husband and reminders of other *Titanic* passengers. Madeleine would find herself revisiting *Titanic* during her time in Bar Harbor both by choice and by circumstance.

Madeleine would often socialize with Mrs. Lois Cassatt, a very prominent summer colonist. Lois Buchanan Cassatt was a niece of President James Buchanan. Her late husband, Alexander Johnston Cassatt, had owned the Pennsylvania Railroad. Lois and A. J. Cassatt's daughter Lois would begin dating *Titanic* survivor Jack Thayer a few years after the sinking, coincidental with Madeleine Astor's return to Bar Harbor. Jack's father, John Thayer, who was lost in the sinking, had served as second vice president of the Cassatt railroad. Jack and Lois Thayer would continue their presence in Bar Harbor, where their family's influence is still felt today.

Madeleine also spent time with *Titanic* survivor Eleanor Widener. At the end of July in 1915, Madeleine would travel to Newport as the guest of Eleanor Widener for a week.

A shocking reminder of the *Titanic* tragedy that season came in the form of a news item from neighboring Winter Harbor, also popular with the summer colony. The Spedden family had been spending their summers in that community for years. Frederic and Daisy Spedden, along with their only child, nine-year-old Douglas, enjoyed the Maine beauty there, but with less of the headline-generating social life that was found in Bar Harbor.

Three years previously, the Speddens had been fellow first-class passengers aboard *Titanic*. Unlike the Astors, the Spedden party had a charmed experience on *Titanic*. The entire party, including Mr. Spedden, all escaped quietly and safely in a lifeboat.

Fate would wait for three years to exact its toll from the Spedden family. Automobiles were new in Maine at the time. What once had been paths for the slow movement of a horse and buggy now became the roadways for much faster and heavier automobiles. Winter Harbor was no exception. While Douglas was playing with a ball on the lawn of the Speddens' summer home that season, the ball rolled through a hedge and out onto the street. An automobile driven by a year-round Winter Harbor resident went by at the same time, striking Douglas. The boy was carried into the cottage, where he lingered for several hours before dying. This was Maine's first recorded automobile accident.

* * *

In July of that summer, a War Relief Committee was formed in Bar Harbor. Madeleine Astor and many of Bar Harbor's summer colony pledged an hour a week to sew items for the Allies. Because there was an overlap of Bar Harbor summer colonists and Aiken, South Carolina, winter colonists, the arrangements were made largely based on work of the Aiken Relief Society, on which many of the Bar Harbor summer colonists served. The Bar Harbor War Relief Committee raised $650 for materials and general expenses.

As can happen in a summer colony with a strong year-round population, there was a mix-up at the beginning of the endeavor. There had been some misunderstanding regarding whether the year-round residents were invited to participate in this effort or whether it was just for members of the summer colony. The issue was quickly ironed out, and the year-round residents were invited to help.

The Bar Harbor War Relief Committee started work on July 11, 1915, with Madeleine Astor and her sister Katherine there. The town's high school building, empty of students for the summer, was used for the work. Desks were removed from the school rooms and tables put in their place, where women and men worked side by side. The group would operate from 10:00 a.m. to 1:00 p.m. every day except for Sundays, making surgical dressings, bandages, and shirts for the wounded, together with garments of all kinds for war refugees.

In the first two weeks of the five-week endeavor, 12,649 dressings and bandages were made, along with a total of 924 garments. The *Bar Harbor Record* noted that Bar Harbor was one of the few summer colonies undertaking such an effort with their seasonal visitors and that interest in the project was growing.

"The noteworthy fact about these figures is that they indicate not a falling off of interest such as might be expected in the gayest week of the season, but a great increase," wrote the *Bar Harbor Record.*

* * *

Reporters would continue to use Madeleine Astor's name to make up stories when the real stories about her were not interesting enough. One such story appeared while Madeleine was in Bar Harbor that summer. Out of New Haven, Connecticut, came a story that waiters at an unnamed local hotel were still discussing the July 10 visit of "Mrs. John Jacob Astor, formerly Miss Madeleine Force." The story reported that during a motor trip through New England, Mrs. Astor's automobile stopped at the hotel for a meal. With Mrs. Astor was her poodle, Mizzie. According to the story, an expensive steak was ordered for Mizzie, along with a request that the steak be cut into small pieces so that Mizzie would be able eat it more easily.

"Mizzie consumed the steak with the usual canine celerity, and the waiter pocketed a substantial tip," reported the International News Service, a syndicate that provided stories to newspapers across the country.

The *Bar Harbor Times* took exception to this story. The story was not only inaccurate but also insulting to a woman who was spending her time in Bar Harbor rolling bandages for the war effort.

"This kind of stuff helps to fill up the columns of the big Sunday editions but as Mrs. Astor has been in Bar Harbor for the past month, the story falls pretty flat to those who know it to be false."

* * *

Madeleine and her family would celebrate John's third birthday in August with a party at Islecote. Later that month, Katherine Force had charge of the fancy goods table on the grounds of Bar Harbor's prestigious Building of Arts at the annual hospital benefit. Toward the end of the month, Mrs. Astor would be entertained at Kamp Kill Kare by her friend Dorothy Sturgess, a future trustee of the Museum of Modern Art in New York, along with thirty-two other guests at a picnic dinner. Also present was William Dick, Madeleine's childhood friend from Brooklyn.

The picnic was held at Beech Cliffs on Mount Desert Island. A large bonfire was built, and it was decided to broil the lambchops over the fire. Madeleine Astor decided to try her cooking skills, thrusting a lambchop over the flames. The lambchop soon started smoking, and the others in the party advised her to thrust her chop deeper into the fire. She did, and the lambchop was soon burned beyond consumption. While others were eating, Madeleine's lambchop was ruined.

Madeleine hurled the lambchop over the cliffs into Echo Lake. She then proceeded to take another uncooked lambchop and again put it over the fire, "and within a few minutes satisfied herself that she could cook," wrote the *New York Times*.

* * *

Madeleine spent much of that summer pursuing her athletic endeavors. In July, she and other socialites were enjoying trapshooting at the Kebo Country Club. Mrs. Force, Katherine, and her fiancé, Henri Harnickell, would participate in that club's golf putting contest at the end of August in mixed foursomes putting, competing against each other. By the end of July, Madeleine and Katherine were back on the tennis courts at the Bar Harbor Swimming Club. They were among eighteen entries for that season's tennis championship tournament.

Tournament play would begin in the middle of August. In the mixed doubles category, Madeleine was playing with Edgar T. Scott of Philadelphia, and her sister, Miss Katherine Force, was playing with Joseph T. Bowen of Chicago. Both teams were victorious in the first round of play and again on August 18, which ensured that the Force sisters would face off against each other in the semifinals.

The following day, the Force sisters were on opposite sides of the tennis court they had commanded for the past nine years, fighting each other for the title of champion. The *Bar Harbor Times* said that the semifinal round of the mixed doubles tournament "brought out the best tennis of the tournament." In the end, rebuffing her sister's challenge, Madeleine was victorious in three matches, 6–4, 5–7, 6–2.

At the end of August, Madeleine and Mr. Scott played in the finals against Miss Eleanor Cary and Richard Harte Jr. of Philadelphia and Northeast Harbor, respectively. The newspaper described the match as "close and exciting . . . the match was about even for the first two sets, but Mrs. Astor and Mr. Scott came back strong on the third set, after losing the second, and won rather easily." The final score was 6–4, 4–6, 6–1.

Madeleine Force Astor continued to be a champion.

* * *

Madeleine would spend much of September into November entertaining at her summer cottage. At the end of September, the *Bar Harbor Record* announced that Mrs. Astor, her mother, and her sister would remain in Bar Harbor until the end of October, when they would travel to New York for the winter. At the end of October, it was announced that the party would extend their stay into November. The newspaper also announced that even though Mrs. Astor had not yet taken a cottage for the following season, it was expected that she would return to Islecote.

"Her cottage was a center of gaiety all summer, and it was not till November, almost Thanksgiving Day, when she went back to New York—almost the last of the cottagers here to close their summer home," wrote the *Bar Harbor Times*. "Bar Harbor was largely devoted to dancing for the past few seasons, and at the regular dances at the Swimming

Club, the Malvern, and various other places where society gathers, she was generally to be found."

* * *

Madeleine Talmage Force Astor truly was victorious in the year 1915, not just on the tennis courts at the swim club but also in Bar Harbor's society. She had proved her worth on the tennis courts when she first arrived there but had been beaten down after her engagement to Colonel Astor. Despite the darkness of that time, it was nothing compared to her experience and loss on *Titanic*. The victorious Madeleine Force who had arrived in 1907 returned in 1913 as the defeated Madeleine Astor. When the summer season of 1915 came to an end, Madeleine Astor was on top. Wrote the *Bar Harbor Times*, "She was the acknowledged leader of society, and both the Swimming Club and the Kebo Golf Club were visited almost daily by her. It was a welcome place into which she came, also. Before her marriage to Col. Astor, the Forces have been coming to Bar Harbor for many years, and she and her sister had grown up here. They had a small cottage in an unfashionable locality, entertained very modestly, and had rather a modest place in fashion's whirl there. Her marriage to Col. Astor, whom she won solely by her beauty and charm, at once placed her in a position to dictate to the resort here and families who would have gladly snubbed her as plain Madeleine Force were forced to recognize her unquestioned social leadership as Mrs. John Jacob Astor, and mother of the heir to the Astor millions. Since her marriage, her social position has been unquestioned here."

Chapter 8

Debs of Other Days

"Debs of Other Days."

—NEWSPAPER HEADLINE FROM 1931 DESCRIBING THE THIRTY-EIGHT-YEAR-OLD MADELEINE ASTOR DICK

HAVING CONQUERED HER TERRITORY OF BAR HARBOR, MAINE, DURING the 1915 summer season, Madeleine now took aim at New York when she chose to revive the Astor family's tradition of a grand event at the Astor mansion to celebrate the new year.

This was only the third time that Madeleine Astor had opened the Fifth Avenue mansion since inheriting its use three years previously. The first two occasions were philanthropic in nature. This would be the first large social event of its kind in the Astor mansion since Madeleine's marriage to Colonel Astor four years earlier. Madeleine sent out invitations to nearly four hundred of her friends, two hundred for dinner and then another two hundred for a reception and dancing after. The dinner was held in the large hall of the mansion, with its white marble water fountain that played music, one of the last features added by Colonel Astor. There were four tables in the center of the hall, each seating twenty, and one table for a party of twelve. The other guests dined at tables in the dining room adjoining the great hall. From the centers of the large tables in the hall sprang tall palms, the branches of which expanded high above the heads of the diners. In the center of the smaller tables was a mound of pink roses. Pink also was the color scheme of the decorations on the tables in the dining room. Large candy baskets adorned the tables. During the dinner the renowned Conrad's Orchestra had played classical selections, and now the program was changed to popular airs for the dancing.

At 10:30 p.m., the additional guests arrived for a reception that preceded the dancing. Then the guests moved to the famed ballroom, the walls of which were lined with the Astor collection of paintings.

"Bar Harbor's summer contingent was well represented at the dinner-dance given by Mrs. John Jacob Astor last week, when for the first time in several years the Astor residence was the scene of an entertainment that recalled the brilliant events given there by the late Mrs. William Astor," wrote the *Bar Harbor Times*.

* * *

Madeleine and John, along with Mrs. Force and Katherine, would spend part of the winter in Aiken, South Carolina. Due to the war and the limitations on overseas travel, the Bar Harbor summer colony was noted to have an unusual number of people wintering at Aiken that season, which was busy with polo matches and golf games at the Palmetto Golf Club. Madeleine and Katherine continued their athletic pursuits in Aiken, winning trophies in foursome golf with a score of 61–65.

Mrs. Astor returned to the Fifth Avenue mansion in New York City in the spring, closing that home on June 10 in anticipation of her return to Bar Harbor, to the same cottage she had occupied the previous season. Madeleine and John arrived in Bar Harbor on Friday, June 16.

Madeleine Astor had her son with her as she traveled to Bar Harbor, but she was also carrying a secret. She was engaged to be married on her arrival in the Bar Harbor she had conquered the year before.

* * *

Bar Harbor was incredibly full of summer colonists during the 1916 season. With war still taking place in Europe, overseas travel was not an option for the members of society, who chose instead places such as Bar Harbor and Newport to spend the season. The *Bar Harbor Times* reported that there were no empty cottages to be had. Madeleine again rented Islecote, arriving in Bar Harbor on Friday morning along with her household staff. They were met at the wharf by a heavy rain, and the party was taken immediately to their cottage, not too far away.

Waiting at one of Bar Harbor's hotel's when Madeleine arrived that season was one of the men who had attended a few of the same summer functions as Madeleine Astor the previous year—William Dick.

William Dick was reportedly a childhood sweetheart of Madeleine Force. His younger sister, Julia Dick, had been in the same debutante circle during Madeleine's coming-out season, and Madeleine was twenty-three, while William was twenty-eight.

Madeleine had been at many social functions the previous season, and while those functions generally had single men as guests, her name was never officially linked in print with any of them. Mr. Dick had been at various dinner parties the previous season and at Beech Cliffs when Madeleine was cooking lambchops. He was noted to be at the Bar Harbor Swimming Club watching Madeleine play tennis and being attentive to her when she was not. He was her guest at dinner parties at Islecote, along with other guests. They took rides together to Jordan Pond House, along with other friends. He had also spent time with Madeleine and her family over the winter in Aiken, South Carolina.

William was the son of John Henry Dick (a wealthy sugar refiner) and Julia Mollenhauer Dick, who were prominent in Brooklyn society. He was born and raised in Brooklyn and had been educated at a school in Connecticut, as well as with private tutors. At the time of the engagement, he was active in financial circles, serving as vice president of the Manufacturers Trust Company of Brooklyn and director of the Broadway Trust Company, among many other business interests, including his father's sugar industry, lumbering, and railroads.

Though not in the league of Colonel John Jacob Astor financially, William Dick was said to be a very wealthy man, worth $3 million to $5 million, not adjusted for inflation. His generation was the third of wealth, with his grandfather making the family fortune in sugar refining and later banking, holding most of the large accounts of the Williamsburg District of Brooklyn. William himself would learn the sugar industry from the ground up, starting in the business at the Williamsburg factory as a boy.

William Dick was different from John Jacob Astor. Mr. Dick was a millionaire, but not at Colonel Astor's level. Though Mr. Dick's parents were socially active, William was not. He worked and spent time at sportsmen's clubs. Rather than holding the Astor Cup for yachting, Mr. Dick preferred to spend his spare time with a rifle in his hand, hunting. His summers were spent in a large cottage, but this one was on Long Island, not in Bar Harbor or Newport. Socially he was quite the opposite of Colonel John Jacob Astor, son of the leader of New York society.

* * *

During the Astor–Force romance, one signal to society that Colonel Astor and Madeleine were a couple was the Astor ball held in January 1911. For the Astor–Dick romance, the signal seemed to come from the grand dinner and dance Madeleine had held in January that year at the Astor mansion, where William Dick was a guest. Only the couple's most intimate friends knew the couple had become engaged, fewer still knew of the approaching wedding, and only the handful of invited guests knew the ceremony was to take place on Madeleine's arrival in Bar Harbor.

"It began to be noticed that he was rather often in her company," reported the June 18, 1916, edition of the *New York Times*. "Still, so carefully was their secret guarded, that when this was commented upon the matter could be turned off lightly as the natural result of old friendship, and society has not suspected ever since they have actually been engaged."

As had happened in Madeleine's first wedding, she tried to find a balance between her privacy and the need for proper social form. For a socially legitimate wedding, notice had to be given beforehand, no matter how big or small the ceremony was going to be. Madeleine Astor and William Dick tried to fulfill the demands of society for publicity and their own desires for privacy by arranging for the release of the news through the *Brooklyn Times*, which William Dick owned. The news was released the day after Madeleine and John arrived in Bar Harbor, allowing her to travel to Maine without the extra herd of reporters that would be following her once the story was released.

On release of the news by the *Brooklyn Times* on June 17, the day after Madeleine's arrival in Bar Harbor, reporters descended on her Fifth Avenue home. The servants there told reporters that she had already left for Bar Harbor. Reporters noted that the servants seemed surprised at the rumor of Madeleine's engagement and were inclined not to believe the news. No one could be reached at the home of Madeleine's parents.

When reporters started asking questions at Islecote, Madeleine's personal secretary said that Mrs. Astor would neither confirm nor deny the rumors but that a marriage license had not been issued.

* * *

The wedding ceremony was intended to be very small and private, and it would have been had it not been for a new Maine law and a town clerk who could not overlook that law regardless of the last name or social position of the person before him.

When Madeleine arrived in Bar Harbor on Friday, she had planned to travel to the Eden Town Hall on Monday to obtain the marriage license. She had made all the arrangements for a simple ceremony on Monday night with twenty guests. Under Maine law at the time, a resident of Maine could obtain a license the same day it was applied for. Unfortunately for Madeleine, despite the fact that she had spent six months in the state the previous year, she was not legally considered a Maine resident. At some point soon after Madeleine's arrival in Maine, it must have been pointed out to her that there had been a change in Maine law three years previously, coincident with the Astor divorce, which required a five-day waiting period for nonresidents to receive a marriage license once the application had been received. On Saturday morning, she arrived at the Eden Town Hall to obtain her marriage license. Because the news had already been released by the *Brooklyn Times*, reporters followed Madeleine Astor to the town office and recorded the conversation.

"You may obtain the license next Thursday—not sooner," the clerk told Mrs. Astor.

"But we must have a license for Monday," replied Mrs. Astor. "We're to be married Monday at Bar Harbor."

"Quite impossible," replied the clerk. "The law is the law, and it can't be done."

Mrs. Astor pleaded with the clerk, telling him of the many plans that had been made—guests were already on their way to her summer home, and the decorations were already in place, including fresh flowers that would not last five days. She also expressed her need for privacy.

The clerk was not swayed. Mrs. Astor would leave the office with a blank marriage license application, which was returned just before midnight filled out in pencil. The earliest now that Mrs. Astor and Mr. Dick could wed would be Thursday. By now the entire world knew of their plans for a private ceremony.

* * *

When news broke of Madeleine Astor's impending remarriage, the general consensus among the Bar Harbor summer colony was that it had always been expected that the young woman would again marry at some point. Long-term romance instead of marriage was not an option at this point in history if one's reputation meant anything, and it did to society's Four Hundred.

Mrs. Astor's mother and sister would arrive by train in Ellsworth over the weekend, motoring to Madeleine's cottage in Bar Harbor. Reporters continued to arrive at Islecote. However, Madeleine was silent about her future plans. Initially there was speculation that Madeleine Astor's disappointment would cause her to return to New York or head to some other place and get married there, where she would not face the legal restrictions encountered in Maine.

On Monday, when the ceremony should have been taking place, instead an announcement came from Islecote that the wedding would be taking place at 2:00 p.m. on Thursday. The location of the ceremony had not yet been decided but would be at either Islecote or Bar Harbor's St. Saviour's Episcopal Church. Madeleine would motor to Ellsworth from Bar Harbor that day to pick up her father at the train station. The following day, William Dick arrived, staying at a private home. On his arrival, he traveled to Islecote, and he and Madeleine took a long automobile ride accompanied by William's brother, Adolph.

* * *

Knowing that Thursday was the earliest Madeleine Astor could remarry, reporters watched every movement into and out of the long, private driveway leading to Islecote and the other two cottages at Pointe d'Acadie over the following few days.

"So far the decision has gone to the alert newspaper men, both local and out of town New York and Boston city staff men, who have been down here and ferreted out practically every detail, even to what the bride would wear, her plans and the legal obstacles in the way of the marriage as it was first planned for Monday," wrote the *Bar Harbor Times*.

Most of the wedding party had arrived in Bar Harbor by noon on Thursday, and at 1:00 p.m. a luncheon was served by Mr. Dick for members of his family at the De Gregoire Hotel. In attendance were his parents, his siblings and their spouses, and a few others. The table was decorated with Killarney roses and white lilacs. At the same time, Mrs. Astor was holding a family dinner at Islecote, her guests including her family and a few others. Both lunches were described as simple.

There had been several changes of plan for the ceremony's location between Saturday and Thursday, so the public was not quite sure where the ceremony would be held. A logical choice would have been Islecote. However, decorum was important to the Force family. After the traditional separate bride and groom luncheons, the separate wedding parties took to automobiles and motored the short distance from the De Gregiore and Islecote to St. Saviour's Episcopal Church in the center of Bar Harbor. The ceremony began at 2:00 p.m.

The wedding was informal considering the couple who was getting married. Madeleine was dressed in a simple suit of blue serge, gray spats, black shoes, a little black hat trimmed with ribbon, and a magnificent set of silver-gray fox furs. William Dick wore the conventional afternoon dress. He was attended by his brother, Adolph, who acted as the best man, while Madeleine was given away by her father.

There was no music, but the cooing of doves in the ceiling of the church provided a natural accompaniment to the socially historic event below. The ceremony was brief, the only feature being the reading of the

Episcopal service by the church's rector, Reverend Mr. Larned, which was said to be done in a most impressive manner. With light filtering in through the church's beautiful stained glass windows (including one dedicated to Astor cousin John Innes Kane), Madeleine Force Astor became Mrs. William K. Dick. At the conclusion of the ceremony, Madeleine Dick was described as looking beautiful and thoroughly radiant and happy.

"There have been few weddings so informal here, especially considering the position of those concerned," wrote the *Bar Harbor Times*.

Having learned of the movements of Mrs. Astor and Mr. Dick in the Bar Harbor village, soon a large crowd was assembled outside the church. As the ceremony concluded inside, outside the front door of the church stood a man named Edward Suminsby, who guarded the church's entrance from the ever-growing curious crowd, which included several hundred residents and summer colonists of Bar Harbor, as well as a battery of moving picture men armed with cameras large and small, all awaiting the emerging of the wedding party from the church.

At the conclusion of the ceremony, there was a rush for the pathway from the front door of the church. No one appeared.

The new Mr. and Mrs. William and Madeleine Dick, instead of emerging from the front door, exited the church from the back, which was not clearly visible from the front of the church. Entering an awaiting automobile, Madeleine and William Dick quickly made their way down Kennebec Street and eventually to a waiting train in Ellsworth.

A look of disappointment came over the faces of the crowd waiting at the front with the realization that they had all been fooled. There was a mad rush for the back of the church, but it was all over. A newspaper photographer penetrated the empty precincts of the deserted church and, throwing up his hands in a gesture of despair, informed the crowd that it was all over. Cameras were thrown into waiting automobiles and chase was given to the wedding party, but it was too late.

"It was the last chapter in a battle of wits which Mrs. Astor-Dick and her friends have waged to keep the details of her wedding a secret from the public, and this last skirmish must be set down to her credit," wrote the *Bar Harbor Times*.

* * *

The remarriage of Madeleine Astor was the story that newspapers had been waiting for since the reading of Colonel Astor's will after *Titanic*'s sinking. The terms of the will helped ensure that outcome. By remarrying, Madeleine forfeited everything—the trust fund she had inherited and its interest income, as well as the use of the Fifth Avenue mansion and the other Astor facilities. The financial aspect seemed to be the angle of the story, but the biggest possession Madeleine would be giving up was the name Mrs. Astor. She was also giving up her claim to the role of society leader that came with the name. By accepting William Dick's name, she was giving up everything Astor.

Money would not be an issue for Madeleine Astor. She had money of her own from her initial financial settlement with Colonel Astor before her marriage, her dowry. Her son had his own trust fund for financial support. After the wedding, the *Bar Harbor Times* ran an editorial putting Madeleine's sacrifice into perspective.

"Mrs. Madeleine Force Astor sacrificed $3,500,000 and a Fifth Avenue home for her love match, probably the greatest sum ever known to be given up for this cause. Still, in view of the half million settled on her by her late husband, the several millions of her second husband, and the interest of her son in his father's estate, which will probably amount to $10,000,000 there's many a poor girl who could manage to worry along on her present fortune, by practicing the strictest economy, anyhow."

In marrying William Dick, Madeleine also was giving up the Bar Harbor society life she had been a part of for the past seven years, since she was a girl of fourteen. Her new husband seemed to have no use for the society pages. He was active in his own social circles, but they were more in Long Island and quiet outdoors activities rather than ballrooms or flower-lined dining rooms with their associated reporters. Madeleine must have realized all that when she made her vows at St. Saviour's Church in the middle of Bar Harbor. She could survive on her own financially, so money was not the motivation for the marriage. In marrying William Dick, Madeleine Astor seemed to be making a conscious decision to walk away from society.

Initially the Dicks were expected to return to Bar Harbor and spend the rest of the summer there. They did return for a two-day stay before traveling to Mr. Dick's country estate in Islip, Long Island.

"The return from their honeymoon this week of Mr. and Mrs. William Karl Dick gave society a fresh opportunity to comment on what for Bar Harbor has been the big piece of news of the summer," wrote the *Bar Harbor Record*.

* * *

Madeleine and William Dick chose California for their honeymoon, traveling there by private railroad car. They stayed at the Hotel Fresno but tried to guard their privacy by registering under a false name. A reporter gave their taxicab driver a 50¢ fare and a $1 tip to find out where they were registered.

While in California the Dicks visited Yosemite Valley. They traveled to Santa Barbara, where they would stay in an attractive rose-covered bungalow that had been placed at their disposal for their honeymoon. The *Placerville Mountain* (California) *Democrat*, in their July 22, 1916, edition talked about three new brides who had visited the area recently, including Mrs. Dick.

"Mrs. Dick is probably the most beautiful. At least she has been most discussed, and those who saw her in San Francisco found her more lovely than her portraits. She is tall and slim and very graceful, with a clear olive complexion, waving light brown hair, violet eyes and classic features, and her charm of manner impressing everyone. The day of her arrival she wore a black cloth tailored suit with rather long skirt and flaring coat and a blouse of finely tucked white handkerchief linen with a V-cut sailor collar. Her hat was a black silk beaver sailor worn low over her hair and circled with goura feathers, across her shoulders was a silver fox fur, and there were black patent leather shoes with light tan spats. The only things that suggested Astor millions were the beautiful pearls. There was a necklace of two long strands of large, pink-toned pearls, and a broach with a huge emerald with set-in diamonds."

Visiting Yosemite National Park, the Dicks tried to escape attention by avoiding the trappings of society garb and leaving their valet and maid at the hotel while going out for their daily activities.

"They dress in the simplest of costume, and even for dinner Mrs. Dick wears sports clothes instead of making any attempt at dinner dress. They take so many of their meals in private and safeguard themselves so carefully from attracting attention that only the more adventurous and curious tourists have been able to get first hand knowledge of them," wrote the *Oakland Tribune*.

The Dicks would fall victim to one tourist who was eager to get a close-up look at the famous Madeleine Astor. The tourist feigned illness by lying prostrate on a trail at Yosemite that the Dicks were enjoying. Madeleine and William, who were on horseback, almost ran over the lady, reining their horses back in the nick of time.

The young, athletic Madeleine Dick was out of her saddle quickly, as was William, who gave the woman a drink of water from his canteen. The woman quickly "recovered," sat up, and said she could catch up with her party, which was not very far ahead. On reaching her friends, the woman boasted to them of how she had accomplished her purpose of "getting a good look at the Dicks" and talking to them before she left the valley. The Dicks, genuine in their concern, saw the woman in the hotel the following day and inquired as to her health.

"Needless to say that while satisfying this cheap curiosity, she lost the respect of all the acquaintances who knew of the affair," wrote the *Oakland Tribune*.

* * *

In Bar Harbor, the absence of Madeleine Astor was noted on the tennis courts.

"The ladies tennis tournament was marked by the absence of Mrs. Madeleine Astor Dick, the present holder of the title, who was not present to defend her title," wrote the *Bar Harbor Times* in their July 29, 1916, edition.

Miss Dorothy Disston, an athlete who would later play professional championship tennis, won the title that year. Katherine continued to play tennis at the Kebo Valley Club in both singles and mixed doubles. Her mother, Mrs. Force, would participate in a putting contest along with her daughter, who came in second.

* * *

Madeleine Force Astor Dick's name would now become associated with a quieter society. After returning from their honeymoon and ending the 1916 summer season on Long Island, the Dicks spent the fall and winter in New York City. They had rented a furnished house at 87 West Fifty-Third Street. William's parents were at 20 East Fifty-Third Street, several blocks down the same street. The house was in the same residential district as the Astor mansion.

Mrs. Dick continued to be active in society for the remainder of the year, though on a lesser scale than in Bar Harbor. She would serve as a member of the Executive Committee of the Lafayette Fund to give a charitable supper and dance at the Vanderbilt Hotel, the proceeds of which were to benefit French soldiers at the war front. In November, she would be a patroness of a charity benefit performance in New York that featured famous actress Sarah Bernhardt, the only one Ms. Bernhardt gave that winter. The performance was held at the Hotel Biltmore for the benefit of blind Allied soldiers.

At the end of the year, Mrs. Dick was a guest in Caroline Astor Wilson's box at the Metropolitan Opera.

* * *

The year 1917, Madeleine's first full year of her second marriage, would be bittersweet, as it was marked by the loss of her father, William H. Force. Mr. Force had been ill for his last few years, spending much of his time at the Bernardsville, New Jersey, country home. He died on May 19 at his New York home at the age of sixty-five. Mrs. Force was staying at the Hotel Chatham on Forty-Eighth Street at the time. She inherited the entirety of her husband's estate. Made up of real estate, personal property, stocks and bonds, and interest in his business, William H. Force's estate was valued at $50,277, or a little over $1 million in today's value.

"Father of Mrs. Dick, Widow of John Jacob Astor," read the sub-headline in the *New York Sun* announcing Mr. Force's passing.

* * *

With the United States joining World War I in 1917, Madeleine Dick continued her duties of conscience. In April of that year, she was noted as a member of the League for Political Education, an organization populated by progressive women and men. Fellow members from Madeleine's Bar Harbor days included Mrs. Fannie Morgan, wife of J. P. Morgan, and Mrs. Louise Carnegie, wife of Andrew Carnegie. Madeleine's husband, William, also did his part for the war effort, serving on the Advisory Board of Managers of the Islip, Long Island, chapter of the American Red Cross.

Despite the countless time and resources donated to charitable causes by Madeleine Astor Dick over her lifetime, she would still lose sympathy in 1917 with the accounting of her son John's trust fund interest.

The year 1917 would see the escalation and expansion of World War I, with the United States joining the Allies. People of the world were sacrificing their everyday comforts for the war effort, while those in the United States also faced increasing taxes to pay for their country's war effort. At the beginning of the year, Madeleine Dick petitioned the Surrogate Court in New York for more money from her son's trust fund to cover his expenses, which she claimed were now $29,000 a year, or half a million dollars adjusted for inflation.

With a world at war, the story seemed to mark a change in attitude on the part of the public toward Madeleine Astor. The child was living a life that most people could not understand in the best of economic times. The public also found it abhorrent that the child was being charged for his own upbringing. The details of Mrs. Astor's accounting would prove embarrassing, as seen in a syndicated news story reprinted in newspapers across the country.

"What Baby John Jacob Astor Paid for Being Born," was the headline in the February 18, 1917, edition of the *Chicago Examiner*. "Being a millionaire baby is not all that it has been cracked up to be. It has its advantages, of course, but it also carries with it certain penalties.

Little John Jacob Astor, who is four years old now and has an income of $140,000 a year, will find that out when he grows old enough to scrutinize the account which will be rendered to him showing how his fortune was expended for him during his babyhood.

"He will find out, for instance, not only that he has been made to pay for every stitch of clothing that he has worn since the day of his birth, for every mouthful of food and drink, for every toy and plaything—even for his own birthday and Christmas presents—but that he also had to pay for the expenses incidental to his coming into the world and for numerous items purchased in anticipation of that interesting event.

"All these things are revealed in a remarkable accounting recently filed by his mother, the former Mrs. Madeline Force Astor, now Mrs. William Dick. . . . She itemizes all purchases made during little John's first three years and goes back almost a year prior to his birth so as to include everything which she thinks ought to be paid for by him rather than by her.

"Indeed, it is doubtful whether John Jacob Astor, when he grows up, will approve of the great sums of money that were spent on him out of his own funds, in his early days."

In Madeleine Dick's accounting, she explained to the court how she had spent the $20,000 yearly allowance she received from her son's trust fund for his upkeep, along with money of her own to make up the difference. This included having charged her son rent to live with her in their Fifth Avenue home.

The establishment so occupied was maintained at great expense. She said she was advised by counsel that it was "proper and reasonable that there should be charged to said infant on account of his share of the expenses, one-third of the cost of maintenance of the establishment and one-third of the taxes paid on said premises."

Mrs. Dick's court accounting showed that she would pay a household bill and then split it in two between herself and her son, regardless of what was purchased. "What will he say when he reads among the items of a druggist's bill rendered July 31, 1912, two weeks before his birth, '1 box wooden toothpicks, 10 cents'? How will he regard another bill amounting to $67, half of which, or $33.89, is charged against him, when he observed that the principal item on this bill is 'one coat and cape, $58'? If the coat and cape were for him, why shouldn't he pay for the whole item, and if they were for some one else, why should he pay any part of it?"

Mrs. Dick's accounting included the many expensive gifts she had purchased for her son, including supplies for his third birthday party, spent in Bar Harbor, which included a floor croquet set, a two-wheeled cart, a seesaw, a magic fishpond, a bubble-blowing machine, and an athletic slide, among many other items. "What is the advantage of being born with a golden spoon in your mouth if you have to pay for the spoon?" asked the *Chicago Examiner*.

* * *

Lost in the discussion was the fact that since John was born, Madeleine had been taking a lesser sum than allowable by the court from her son's trust fund to cover his expenses so that he would have more money from interest when he turned twenty-one. She had been paying part of his expenses out of her own pocket for the past five years. Still, everything is relative.

* * *

Madeleine and William would have their first child that year, with William Henry Dick Jr. born on April 11, four days before the anniversary of *Titanic*'s sinking. The child was born at the Dicks' New York City home. The birth of Madeleine's second child brought out scores of congratulatory telegrams and phone messages. Mr. Dick spoke to a reporter for the New York Evening *World*, saying no name had yet been chosen for the boy.

The Dicks would travel to the countryside of Islip, Long Island, that summer. A photograph that ran in the newspapers was of "Former Astor Widow, Now Mrs. Wm. K. Dick" at the Red Cross horse show at Islip, a charity event and one of the most important social events for the summer colony of Long Island. Mrs. Dick was photographed on her favorite horse. Five-year-old John Astor would also be photographed in his mother's box at the horse show.

Mrs. Dick would begin the process of instilling social responsibility in her oldest son early, enrolling him in the *New York Evening World*'s Kiddie Club. The children would "adopt" orphans or children in France who had lost their fathers in the war. "And the mother of little John Jacob Astor, Mrs. William K. Dick, gave a whole lot of money in his name," wrote the *New York Evening World*.

Ending a year of great change for Madeleine Astor Dick was the absence of her sister, Katherine, who suddenly traveled to Europe to work in the war relief effort. No longer satisfied with just wrapping bandages in polite societal gatherings, Katherine had decided to go to where help was needed even more. With her engagement to Henri Harnickell seemingly forgotten (still no wedding ring on her finger) and her father recently deceased, Katherine left the United States with her friend Miss Phyllis J. Walsh, their destination being "somewhere in France." The two women were among a contingent of young women who had dedicated themselves to overseas war relief work.

This must have been one of the biggest adjustments for Madeleine Dick in that year of changes. Katherine had been at Madeleine's side for all of Madeleine's twenty-four years, and now she was gone at a time of further change for Madeleine and would be for approximately two years. They had grown up in Brooklyn together, gone to Europe and Bar Harbor together, and played together and against each other on the tennis courts. Katherine had been at her sister's side through the criticisms of Madeleine's marriage, the savage attacks in the press against their parents, the loss of Colonel Astor, the birth of John, and the return to Bar Harbor. Now the Force sisters appeared to have gone their separate ways.

* * *

Madeleine would mark the 1918 New Year's season as a patient in Johns Hopkins Hospital. In early January, Mr. and Mrs. Dick, along with Dr. H. M. Briggs of New York and a trained nurse, traveled to Baltimore, Maryland, arriving there on January 10. They registered at the Hotel Belvedere and then checked out shortly thereafter, saying they were going to visit a sick relative at Johns Hopkins. Later it turned out that Mrs. Dick was, in fact, the patient. Her undisclosed condition was reported to not be serious, and it was said that she might or might not have to undergo an operation.

It was reported that the Dicks would summer in Bar Harbor in 1918, with the *New York Sun* running an item in its August 13, 1918, edition that Pointe d'Acadie had again been leased by Mrs. Dick for the season. It would appear instead that they spent their summer in Islip, Long Island.

* * *

In May 1919, the youngest of Madeleine's three children was born: John Henry Dick, named after William Dick's father.

In the summer of that year, Madeleine's older sister, Katherine, returned to the United States after two years of war relief work in France. Though she had not spent much time near the trenches, she was diagnosed while there with "trench sore throat," a disease commonly contracted by soldiers at the front. She underwent an operation on her return to the United States and was confined to her apartment at the Ritz-Carlton in New York.

"She went through the ordeal of shell fire and other war risks without injury or illness, but developed tonsillitis on her return," wrote the *New York Evening World.*

The Dicks would spend part of their summer in Islip, Long Island. In July, they attended the Islip Polo Club Horse Show, which boasted more horses entered that year than ever before. There were nineteen separate events, and society was described as being out in full force. Mr. Dick was a member of the committee organizing the event. John Astor and his stepfather, who was also an exhibitor, were photographed together at the event, with John dressed in a white sailor suit and shorts and Mr. Dick in a wide-brimmed white hat and suit, watching the race while standing against the front of the grandstand. John's facial features had the look of his mother's but the shape of his father's.

The Dicks would spend the latter part of their summer in a camp on the lower St. Regis Lake in the Adirondacks. Returning to New York at the end of the season, Mr. Dick would be appointed to a committee to protect stockholders of the recently defaulted Brooklyn, Queens County, and Suburban Railroad Company.

* * *

The following summer would see the first public cracks in the Dick marriage with the publication of a story that was reported across the country.

"Mrs. Dick Is Domiciled in Reno. Takes Residence There for Usual Purpose, It Is Believed," read the headlines of the June 20, 1920, edition of the *New York Herald*. "The fact that she has gone to Reno is almost as great a surprise as was the announcement of her engagement to Col. Astor."

Madeleine's sister quickly came to her sister's defense, indignantly denying the report. "Absurd, ridiculous and malicious," was the way Katherine Force characterized the story. "It is absolutely untrue. Mr. and Mrs. Dick are out on their boat together or they would deny the story."

Madeleine Dick did arrive in Reno, Nevada, on June 19, 1920, renting a residence there. Mrs. Dick would say nothing concerning her reason or how long she intended to remain. A several-month residence was required in Reno before a divorce would be issued.

"Friends of Mr. and Mrs. Dick said last night that the marriage has not been unbroken happiness for either of the couple. Their tastes, it was said, differed radically. He was a quiet, unassuming person who cared nothing for society, she was brilliant and popular wherever she went," wrote the *New York Tribune*.

Reporters checked at the Dick home at 7 East Eighty-Fourth Street, where it was said that Mr. Dick was spending the weekend with his family at Islip, Long Island. Reporters contacted Madeleine's mother, who declined to discuss the presence of her daughter in Reno. Rumors concerning the impending divorce seemed to end when the Dicks arrived in Islip later in the summer, denying reporters' questions about the rumors.

"There is absolutely no truth in the reports," said Madeleine Dick, "and I cannot imagine where they came from."

"Have you read the dispatches in the morning papers?" she was asked.

"I have, and they are absolutely untrue. I do not know who started them. I cannot imagine who would say such things about me. You can say for me that there is not a word of truth in them."

That summer's newspapers featured pictures of the Dick family in attendance at Long Island's eighth annual horse show, where the weather was perfect and the attendance large. Society was well represented, and there were now twenty classes of horses. Mr. Dick, who continued his membership on the show's executive committee, took his wife and children specifically to see the ponies.

* * *

Madeleine's sister, Katherine, having returned from Europe, made her way back into the headlines. Katherine Force had taken a different path than her sister. Madeleine's first announced engagement was to Fifth Avenue's Colonel John Jacob Astor, and Katherine's first fiancé was Brooklyn's Henri Harnickell. Madeleine's first marriage was at age eighteen and she was now on her second marriage, while Katherine was thirty and unmarried. Madeleine had sewn bandages in Bar Harbor for the war effort, while Katherine spent two years where the war was taking place.

Now Katherine was taking yet another divergent path. While Madeleine had never worked in her life, as was traditional for women of the time, Katherine had taken a job selling real estate. Her story was featured in a headline in the July 25, 1920, edition of the *Philadelphia Inquirer*: "Rich Girl, Rejecting Marriage, Going to Work."

"Katherine is today an older and wiser girl than in that faraway time when for a short dream period the drab Brooklyn days were turned into glittering Arabian nights. And even then she had a mind of her own. Though Katherine, in spite of engagements and rumors of engagements, is still plain Katherine Force, still subject to the absolute dictation of Mama Force and obliged to bask, if at all, in the reflected glory of her twice married younger sister. . . . Nor is she going to pour pale tea in pink cups, modestly garbed in cap and apron, for her erstwhile chatty friends. Neither is she going to 'do' their rooms in hectic mauves or citron greens. She is dealing in the raw article, so to speak; that is, she is buying and selling land and houses, at an enormous profit, and letting the other fellow do the rest. And if her kindly friends and admirers are carried away by a pardonable enthusiasm when they declare that she is causing the oldest and best established real estate firms in New York to tremble in their boots, it is certain that she is making a great success and is showing a shrewd understanding of the valuation and profits open to a clever manipulator that signals well for a greater degree of financial independence than she has ever known."

The *Philadelphia Inquirer* questioned the need for Katherine to go to work. For the newspapers, the Astor storyline always boiled down to money. Certainly the motivation must be money, not personal satisfaction.

"Has sister's generosity failed? Is Mr. Dick, whose ancestry is more immediate than the Astors, who also hark back to Germany, running true to frugally Teutonic form, and has he, perhaps, vigorously suggested that his wife is now a Dick and no longer a Force? And does he find the prolonged Force presence to his home a bit too forcible for comfort? Once more society is agog about this family, which in one way or another seems never to be far out of the spotlight, in spite of Katherine's declaration that she 'loves life but hates publicity.'"

* * *

With the divorce rumors put to rest, and the Dick marriage seemingly in good shape, the years progressed for Madeleine, who was now out of society but not out of the limelight. Her name, as well as those of her mother and sister, continued to appear on the society pages, though perhaps less often. Madeleine and Katherine continued to play "aggressive, hard-hitting tennis," reported the *New York Herald* in 1921.

One of the quietest events of that year, which would have a long-lasting effect on the relationship between Colonel Astor's two sons, was the application of Madeleine Dick to give up financial guardianship of her son John Jacob Astor VI. Vincent Astor, who already served as his sister Muriel's financial guardian, was appointed by the court as his brother's guardian as well.

* * *

Katherine Force's career in real estate would last for only one year. She gave up her interest in work outside the home in 1922 on the announcement of her marriage to a respected man of society. Katherine and her mother had traveled to Europe that year, returning early in November aboard the *Aquitania*. On their arrival, they were asked about published reports that Miss Force's engagement would soon be announced. Both women denied the rumors. One month later, Katherine Force was Mrs. Lorillard Spencer Jr.

Major Spencer was much higher on the social scale than had been her first fiancé, Henri Harnickell. To the extent that Mrs. Force cared about the marriages of her daughters, Katherine seemed to have chosen well, despite the fact that Major Spencer was divorced.

Katherine Force and Major Spencer would be married just before Christmas at the home of Madeleine Dick at 7 East Eighty-Fourth Street in New York. Only members of the two families were in attendance. Katherine was given away by her godfather, and Madeleine was her only attendant. John Astor and William Dick served as pages for the ceremony. A reception followed, with a few guests invited.

Titanic always had a way of following Madeleine Astor, and this was true in the case of her new brother-in-law. Major Spencer's uncle, William Augustus Spencer, had been a passenger on *Titanic*. He died in the sinking, and his body was never recovered.

* * *

Much as she had with the marriage of her daughter Madeleine, Mrs. Force would again come under criticism with the marriage of her daughter Katherine.

"Katherine Force's 'Dutiful Daughter Romance,'" read the headline of the January 14, 1923, edition of the *Cincinnati Commercial Tribune*. "How She Turned Her Back on the Joys of Bachelor Maidenhood Rather Than Let Ambitious Mother Be Cheated a Third Time of What She Has Long Wanted So Badly—a Rich and Fashionable Son in Law To Help Her Get Still Higher Up the Social Ladder."

"No statistician has told us how many mothers were made supremely happy during the past holiday season by acts of thoughtful kindness on their children's part. But no matter how many millions there were of them, it is safe to say that none had better cause for the blessing of a gift of a dutiful daughter than Mrs. William H. Force. For Mrs. Force's daughter Katherine gave her what she had been longing—yes, struggling—for years to have—a rich and fashionable son-in-law.

"When Katherine walked to the altar to become the wife of Major Lorillard Spencer, Jr., the millionaire war hero and member of one of New York's proudest families, what a splendid Christmas present that was for ambitious Mrs. Force! It brought satisfying reality to all her dreams—dreams which have so often been shattered by the strangest mischanges.

"According to the stories society gossips tell, few mothers have ever been more ambitious for their daughters to make successful marriages than Mrs. Force. The ambition began about the time when the late Mr. Force's trucking business started paying so handsomely that the family could afford to have social aspirations. It took more and more of a hold on her as she saw what attractive girls her two daughters, Madeline and Katherine, were growing to be.

"And what ambitious mamma would not have been delighted with such a match as Mrs. Force had so skillfully engineered for Madeleine? . . . On neither side of the Atlantic was there a drawing room that would refuse to welcome the woman who bore his name—and, also, of course, her mamma.

"All her friends said, she [Katherine] was distinctly 'not a marrying girl.'"

Madeleine was drawn into the story with the implication that her marriage to the socially unambitious William Dick had been a disappointment to Mrs. Force.

"Mr. Dick positively refused to play the role of fashionable son-in-law. He let it be known that he much preferred the quiet life of the prosperous country gentleman to any of the allurements Fifth Avenue and Newport have to offer. And what made the situation quite hopeless from Mrs. Force's viewpoint was the fact that he had won his bride over to his way of thinking.

"Can you imagine what a disappointment this was for Mrs. Force?

"The gossips who have been watching the progress of this romance think it no disparagement of the gallant Major's ability as a lover to say that the duty Katherine felt she owed her mother played an important part in her decision."

* * *

One significant, very symbolic change in the Astor family was the loss of the Astor mansion on Fifth Avenue. Vincent sold the Astor home on May 5, 1925, to a real estate operator and builder. The home had been in the Astor family for thirty-three years at the time. Vincent, who had his own home in New York City by the time his father married Madeleine Astor, never lived again in the mansion even though he would receive ownership of the historic building after his stepmother's marriage to William Dick. The real estate developer who purchased the mansion announced plans to demolish the structure and build a twenty-story apartment building on the site.

"Upper Fifth Avenue to House the 4,000," read the headline in the *New York Times*. "Demolition of the Astor mansion will mark the passing of one of the most famous social landmarks in the country. . . . It was the citadel of society. . . . It was for many years the social centre of the city and was the scene of many of the most brilliant functions given in New York."

By then, many of the mansions on what was called "Millionaire's Row" were being lost to time and progress. Society was not as important now, its grip on the imagination of the public slowly eroding. The Astor mansion, which had seen so much of the family's history, was gone.

"The Astor sale merely emphasized the passing of a scepter from one dynasty to another and underscored the record of a social revolution which has long been going on. It was a symbol of the passing of the old and the coming of the new. It reminded a busy city, which is so intent upon the future that it has little time to think about the past, about the gracious and spacious days when Mrs. Astor held court for the Four Hundred."

* * *

In 1925, a picture was taken of brothers John Astor and William Dick Jr. at Atlantic City, where they were enjoying the spring sea air with Madeleine and William. The following month, John would be featured in a newspaper story headlined "Three Poor Little Rich Boys" ("What They Have and What They Miss in Cloistered Seclusion"). In November of that year, a picture of Mr. and Mrs. Dick ran in newspapers across the country accompanied by a story stating that they were considering divorce, this time to be obtained in Paris. Friends denied the rumor, and nothing more happened in that direction.

In 1928, a picture of Mrs. Dick wearing tweed ran in newspapers. The story extolled the virtues of the fabric, saying that it was practical for suits and coats, being very popular and smart. Mrs. Dick was photographed walking on Park Avenue in New York wearing an ensemble of heavy tweed in black and white check, with an inset vestee of white crepe. The suit was belted and the skirt bound around the hem with the tweed.

That same year, Madeleine and John would be guests of her sister at Chastellux, where Madeleine and Katherine joined the tennis players at the Casino.

In 1929, it was announced that, in the future, the Dicks would spend part of their summer season at Southampton, New York. They had leased one of the popular summer colony's most handsome villas for their entry there. "And, I need hardly add, the colony out on the south shore of Long Island is duly impressed, for Madeleine Force Astor Dick's pearls are, indeed, eye compelling and in manner she has become grander than those born to Astor prestige and millions," wrote the *San Antonio Light*. The newspaper noted that Mr. and Mrs. Dick had been married at that point for thirteen years. "How time flies."

The newspaper took Bar Harbor to task for losing Madeleine Astor from its summer colony, though the decision had been Madeleine's. "The dull, stiffed-shirts who compose the Mt. Desert Isle colony could not forget that Madeleine became Mrs. Astor via the Brooklyn Bridge. At Southampton, Mrs. Dick undoubtedly will have the success that was denied her in Newport and Bar Harbor."

* * *

In January 1930, the first Mrs. Astor paid a visit to the United States. She was now Lady Ribblesdale. She had been out of the picture for quite some time. It was noted that both she and Madeleine Dick had eaten at the Colony Club at the same time, though at different tables. "There was no sign of recognition," said reporters.

In Bar Harbor that summer, Vincent Astor was showing off his new yacht, the *Nourmahal*, namesake of his father's and grandfather's yacht.

* * *

In August 1931, a picture of Madeleine Dick and her son John taking an open carriage drive in Bermuda while on vacation made its way across the country in newspapers. "Today Mrs. William K. Dick leads a quiet existence, a tall, slender woman still with much grace and manner, who spends her summers at Southampton and her winters in Florida," read one newspaper. The headline of the story was "Debs of Other Days."

As the years had gone on since Madeleine Astor's departure from Bar Harbor, the lessening of her name in the newspaper headlines made it appear that she was headed for social obscurity.

So it would seem.

Chapter 9

This Terrible Thing

I suppose there must be some basis to the rumor—unfortunately! But I resent having anything to do with such a thing. I have repeated arguments with my mother about this terrible thing that threatens us all, but apparently it is of no use.

—John Astor on the engagement of his mother to young, penniless Italian prizefighter Enzo Fiermonte

Without a word of explanation, Madeleine Astor Dick swept into the lobby of the exclusive Riverside Hotel, where she had reserved a suite, according to awaiting reporters. With her were two of her sons and a maid, along with a very handsome young man. Because the reservation was under the name of Mrs. Dick and party, the individual names were not available to reporters, including the mystery man's name. The man was described as young, slender, smartly dressed, and dark-eyed, with black hair. He appeared bored as Madeleine registered for her rooms.

By the year 1933, society was changing, both high society and society at large. The world had been changed by its first world war, and the economy had changed to pay the associated high war costs. When Madeleine Astor Dick checked into the Reno hotel that summer, America's economy was crumbling. There had been four years of runs on banks, signaling the beginning of the Great Depression. The sense of wonder that the general public had felt in reading of the adventures of high society turned into resentment from those who now found themselves with nothing.

The means by which the public at large received news was also changing. Newspapers were no longer the only way to keep up with those members of society. Now there were radio and magazines. The competition for stories and the attention of the public had increased, while the standards of decency and the lines between private and public had decreased.

* * *

Madeleine Astor Dick's life could be described as quiet for the past seventeen years of being Mrs. William Dick, especially in relation to her Astor years. Rumors of a divorce between the Dicks had been in circulation since just a few years into their marriage. Now, in 1933, the children were older, with Jack, twenty, an adult in practice (though not yet by law) and William and John Henry sixteen and fourteen, respectively. Rumors of a divorce had resurfaced that spring. Shortly before Madeleine left for Reno, a reporter would arrive at the Force home in New York City to ask about the stories. In the spacious lobby of the mansion were fourteen pieces of luggage, all marked "Reno, Nev." Young John Astor was supervising the assembling of the luggage. His mother made an appearance in the lobby.

Mrs. Dick was described by the reporter as having preserved a youthful appearance despite what he called "the tragedy of her life." She was dressed in a blue woolen traveling ensemble, which the reporter called stunning. Although she refused to say when she was leaving, it was learned that it would be soon. The reporter asked Mrs. Dick about the rumored impending divorce. Mrs. Dick said she had no statement to make. "You will have to see my attorney about that," she replied.

Joseph R. Truesdale, Madeleine's lawyer, asserted he would make no statement concerning possible divorce proceedings but admitted the Dicks were living apart. "They are legally separated."

"You mean they have obtained a separation in the courts?" the reporter asked.

"No. I mean they are definitely separated. Mrs. Dick has been living at her home here and Mr. Dick has been living at their estate in Islip, Long Island. She has custody of the children."

The lawyer declined to say whether his client was headed directly for Reno. "I understand she's going to a ranch out west," Mr. Truesdale told the reporter.

* * *

Enzo Fiermonte, twenty-four, had been born in Casamassima, a rural village in southern Italy. He first started boxing in Rome at the age of sixteen and found success there. He had been professionally boxing in the United States for two years and was working his way to a national championship before he met Madeleine Astor Dick. When he officially retired from boxing in 1943, his record was forty-seven wins, eleven by knockout; seventeen losses, ten by knockout; and two draws.

Madeleine met Enzo Fiermonte while they were both sailing to France aboard the *Vulcania* early in 1933. Enzo would be appearing in a boxing match in Paris; Madeleine was traveling to Europe for her health. Enzo knew no one on the ship other than a doctor traveling in first class, who he knew was a boxing fan. The doctor invited Enzo to his table in the first-class dining room for dinner. When Enzo arrived, he found that the doctor was not alone but had been joined by a woman, whom Enzo described as tall and broad shouldered, with big, cold blue eyes. He said she looked at him differently from any other woman, seemingly looking right through him.

"She was different in a peculiar way," said Enzo. "I could not decide how old she was. When she smiled she looked extremely young, and when she was serious she might have been past middle age."

Enzo, whose English was not good, said the doctor and Mrs. Dick seemed to be speaking a foreign language. The next day, the doctor invited Enzo to a cocktail party Madeleine was giving, saying that Mrs. Dick had specifically asked for him. Enzo replied that he did not drink because of his training.

"But she's expecting you, my lad. You ought to come. You can't afford to turn down her invitations."

At the party, Madeleine broke away from a crowd of people to greet him formally and then returned to the conversation with her other guests.

Enzo chose to sit in a corner, not knowing anyone. Soon he was aware of Madeleine sitting at his side. She took his hand in hers.

"I hope we'll see each other tomorrow, Signor Fiermonte, you're quite the most interesting person I've met for a long while," Madeleine said to Enzo. "My dear, I don't think we realize how bored we are until we meet some real people."

* * *

Enzo could not get Madeleine Astor Dick off his mind. The next morning, they met on deck and played deck tennis. They would spend the day together, playing backgammon in her stateroom that afternoon. She would tell him that her nerves had been ruined by the *Titanic* ordeal, which was why she was sailing to Europe. He wondered how she dared to travel on the ocean again after the *Titanic* disaster. Enzo had wanted to compliment Madeleine all day but had been afraid. That evening he told her she was beautiful.

"I suppose you tell all women that—I know I'm very ordinary," replied Madeleine. "They say I was quite good looking once, but I've had too much trouble in my life to keep my good looks."

That evening they had dinner together. Madeleine wore orchids, which had been brought on the ship specially for her. She was adorned with diamonds on her fingers and pearls around her neck. Other first-class passengers stared and whispered when Madeleine arrived in the first-class dining room on young Enzo's arm. After dinner they would go on deck, where they held hands and looked up at the moon. They exchanged a kiss.

"It's a pity we did not meet before," Madeleine told Enzo. "I've enjoyed myself so much—the first time perhaps for years. It's been a lovely evening."

The following morning, they had breakfast in her suite. Madeleine asked Enzo to continue to travel with her, but he said he could not.

"She reacted like someone who had never been refused anything," said Enzo.

"Of course you're coming. I shall be terribly unhappy without you—and I don't intend to be unhappy any more in life. I've had my share."

Despite Madeleine's disappointment and his growing feelings for her, Enzo stuck fast to his rejection of her invitation. Enzo could not travel with her because he had a secret—he was married, with a wife and child back in Italy.

* * *

Madeleine Astor Dick and Enzo Fiermonte parted when the ship landed in Europe, and Enzo was soon with his wife, Tosca. In Rome he was praised for his New York boxing by reporters interviewing him. He was preparing to go to Paris to resume training when he received a telegram from Madeleine. She was inviting him to come see her, and if not, she would come to Rome to see him. He agreed to meet her, intending to tell her that he was married and then say goodbye.

They met at the famed Excelsior Hotel in Rome. They had dinner, followed by a gondola ride. They spent the next few days together. Madeleine confided to Enzo that she was already being made fun of because of her feelings for him—by the doctor who had introduced them.

"It's the usual thing—every one is unkind to me. People will not mind their own business. I can never do what I like. It's just as if I were a child and didn't know my own mind. The doctor has been telling me that I'm making a fool of myself with you. He knows that I'm in love with you, and he says I'm too old for you."

Madeleine would tell Enzo she had been to only one boxing match in her life and asked him to fight for her entertainment. Arrangements were made with the manager of the hotel for Enzo to fight in the hotel's attached nightclub. The dance floor was cleared and a ring brought in. Madeleine, dressed in white, wearing her famous pearls and diamonds, was hostess to a party of twenty guests for the event. At her side was a vacant chair for Enzo. The show was a success, with every table in the nightclub booked. In the ring he sparred with four local boxers, one round each.

After the match Enzo changed his clothes and joined Madeleine and the others at her table. He found her in a terrible state. She told Enzo that people at her table had told her she was foolish for associating with Enzo.

"Take me out immediately, Enzo. I will not stay here another minute," she said tersely.

Back in her hotel room, she told Enzo of her life from the day she married Colonel Astor, telling him of the tragedy of the *Titanic*. She told of how her life had become haunted by reporters ready to invade her privacy from the time she met Colonel Astor until she married William Dick. Though she had found seclusion in her second marriage, she told Enzo, the marriage was a disappointment. "Life is hell!" she exclaimed.

* * *

In Europe, Madeleine would take a cottage and was soon joined by her sons William and John Henry, along with their tutor. They never left their mother alone. She was so busy entertaining them that she forgot Enzo a little, though they continued to secretly date while her sons were there. During this time Enzo finally confided to Madeleine that he was still married.

"My dear, so am I. And I have three sons. Is that all?" replied Madeleine. "[T]he marriage I want to escape from now was a big mistake in my life."

Madeleine told Enzo that he could divorce his wife and marry her, but he replied that he could not because he was Catholic. Madeleine called him a cad. Madeleine told him she never wanted to see him again, and he left.

Eventually Madeleine would phone Enzo, who was now staying at his mother's home in Rome, and soon they were traveling together in a suite aboard the *Olympic*. They went to dinner on the ship and met people. In the evening they danced.

"That trip was a step up the ladder for me, the first taste of luxury life, where money was never counted, and where comfort mattered before everything else," said Enzo. "It was amusing to meet people who seemed to have nothing to do but to laugh and play."

Madeleine told Enzo she wanted to marry as soon as possible. She had been planning on divorcing Mr. Dick anyway, she told him, and now it was worthwhile to go through with it. The only difficulty, she said, would be her family.

"It seemed she was used to being criticized and attacked by her various relatives," said Enzo. "Her son, John Jacob, meant more to her than anyone else. I suppose if she ever devoted herself to anyone, it was to him, and she did not want him to be angry with her."

Part of the difficulty with Madeleine's family would be Enzo Fiermonte's profession of boxing, which was not a suitable profession for what was quickly becoming the remnants of the Four Hundred, desperate to hold on to what social standing they still had. She said he would have to quit boxing. He told her that marriage would be impossible. They parted when the ship docked in New York.

Two weeks after arriving back in America, Enzo was again in the boxing ring fighting professionally when his jaw was broken. He spent the next three months recovering. He was training for his comeback fight when he received a phone call from Madeleine, who told him she would be in attendance at the match, along with friends. They had ringside seats, and she had planned a large celebration after the match, at which she would like him to be the guest of honor.

Enzo knocked his opponent out that night. After the match, he went to Madeleine's house in New York, which was filled with flowers for the reception. Enzo stayed among the guests, leaving when they did. He then secretly returned, as had been prearranged. She told Enzo that night that the fight she had just watched was nothing like the exhibition match she had arranged for Enzo in France and that she was unhappy with him boxing.

* * *

Madeleine and Enzo remained a secret couple until she could make arrangements for a divorce, though gossip was quickly spreading. Madeleine would travel to Reno, accompanied by her two youngest sons. Her oldest, Jack, was with his aunt, Katherine Spencer, who had three children of her own by then, at her home in Newport. Enzo traveled separately by automobile to Reno to be with Madeleine. By now the rumors of a romance between the boxer and Madeleine Astor were receiving some level of confirmation when Tosca Fiermonte, Enzo's current wife, talked to reporters in Italy. She was quoted as saying that her husband was seeking a divorce so that he could marry Mrs. Dick. Tosca Fiermonte added that she would not contest the divorce provided she received $30,000 to educate her and Enzo's son, Gianni.

* * *

When Madeleine Astor Dick checked into the lobby of the Riverside Hotel in 1933 to finally obtain her divorce from William Dick, Enzo was with her, and reporters following her noted the presence of her traveling companion. Although the man fit Enzo Fiermonte's description, Enzo was not well known enough in the boxing world to be recognizable. Though the man's presence was reported, his suspected identity was not and could not be until there had been some confirmation of who he was.

Mrs. Dick's first act in Reno was to engage Robert M. Price, a local attorney, to steer her swiftly through Reno courts, where she reportedly hoped to end all ties with her second husband. Madeleine would have to live for six weeks in Reno, Nevada, to be able to legally take advantage of that state's simple divorce laws.

She spent the first few days in Reno quietly, with no public confirmation of the mystery man's identity being Enzo. The scene would change quickly, however, when Madeleine read the morning newspaper to find a story that she and boxer Enzo Fiermonte were in Reno together. Enzo said she threw the newspapers at him in confrontation, accusing him of having tipped off the press.

Enzo told the furious Madeleine that he had been tricked into confirming the story. He said he had received a telephone call in his room at the hotel from a New York reporter, who asked Enzo whether he would be returning to New York to compete in the middleweight boxing tournament. Enzo replied that he was not sure.

"You are Mr. Fiermonte, aren't you?" asked the reporter. Enzo confirmed that he was. The reporter then asked whether he was having a nice holiday in Reno and subsequently hung up the phone. The next day, the story was in the headlines across the country.

Accompanying almost every news story regarding Madeleine Astor Dick was a retelling of the *Titanic* story, especially when the news story advanced that still-popular storyline. This was fresh meat, and it was prime. In black, bold print in headlines across the country, it was reported that Colonel John Jacob Astor's forty-year-old widow was with an "Italian Adonis" in Reno, waiting for a divorce.

Reporters descended on Reno. At this point Madeleine was still denying the romance, but, much like Madeleine and Colonel Astor during their courtship, the couple were not making a great effort to hide their relationship. Madeleine and Enzo were seen together almost daily on the bridle paths and on the beaches of Lake Worth, where they would rent a cabin. Reporters asked Madeleine about the rumors. She described Mr. Fiermonte as "a nice boy" she had met over the summer on a steamer in Italy. It was at that time she engaged his employment for the instruction of athletics for her three sons, teaching them "the manly arts," she said. Madeleine continued to deny rumors of a romance or an impending marriage, saying those rumors were very upsetting to her and that she was considering leaving Reno and obtaining the divorce someplace more private.

"You are authorized to say I will leave Nevada in a few days and seek a divorce somewhere in the East," she told reporters.

"Yes," her son William added. "You may say my mother will get her divorce in New York."

"Billy, I didn't tell you to say that," his mother rebuked. Reporters said Madeleine seemed greatly disturbed by William Jr.'s remark.

Shortly arriving in Reno, Madeleine told her two younger sons she intended to marry Enzo. The boys laughed at her, according to Enzo, with William ridiculing the idea and telling his mother that she was too old for the prizefighter. Madeleine told her son that Enzo had made her young again.

At his aunt Katherine Spencer's home in Newport, John Astor was asked by reporters for confirmation of the romance between his mother and Enzo Fiermonte.

"I suppose there must be some basis to the rumor—unfortunately!" said John. "But I resent having anything to do with such a thing. I have repeated arguments with my mother about this terrible thing that threatens us all, but apparently it is of no use. Until I read the story in the newspapers, however, I was under the impression that she had given up her ideas of divorcing my stepfather.

"Enzo did give me a few boxing lessons, but that was quite some time ago. After my mother began taking such an interest in him, I quit associating with him for good. I no longer consider him my friend. There were certain things about him I didn't like. I haven't seen him for months."

* * *

Madeleine and William Dick's divorce was granted on July 21, 1933. The grounds were extreme cruelty.

"Childhood Sweetheart Fails Her," read the headline of one newspaper when the divorce action was officially filed.

The tradition in Reno at the time was for the newly divorced person to throw their old wedding ring into the Truckee River as soon as the divorce was granted. At their Lake Worth bungalow, Madeleine would have Enzo throw the ring for her.

The ring for which she had so sensationally given up everything Astor, including her leadership of Bar Harbor society (arguably with later regret), was gone forever.

* * *

After Madeleine obtained the divorce, she, along with Enzo, the two Dick boys, and her doctor and nurse, traveled to Palm Beach, where Madeleine had rented a large fifteen-room cottage on the water. The family would spend their time fishing and playing tennis.

Madeleine had obtained her divorce, but Enzo's divorce was not as easy. In Italy with Enzo's son, Tosca Fiermonte was refusing to grant the divorce.

Madeleine and the family would be visited in Palm Beach by Madeleine's son John, just about to turn twenty-one. According to Enzo, John had a secondhand Rolls Royce, in very bad shape, and he wanted Madeleine to advance him the $6,000 to pay for it against his trust. Madeleine refused. John said he would simply make arrangements for the money to be paid when he came of age. He and his mother fought over the issue, with Madeleine in tears for two days afterward. She told Enzo she would write Vincent Astor and ask him to lecture his younger brother.

The fight between Madeleine and John, along with Enzo's general presence in Madeleine's life, caused tension in the Palm Beach house. With Enzo having no real claim there, he volunteered to return to New York to resume training while he awaited his divorce from Tosca. Madeleine agreed, and she initially volunteered to go with him, but the threat of newspaper coverage helped change her mind. After a few days staying at a New York hotel, Enzo was surprised one evening by a car approaching him as he was leaving the gym on Sixty-Sixth Street. The window was lowered, and a white-gloved hand emerged, beckoning Enzo. The chauffeur opened the door so that Enzo could enter the vehicle.

"So you thought you'd let me drop! I wonder how many more times you're going to try to get away from me?" Madeleine said to Enzo.

The couple would go to her Eighty-Fourth Street home, which she had purchased from her now former father-in-law. Enzo described the home as a gloomy six-story building that was more like an antique shop than a home, owing to Madeleine's hobby of collecting furniture.

"The place depressed me," said Enzo. "It seemed like a dull mirror that reflected the cares of its owners. Madeleine was a changed woman in that house. I could hardly believe she was the same woman with whom I had fallen in love in Venice."

With their romance an open secret, Madeleine would invite small groups of friends into her New York home to socialize with her and Enzo. The conversations centered on finance or society scandal. Enzo found he had little in common with Madeleine's friends, finding them either very frivolous or deeply morose.

"Most of them came because an invitation from Mrs. Dick was a social command," said Enzo.

In New York, Madeleine seemed to be grooming Enzo for his future station in life, trying to arrange a job for him with her cousin Lyndon Dodge, who also handled her finances. Though Madeleine discouraged any plans for a return to boxing, a few weeks later Enzo Fiermonte had a contract for a match in New York City. Madeleine did not attend.

* * *

Along with Enzo's return to the ring, the stress of Enzo's inability to obtain a divorce worsened the conditions of his and Madeleine's relationship. Madeleine made Enzo an offer to finance a cash settlement for Tosca in exchange for her signature on his divorce papers. Enzo refused, citing his pride.

The newly divorced Mrs. Astor-Dick was off the social radar for a few months. In August, she and her sister Katherine would visit Bar Harbor with Mr. Thomas Le Boutillier, noted socialite and polo player, on their way to Newport. They stayed at the Malvern Hotel. At Newport they quietly celebrated John's twenty-first birthday at a small family dinner at Chastellux, Katherine Spencer's residence. John Astor would spend the rest of the summer in Newport, which would become his base of operations as a young adult. This was his first full season in the still-popular summer resort, where he was active in the younger set of the summer colony.

* * *

Mrs. Astor-Dick's name would come up again in October when rumors began to spread again that she would be marrying Mr. Fiermonte. The rumors would fit into a current trend of prizefighters marrying social debutantes.

Wrote the *San Antonio Light* on October 15, 1933, three months after Madeleine's divorce: "Another Prize Fighter to Marry a Rich Society Woman?"

The story told of how former boxing champion Gene Tunney, who had a summer home in Maine, had married Miss Josephine Lander, Social Register heiress, and how boxer Jack Dempsey had been "lured by a movie siren."

"High society and even royalty tumbled over each other to welcome the pair," according to the paper. "But for Mrs. Madeleine Force Astor Dick, the same sort of thing seems to be K.O. with loud boos and raspberries. Why cheers for Polly and Bronx cheers for Madeleine?"

This news story would give a chance to mix Madeleine Astor's names and the proper words of society with the gritty world of New York boxing. Enzo Fiermonte's boxing manger in New York was "Knobby" Johnston. Reporters would soon find Knobby, and he was happy to talk.

Much of the world of boxing was about promotion, and pithy comments helped bring people into Madison Square Garden. At the same time, Madeleine Astor hated publicity, and certainly publicity that linked her to the sport of boxing. Asked about the string of boxers marrying society women, and specifically whether Enzo should marry Madeleine, Knobby Johnston was in support of such a marriage.

"Sure, I've seen photos of this Astor-Dick dame," Johnston told reporters. "She looks like a real swell to me. She ought to handle my kid like a mother. Keep him out of trouble with Broadway gold-diggers and all that. I'm all for it.

"The way I figure it, the kid's on the level with his new headache—the lady with all them ritzy names. And, being on the level, he doesn't want to give up the situation by letting the lady pay his old bills. No sir. This Enzo person isn't the kind to throw a fight or live off a dame.

"Look at some of those other swabs. I could name a dozen. Good fighters just went wrong over women. Chippy chasers. Can't stay in training long enough to make a good fight. Can't stay out of the night clubs. Guzzle booze when they ought be doin' their road work. And when they do marry—huh! Always get tied up with some skirt that drives 'em nuts for money.

"Diamond tiaras. Diamond necklaces. Diamond rings. Swell dresses. Can't satisfy 'em. Gold diggers, every one of 'em. Long comes some third rater and throws the boy for a loop. Wife's fault. Makes 'em so dizzy from money jitters they don't know enough to hold in the clinches and throw their weight on the other guy. Just makes 'em crazy and they can't help but slip.

"Now look at Enzo—if he marries this society frill. She's got diamonds, plenty of 'em. And she's old enough to wear her carpet slippers when her old man's in training instead of gadding around like these Broadway Jezebels who are always trying to grab off these young fellas trying to work their way up.

"Yes, I'd heard all about the wife and bambino in Rome. That's one thing you can say about Enzo. He ain't like those other palookas that go 'round throwing sand in the eyes of their managers. No, sir. He's 10-carat gold, that kid is—he'd tell the truth if it killed him. Good fighter. A man's man; none of this here gigolo stuff about him.

"No sir, I won't kick if he marries this Astor-Dick dame. I'm all for it, myself. Course I don't know what their sentiments are, but they can have my blessings any old day."

* * *

Madeleine Astor would travel to Bermuda, while Enzo would travel to Reno, having received word that Tosca would sign the divorce papers. He would join Madeleine after having established residency in Reno and the divorce had been granted.

Madeleine was waiting at the dock in a horse-drawn carriage for the newly divorced Enzo when he arrived in Bermuda, along with reporters who had sailed on the same boat in pursuit of the Astor-Fiermonte story, with a wedding expected at any time. The same chase Madeleine had been at the head of in her relationships with William Dick and John Jacob Astor was now in effect for a third time.

Madeleine and Enzo stayed at a vast mansion in Bermuda called Bellevue, on Grape Gyay, one of the most beautiful spots on the island. The outside walls of the mansion were white, with flowers of every color surrounding it. The estate was filled with gardens, and each one was different. There was a private beach, a natural swimming pool cut out of rock, and a path that led through the dark, cool woods. The next day, one of the reporters arrived at Madeleine's rented cottage.

"We are not engaged," Madeleine said to the reporter, with a smile on her face. "If anything happens, we'll let you know. In any case, we are great friends."

* * *

Enzo had spent his time waiting for his divorce in Nevada reflecting on his obligation to Madeleine and thinking about her cold blue eyes. He thought about the lack of joy he felt with Madeleine, the dullness of her house on Eighty-Fourth Street in New York City. He remembered all the times he had seen Madeleine brood and cry and then challenged himself to try to remember a time she had laughed. He wondered about the lack of spontaneous joy on her face.

"The life she led; the everlasting hours of worry about trivialities, her medicine, her boredom, the complete lack of gayety in her life—all united against her. I did not kid myself. When she was with me, and conscious of me, she looked younger, but I realized the difference in age."

Also in Enzo's mind lingered the memory of a young woman he had fallen in love with in New York before he met Madeleine. He still had feelings for her, but he also recognized his obligation to marry Madeleine.

Enzo had arrived in Bermuda a conflicted man. He still wanted to box but knew Madeleine would never accept that career for her husband. He was not sure marriage was the best next step. Over dinner one evening, Madeleine told Enzo that she felt he had changed. He took her two hands in his and told her he had decided not to marry her, that they could not be happy together.

"We're not even happy when we are alone, and we even fight before other persons," Enzo said to her. "We can't go and live on a desert island, and that's the only way we could be happy. If you're tired of seeing people, I'm not—I want to live. I've been dead for a year, and I can't live in a grave. Let's be reasonable, part friends and give each other a chance. You should marry someone in your own circle and of your own situation."

"You mean I'm too old?" Madeleine replied.

Enzo said Madeleine's eyes looked frantic. Their discussion escalated into Madeleine revealing that she knew about the young woman back in New York, though it did not occur to him yet that Madeleine had been having him followed since she had met him.

"You're going to marry that little tramp in New York. That's how it is! I give you background, I teach you how to behave, and you're going to marry a common little chit in New York?"

According to Enzo, Madeleine then slapped his face. He said he grabbed at her hands, telling her to stop, feeling his dignity injured.

"Stop it indeed! After you've ruined my reputation and let me make a fool of myself! The whole world is laughing at me."

Enzo released her hands and headed for the door. As he was turning the handle, he said Madeleine grabbed his ample black hair with both hands and pulled, screaming that he could not go. Enzo said the pain was awful. He said he brought both his arms down to make her release her grip. She fell. All he could remember after that was seeing her lying injured on the floor of the Bermuda mansion.

Enzo picked Madeleine up and carried her to her bed. He worried that she was going to die and quickly ran to get the doctor. Enzo fled the cottage when the doctor arrived.

According to Enzo, after a while the doctor came out and found him on the grounds of the estate. The doctor said that Mrs. Dick had fractured her arm when she fell. Enzo said that it was his fault.

"It was fine of you to tell me, I appreciate it, but don't tell anyone else," replied the doctor. "Madeleine doesn't want it known."

At the hospital, Madeleine would not speak with Enzo. Two days later, she called him and asked him to visit, which he did, carrying gifts of flowers and fruit. He begged her forgiveness. He did not leave her side. Madeleine Force, who had earned her name on the tennis courts in Bar Harbor, had suffered nerve damage, and a specialist had to be called in. Her recovery was slow.

As soon as Madeleine did recover, she and Enzo again began to quarrel. Madeleine could not forget the girl in New York, whom the press had found out about and was calling Enzo's next wife. Despite Enzo's efforts to convince Madeleine that was all in the past, she refused to believe him. Enzo knew she would never believe him and that she would never be happy with him out of her sight, at a point in his young life when he wanted to live. He left Bermuda and returned to New York without her.

Enzo had just checked in at the Commodore Hotel when he was approached by a man who identified himself as a doctor. The man said he had been instructed by Mrs. Astor to impress on Enzo the importance of returning to her side in Bermuda. Enzo listened to the man for half an hour before promising to return. The episode impressed on Enzo Fiermonte that he would never be free of Madeleine Astor, no matter where he went. The ship on which he sailed back to Bermuda was full of reporters and photographers following Enzo. Every time they saw him, they would ask him whether he was returning to marry Mrs. Astor.

Landing in Bermuda, Enzo was surprised when he was refused permission by British authorities to enter the same country that he had just left a few days before. They explained that they had received instructions by telephone from New York that on no account was Enzo to be allowed to set foot on the island. They provided no explanation as to why. At the time, the president of the United States was Franklin D. Roosevelt, half brother to John and Vincent Astor's uncle James Roosevelt. Enzo appealed to the ship's captain and the police chief, but to no avail. He then telephoned Madeleine, who was furious. She told Enzo that the orders must have come from her family, who was opposed to a wedding between the two, which would have social implications for the entire family.

On board the ship, a guard was assigned to Mr. Fiermonte. Enzo was able to escape detention one evening by purchasing a sailor's uniform shirt and sneaking off the ship. He headed to the hospital to pay a secret visit to Madeleine. They made plans for Enzo to go to Paris, where she would join him. Before the ship left, she sent him a note saying she looked forward to starting their married life together. Enzo would return to New York first before heading to France. He was met by reporters. Enzo's rant against Bermudan officials went unheard; instead, the reporters were asking when he was going to marry Mrs. Dick.

Instead of meeting in France, Madeleine would dramatically return to New York on a stretcher for medical care. Arrangements had been made for her, along with her maid and personal secretary, to sail on the *Monarch of Bermuda*. During the voyage from Bermuda to New York City, reporters continually tried to obtain an interview with Mrs. Astor, which she continually refused. Madeleine's personal secretary, Miss Edith Searle, objected vehemently to the efforts of reporters to interview Madeleine, saying they were "torture and persecution." Madeleine was met at the pier in New York by her son John and others. A close-up picture of a pathetic-looking Madeleine Astor appeared in the *New York Times* and other newspapers across the country.

Madeleine's doctors would send a cable from the New York hospital to the hotel where Enzo was saying. He took a cab there directly. Enzo found Madeleine looking radiant, with the tired lines gone from her face.

* * *

Now that they were reunited, the couple made plans to get married as soon as Madeleine was released from the hospital. The doctors refused to release Mrs. Dick, so plans changed to a bedside wedding. The next obstacle was Madeleine's son John, who was quite opposed to a wedding and had not been shy with the reporters following him. John Astor reportedly said that if Madeleine married a boxer, he would marry a shopgirl.

The other complication was a prenuptial agreement. At one point during this time, while away from the hospital, Enzo was approached by a man who had papers for him to sign. The man told Enzo he would entertain the amount of money requested as a marriage settlement—Enzo's dowry. At first Enzo refused to sign the papers, but he soon relented. The couple were married the day after.

* * *

The ceremony was held at 5:00 p.m. on November 27, 1933, in Madeleine's New York City hospital room. Though this wedding was the story that reporters had chased for four months, Madeleine attained some privacy, with the staff of the hospital being loyal to her and not tipping off reporters. Madeleine had arranged for the license and the invitations to her family. She told Enzo she was not sure whether they would attend the ceremony.

Madeleine's room was filled with flowers. In an adjoining room a champagne buffet had been set up. Twenty people would arrive for the ceremony, including Madeleine's mother, who greeted Enzo warmly with a kiss. Enzo said that she and Madeleine's sister, Katherine, were the only guests to greet him with anything more than a formal notice. John Astor arrived late, kissed his mother, and shook Enzo's hand. William and John Henry Dick were also there but showed that they were not pleased with the occasion. The other guests seemed simply uninterested.

When it came time in the ceremony to exchange rings, Lyndon Dodge slipped Madeleine's ring into Enzo's hand. After the ceremony there was an awkward silence at the point when the groom is supposed to kiss the bride. The Italian Enzo was not aware of the custom.

"Aren't you going to kiss the bride?" asked the court official performing the ceremony, with a broad smile.

After the traditional kiss, the wedding guests came to life. One by one, they solemnly congratulated the new couple. Champagne was served to the couple's health. After the ceremony, Madeleine authorized Lyndon Dodge to make a statement to the press announcing the marriage. The guests left, with only Mrs. Force wishing the couple happiness.

"It [the wedding] made much agitated conversation around Madison Square Garden and in other circles quite a cut higher in aristocracy," wrote the *Indianapolis Times.*

Madeleine wanted Enzo to spend the night with her, and the hospital's superintendent found a room on the building's fourth floor. Enzo would spend the night with a patient in the throes of delirium in the next room. The following morning, Madeleine and Enzo had breakfast together at her bedside. That afternoon the wheelchair-bound Madeleine was taken to a private railroad car that John had chartered, and Madeleine and Enzo left for Palm Beach. A doctor and nurse accompanied them.

The villa at Palm Beach was a high, red-brick building situated on Ocean Boulevard. The place had not been occupied for some time. To Enzo, the place had more of the look of a mausoleum of some long-dead millionaire than a honeymoon spot. On the newlyweds' arrival, the accompanying doctor ordered Madeleine directly to bed.

Enzo would find the swimming pool outside, where he would spend much of his time. He feared going out on the town alone because of the reporters and how Madeleine would react if his name appeared in the newspapers. When Madeleine did recover, the two would spend their time fishing or going for drives in an automobile. At one point Madeleine hosted a cocktail party for twenty-five guests.

"Madeleine gave parties that were packed with the personalities who were always in the newspapers," said Enzo. "She went to the smartest places, and she moved always with a mantle of glamour about her."

Enzo would soon find himself short of money. The few times the Fiermontes had gone out while in Palm Beach, the generous tipping and coverage of other expenses expected of a man in Enzo's new social situation soon cut him short of cash. At one point Madeleine asked him to buy her flowers. He said he had no money. She walked to her desk and came back with a check she had made out for $1,000. She put it into Enzo's hand.

"I'm sorry, sweet lamb—I forgot! I intended to give you this as an allowance for the month. You should have reminded me."

Enzo was shocked and embarrassed. However, due to the expense of being Madeleine's husband, the money went to the purchase of a dozen suits and other necessities, as well as to pay the expenses when the couple went out. Madeleine continued to pay all the household accounts.

The following month, when Madeleine presented Enzo with his second allowance check, she also presented him with an itemized account of the deductions she had made from it. The largest expense was the laundry and cleaning bill of Mr. Fiermonte's new suits and other clothing.

"I soon began to realize that the position of being a paid husband was far from enviable," said Fiermonte. "I was a showpiece, and in the household I rated with the nurse and the doctor, except that they were at liberty to go out when they were not needed, and I was expected to stay in the house."

Enzo was not allowed to go anywhere without his wife. Madeleine would tell him she was sure he would fall in love with some young girl just as he had in New York if he did. Enzo saw Madeleine as someone who thought everyone dishonest until they proved their honesty.

"She had been so hurt and disillusioned by life that she could not understand that some people were naturally upright," said Enzo.

* * *

The monthly allowances continued to be an insult to Enzo's pride. His father had died young, leaving Enzo to help with the support of his mother and two brothers back in Italy, and he did not feel right using Madeleine's money to do that, though there would be nothing left over at the end of each month even if he had wanted to. Enzo told Madeleine he was thinking of returning to New York to resume his boxing career and earn his own money. Madeleine told Enzo she wished he would not do that, and she said that she would write to her cousin Lyndon Dodge to take him up on the promise to take Enzo into his brokerage firm, a necessity to secure a seat on the New York Stock Exchange. Madeleine Astor married to a New York Stock Exchange stockbroker, as her sister Katherine had been prepared to do so many years ago with Henri Harnickell, was much more acceptable than Madeleine Astor being remarried to a boxer.

Though letters were exchanged between Madeleine and her cousin, the position on Wall Street never materialized. Enzo began to mope. Madeleine noticed the change in him and started inviting friends to their Palm Beach villa. They went out more. The socialization itself soon became boring to Enzo. At last Enzo had enough and decided to travel to New York to talk to Lyndon Dodge personally. Madeleine said she did not like the idea of Enzo going there alone and that she would accompany him. The night before they were to leave, however, the doctor advised Madeleine that the New York climate would not be good for her health, and the trip was postponed. A few months later, a frustrated Enzo traveled to New York City alone in search of Lyndon Dodge.

An hour after arriving in New York City, Madeleine would telephone Enzo at the hotel into which he had just checked, telling him she would soon be joining him. At this point Enzo figured out that Madeleine had him shadowed by detectives and had been doing so since shortly after the two met.

Madeleine and Enzo walked to Lyndon Dodge's office, where they talked for an hour. As it would turn out, Lyndon Dodge did not have room for Enzo Fiermonte in his office. Lyndon explained that because of the unsteadiness of the stock market, which had recently crashed, he had to cut his own staff and that he, himself, was working under such pressure that he would have very little time to show someone new the ropes.

Enzo offered to work for Lyndon for less money. Lyndon did not say no but said he would figure out something to do for them and would be in touch. Fifteen days passed without word. Fed up, Enzo did not return to see Lyndon Dodge, instead going to see his old boxing manager,

Knobby Johnston. Johnston told Enzo he could earn cash fast if he was willing to return to the ring. Knobby knew that the new husband of Madeleine Astor would draw many spectators into Madison Square Garden, with the added unspoken promise of Mrs. Astor-Fiermonte also being in attendance. The news was announced in the June 5, 1934, edition of the *New York Times*: "Fiermonte to Fight Maxie Rosenbloom."

The story told how negotiations were being made for a match at Madison Square Garden between "Enzo Fiermonte, the Italian boxer who married Mrs. William K. Dick, the former Mrs. John Jacob Astor," and Maxie Rosenbloom, the current titleholder of the light heavyweight belt. The match was being planned for September. Though Enzo was returning to boxing so that he could have his own money, he announced he would donate his winnings to charity.

Madeleine did not like the idea of the boxing match, but she took the news surprisingly well, as she thought that idleness was worse for Enzo than the negative publicity would be for her and the Astors. She had one condition for accepting the fight, however: Enzo had to train in the Hamptons, New York, where she would rent a cottage. She said this was necessary because her doctor had advised her to live by the sea for a time.

It was July 1934, and the Hamptons were packed with socialites. A boxing ring for training was built on the private beach of the cottage Madeleine had rented for the summer. Enzo's hired sparring partners were housed in the cottage's servants' quarters. The brother of Enzo's manager was allowed to live in the house. Enzo did his roadwork on the grounds of the cottage and arranged his schedule so that he could eat lunch with Madeleine every day.

The idea of a boxing training camp on the beach at East Hampton caused quite a stir. The camp soon became the center of attention there. Still, all went well—for a week. Then there was trouble.

The problem was the newspaper reporters. The boxing world thrived on publicity to put people in the seats at any arena, especially one as large as Madison Square Garden. Enzo's bout especially thrived on publicity. Yet despite the sensation of the upcoming match and the training grounds in the middle of the Hamptons, no one was coming to Enzo for interviews. He had spent the last year being followed by reporters and photographers, but there was not a single one around now.

Enzo soon found out why. Madeleine Astor did not like reporters, and she had instructed her staff to turn any reporters away. For sports reporters, traditionally an interview with the participants of an upcoming event was a given, but they were now having the door literally closed in their faces. Enzo Fiermonte's return to boxing, and his quest for independence, became a running joke in the newspapers.

Enzo quickly went to work trying to repair his relations with the press. He was able to get Madeleine to agree to allow him to host a press conference, but only in the training area of their summer home, not in the house itself. Reporters described the training headquarters as extravagant, including a living area. Boxing gloves rested on the same table as a crystal vase with a fragrant rose. The reporters found that Enzo talked more about his marriage to Madeleine Astor than he did the upcoming boxing match. He denied stories that his wife did not want the fight to happen.

"Please let us get this right first, we are happy," Enzo told reporters. "The story that Mrs. Fiermonte objects to the fight is equally absurd. Mrs. Fiermonte and I are perfectly agreed that I fight this one fight. It is scarcely reasonable that a man in love, married for little over six months, would set his heart on doing something his wife objected to."

Though having his own money was important to Enzo and was one of the reasons for the boxing match, he denied that to reporters. He said his finances would be taken care of with a future on Wall Street, which he knew by now would probably not materialize. Enzo did acknowledge that part of the reason for the boxing match was so that he would not lose his own identity to that of "that young boxer Mrs. Dick married," as he was being portrayed in the press.

The press conference would backfire on Enzo. One of the stories that would come out of the press conference quoted Enzo as comparing Madeleine's physical charms to that of his younger first wife, Tosca. Madeleine was outraged and forbade any further reporters at the summer home, hiring two guards specifically to keep reporters away. By now Madeleine's society friends had tired of the novelty of the training camp on the beach and stopped socializing with the couple. Madeleine stopped sending out social invitations.

Ultimately the boxing match was never held. The New York State Boxing Commission announced that it would ban the scheduled bout between Fiermonte and Slapsie Maxie for the light heavyweight championship. They said that Enzo Fiermonte did not have enough experience in the ring to be considered for a title fight. Enzo abruptly ceased his training at the East Hampton estate and chose to give up boxing.

"Rather than go through the publicity that has been given us, I have decided to hang up the gloves forever," Enzo announced to reporters.

Seven months into the new marriage, Enzo Fiermonte found himself penniless, friendless, and now without a career.

* * *

Madeleine Astor's complicated marriage was also causing problems for her oldest son, who was now of marriageable age. John Astor had reached the age of legal maturity, twenty-one, and laid claim to what was his from his father's will.

John Jacob Astor VI had spent much of his young life with his aunt Katherine Force Spencer. Katherine had been living with her husband in their mansion, Chastellux, raising three children of her own. Newport would become home base for young John Astor, who was becoming quite active in the younger social set, full of young, socially suitable debutantes. This is where John was spending much of his time during his mother's courtship and wedding to Enzo Fiermonte.

Along with his new position in society, John Jacob Astor VI also had a new name. His father had been Colonel John Jacob Astor IV, and an Astor descendant in England had taken the title of John Jacob Astor V before Colonel Astor's son was born, making Madeleine's son John Jacob Astor VI. Over time the English branch of the Astor family was disregarded by the American press when it came to the numbering of the name John Jacob Astor, and John Jacob Astor VI would commonly become known as John Jacob Astor III.

The name John Jacob Astor in a headline would always sell newspapers, and with young John about to reach the age of twenty-one, he began to receive more newspaper coverage. His birthday would be a milestone in the story that had been building for the past twenty years—heir to the richest man on *Titanic*, whose lavish life had been followed by the general public across the country for twenty years. John Jacob Astor III had also received an unequal share of his father's fortune compared to his brother Vincent, who seemed to be giving the money away to everyone but his younger brother.

At the end of January 1933, a few months before news broke about Madeleine and Enzo dating and Madeleine's divorce from William Dick, headlines announced the engagement of John Astor and Donna Cristiana Torlonia, daughter of a Roman prince. The news story said the engagement had been revealed in a letter.

"Absurd," said the young woman's mother, Mrs. Elsie Moore Torlonia of New York. "I want to deny it emphatically. I cannot understand how such a rumor could get started. It is the most absurd thing I ever heard of."

If there had been an engagement at all between John and Cristiana, a wedding never materialized. Instead, as John approached his twenty-first birthday in August, he spent the early summer season in Newport, attending many supper dances and other events organized for the younger set, sponsored in part by John's aunt Katherine. Just two weeks before his twenty-first birthday, John hosted a dinner party for about forty friends, one of the largest parties given in Newport that summer.

Though there had been great buildup to John Jacob Astor III's twenty-first birthday, the day went by quietly, with John motoring from New Hampshire to Newport with his aunt Katherine. There was no special birthday observance. John would spend the rest of August in Bar Harbor as a guest at the Malvern Hotel. While there, his brother Vincent and his wife arrived in Bar Harbor aboard the *Nourmahal* to watch the close of the tennis tournament.

* * *

By the time of John's twenty-first birthday, Madeleine had just divorced William Dick and the rumors about Enzo Fiermonte and Madeleine being a couple were shocking society. During John Astor's twenty-first birthday summer, besides the time he had spent at evening social events, he was spending much of his days at the tennis courts in Newport watching two sisters who were described as "outstanding" players. As his father had done twenty-two years ago in Bar Harbor, now John was watching one of those players with special interest—Miss Eileen Gillespie.

Eileen came from a very socially prominent family. Her grandmother's Newport estate was across the street from the Astors' Beechwood estate, now in the possession of Vincent Astor. Eileen's parents, Lawrence and Irene Gillespie, were from two of the oldest families in the United States. Through her father, Eileen was a descendant of Roger Williams, colonial patriot and a founder of Rhode Island.

Eileen had graduated from Miss Hewitt's School, which was as fashionable as her fiancé's St. George's School. Active in the same social circles, the two would meet often in Newport and in Manhattan society. Eileen Gillespie was in the Social Register, as was John Astor. Both were described as active in outdoor sports, and Eileen Gillespie, much like John's mother, had won several tennis tournaments, though her victories were in Newport, not Bar Harbor.

Soon John and Eileen were dating. They were described by friends and reporters as being happy just because they were together. The new couple were starting to be seen together at more and more social functions, and soon they were everywhere together. Eileen Gillespie made her debut to society at a dance on December 15, 1933. One week later, her engagement to John Jacob Astor III was announced.

Madeleine and Enzo had been married for almost two months at the time of the engagement announcement. John, now in control of the twenty-one years of interest from his $3 million trust fund, began preparing to be a married man. He rented a five-story home at 7 East Ninety-First Street in New York for the marriage. In January 1934, ahead of the planned February wedding, John would purchase a summer home in Newport, the mansion Chetwode, which was reportedly planned as a wedding present for his fiancée.

As an engagement ring, John gave Eileen a thirty-two-carat diamond valued at $250,000, not adjusted for inflation. The historic ring had once been the property of Empress Eugénie of France, wife of Napoleon

III. The mother of the original John Jacob Astor had purchased the ring after the collapse of the Second Empire.

The ring held more value than just its history of financial value. With Vincent Astor having inherited all their father's possessions after his death, the fact that the ring was in John's possession suggests that Vincent had given the ring to his brother to offer to his new bride. Though the brothers' relationship would sour over time, there was a time when they had been close. Vincent was to serve as best man at the wedding. By now Vincent had been a responsible, married member of society for several years. Perhaps he envisioned a married John Astor as a more responsible John Astor, as their last name demanded. The ring seemed to symbolize a faith that Vincent Astor once had in his younger brother.

The wedding was set for February 6, 1934. The guests had been invited, and the bridesmaid dresses were ready. As the date approached, John and Eileen went to a society dance one Saturday night. As the story goes, several people noticed that John was spending much of his time there dancing with another girl. The next day, the following news item appeared: "Mr. and Mrs. Lawrence Lewis Gillespie of New York City and Newport announce that the engagement of their daughter, Miss Eileen S. S. Gillespie, to John Jacob Astor, III has been cancelled."

"As a result of the crispy term used by the Gillespies in breaking the news, Park Avenue was soon to be overrun with social snoopers, all seeking to learn just what preceded the wrecking of the youthful romance," wrote the *Syracuse Herald.*

With a broken heart, like his father before him, John Astor turned to a trip on the sea, taking the honeymoon cruise that he and Eileen would have taken as a married couple. Before embarking on the steamship, at the pier John was asked about the reasons for calling off his engagement.

"They are very, very personal. I feel very badly over the thing. I still care very much for Eileen. She is a very fine girl. You may be sure that the breaking of the engagement was entirely her idea."

In Shanghai, China, where John spent much of his time in his hotel suite, he told reporters he had not gone there for pleasure but to try to forget Eileen. "I don't like to discuss it. What more can I say?"

On returning to the United States a few months later, John again talked to reporters at the pier. He blamed Eileen's parents for the breakup, stating that they had insisted on accompanying him and Eileen on their honeymoon. "The situation was confused. But it was she who broke the engagement. I was willing to marry her, and if I were to think about it, I might still be willing to marry her."

During John Astor's impromptu remarks, he revealed to reporters that the historic, valuable engagement ring was still in the possession of Eileen Gillespie. "I hope it will be returned," John told reporters before traveling to the Manhattan town house he had rented as a home for him and Eileen.

* * *

The story of the cause of the wedding's cancellation was enough of a story on its own, but the fact that the historic engagement ring had not been returned took on a life of its own. Early that summer, negotiations began between John Astor and the Gillespie family for the ring's return. In June, the Gillespies returned the ring to John through the offices of Cartier, Inc., Fifth Avenue jewelers. Accompanying the ring was every other article received by Miss Gillespie from Mr. Astor.

By now John had written a letter of apology to Eileen and her parents and included a promise never to speak of the Gillespies except with respect. In exchange for the apology and the promise, the ring was returned.

"Should Mr. Astor after having received these articles fail to comply with his promise, it will rest in the discretion of Miss Gillespie's parents whether they shall then feel compelled to make public the entire correspondence which took place between Miss Gillespie's parents and Mr. Astor during January 1934 so that those who may be concerned in the matter may be able to judge fully and thoroughly the reasons why these articles have been held until this time," the Gillespie family announced to the press.

John Astor would continue to make off-the-cuff remarks to reporters after the ring was returned, leading the Gillespies to release one of their letters from John Astor, perhaps in an effort to let him know they were serious about their threat.

"Owing to interviews attributed to Mr. Astor by the press and uncontradicted by him, which were not in accordance with the truth, it has been felt necessary to state these facts," announced the Gillespies.

On June 17, 1934, the *New York Times* printed the contents of the released letter.

"Dear Miss Gillespie: I willingly withdraw anything I may have said to you in the corridor of the savoy-Plaza hotel on Sunday, Jan. 21, 1934, which may have hurt you, and I apologize.

"I assure you that if I have occasion to speak or write of you or your family it will be only with respect, for as you know, I have always held you in the highest esteem. Sincerely, J. J. Astor."

In the course of the story about the engagement ring, other stories came out about the Astor–Gillespie engagement. It was reported that John had originally offered a $1.5 million trust to Eileen Gillespie as a wedding present, with her parents saying the amount was too much. Eventually $500,000 had been the trust settlement. With the matter now behind them, the Gillespies attempted to put the unpleasant situation to rest.

"We have nothing to say, and unless we are attacked we'll have nothing further to say," said Mrs. Gillespie.

* * *

The story of John Astor's broken engagement gave reporters a chance to raise the question of what effect Madeleine's recent remarriage had played in the parting of John and Eileen. Though the reason for John's broken engagement seemed to be a quarrel, it is reasonable to think that the Gillespies might have been relieved not to have been in-laws with a boxer. Friends of the Gillespies privately said that they were afraid of being taken out of the Social Register if the marriage had taken place.

"And squarely upon the shoulders of Mrs. Madeline Force Astor Dick Fiermonte did these whirling imps and gnomes of gossip place the blame for the breaking of the engagement between Eileen S. S. Gillespie and Astor," wrote the *Syracuse Herald*. "They said that the recent marriage of Astor's mother, which, if Astor and Miss Gillespie had married, would have given the aristocratic Eileen a former professional prizefighter for a stepfather-in-law, was primarily and directly the cause of the rift between the young people."

The entire engagement episode, combined with the headlines created by John's mother and new stepfather, resulted in ridicule for young John Astor. In July, just after the engagement ring had been returned in a messy exchange, a syndicated news story would appear in newspapers across the country: "Trouble of America's Richest Young Bachelor in Finding a Wife."

"Nobody could be more eligible than the fifth John Jacob Astor, but his first two romances faded even though one of them was sealed with a $250,000 diamond ring."

The story described John as a slender, dark, shy boy who was well behaved and reserved. "He never went to speakeasies, though he could have tipped the musicians incredible amounts and had the toast of Broadway beauties arranged around his table. Instead he went in for athletics and attended school regularly. He is a graduate of St. George's School, at Newport, Rhode Island. His taste leans toward mechanics."

* * *

The stories of John Astor's broken engagement and the engagement ring, along with the social complications caused by Madeleine's remarriage to Enzo Fiermonte, would not have a chance to settle. Instead, they would be enhanced by the announcement of John Astor's second engagement—to one of his first fiancée's bridesmaids.

Ellen Tuck French ("Tucky") was the debutante daughter of the socially prominent Mr. and Mrs. Francis and Eleanor French. The French family symbolized what was happening to society at the time. The depression and stock market crash had taken the money and resources of many of society's good families, including the Frenches. Ellen's father lost his fortune in the stock market and went to work as a New York City taxicab driver. Ellen's mother divorced her husband and married a rich man from Park Avenue.

John and Ellen's wedding was planned for late June. As the date approached, there was more speculation regarding whether John's mother and stepfather would attend the ceremony to be held in Newport.

At this point, Madeleine and Enzo were still in the Hamptons, with his championship match having just been canceled. Enzo, and his relationship with Madeleine, was now a point of ridicule for sports reporters, whose stories caused increased friction between the couple. The training camp on the beach in the Hamptons had gone from interesting spectacle to eyesore for the members of society who summered there, and the Fiermontes were finding themselves socially ostracized, a position that Madeleine never seemed to enjoy. Privacy and social ostracization were two very different things.

The story of the wedding was being pursued heavily by reporters, and a few days before the event, John Astor would hold a press conference.

"I desire to cooperate with the press in any and all matters of legitimate news value. I regret, as does Miss French, that stories have been issued without foundation in fact or reason," John Astor told reporters. "I will be glad to answer questions that I consider proper if they are submitted in writing at this time. Any questions not answered are not to be repeated."

John answered questions about his future, which, he said, included a desire to learn some business and later establish a business of his own. He was asked about his relationship with his brother Vincent, which presumably had suffered from the dramatics and the headlines surrounding the Astor ring and the loss of its possession by the Astors, even if briefly.

"I have always been most friendly with him and still am," John declared.

At the end of the press conference, John invited the gathered reporters to the wedding rehearsal. Miss French's mother soon rescinded the invitation and changed the time of the rehearsal.

* * *

Though it was never said publicly, Enzo Fiermonte did not seem to be invited to the Newport wedding. His exclusion had cast doubt on Madeleine's attendance.

"Mrs. Fiermonte Is Seriously Ill Today," ran the headline in the *Rhinelander Daily News*.

It was four days before the ceremony, and Madeleine Fiermonte announced from the Hamptons cottage that she was not physically able to travel to the ceremony. She was reported to be very ill, though servants at the Southampton cottage could give no explanation as to her sickness. They said she was prostrated.

Then came the announcement from the boxing commission that Enzo could not fight in the boxing match. He was seen leaving the Southampton estate with five pieces of baggage. He said he was traveling to New York on business and told reporters he did not know how long he would be gone. The day before the ceremony, Enzo Fiermonte announced that he would not attend the wedding of his stepson. Enzo told reporters in New York that society held no interest to him.

"I am not planning to attend that wedding tomorrow," he said, "and that is absolute."

He denied that there had been a family rift over his career as a boxer. He said he had not been snubbed by the Astors or by his stepson in particular. "Jack Astor and I are good friends. I had another date, that's all."

By now rumors were circulating that Madeleine and Enzo had separated, the rumor reinforced by Enzo's trip to New York. Asked about a separation, reporters noted that Enzo perspired freely as he answered the question.

"Anything like that will have to come from my wife," said Enzo. "My marriage was no Aladdin's romance. It was based on love, pure love, with money and position left out."

Enzo then implicitly confirmed the separation story, telling reporters that he was dead broke. "I have just $7. That doesn't look as if I got anything out of the marriage financially. I still love my wife deeply. Maybe that's the trouble."

* * *

Madeleine's own marriage drama, unfolding in the last few days before John's wedding, added another ring to the three-ring circus that was the Astor–French wedding.

"Wanted: One genealogist and a Hollywood Hostess to complete arrangements for the Astor-French wedding," ran one New York newspaper story.

"Society has developed a headache from trying to find out what relation Enzo Fiermonte, boxer husband of Mrs. Madeleine Force Astor Dick Fiermonte, will be to Ellen French when she becomes the bride of John Jacob Astor, III, whose half-brother, Vincent Astor, was to have been the best man at the wedding of the former Mrs. Dick's son to Eileen Gillespie, whose grandmother, Mrs. Sherman Watts, lives four doors away from where Mr. and Mrs. John Jacob Astor, III, will make their summer home.

"Indeed, society is finding it all just too, too vex-making and would be glad to swap several lorgnettes [opera glasses] and six shooting sticks [guns] for a little of Hollywood's savoir faire. Why, in Hollywood, the Astor-Force wedding would call for no more than a buffet supper and a Gypsy band. But in Newport they haven't had enough experience with the 'divorce and be friends society' to know just what to do.

"The Astor family tree has spread itself out from one conservative highly prized tree into a family forest. Some of the roots are still deep in the Social Register and some of the roots were yanked right out. A genealogist would probably get sap-poisoning before he was through weaving around the new branches."

* * *

Controversy over the wedding, ensuring additional newspaper stories, also came from the bride's side of the family. One of the invited guests of the bride's father would be Ernst Hanfstaengl, aide to German chancellor Adolf Hitler. Mr. French would cause further controversy when a front-page news story in the *New York Times* announced that he had asked a relief agency for charity: "Mrs. J. J. Astor's Father Asks WPA Relief; F.O. French Says He Is 'Down to Last $15.'"

Mr. French was asked whether he had asked his daughter's fiancé for financial assistance.

"Help from Astor? No sir! I'm well and strong and I'm not too old yet. I don't intend to abjure my principles by taking things from anybody."

* * *

The day before the wedding, John Jacob Astor III and Miss Ellen Tuck French were entertained at a round of Newport parties. Reporters described that there were so many entertainments for them that they barely had time to rush home and adorn themselves in their formal attire for the wedding ceremony.

By the day of the ceremony the guests had all arrived in Newport. The older members of the Astor and French families and others, about eighty in all, were entertained at Chastellux by the Madeleine's sister, Katherine. Madeleine would stay at her son's cottage, Chetwode, along with former sister-in-law Caroline Astor Wilson.

John Astor and Ellen French were married on June 30, 1934. The ceremony had the country's attention. A short newsreel was made of the wedding and is still in existence.

"Seldom outside book covers, and probably never within range of Newport's cliff walks and 10-mile drive, has there been more drama in a wedding; a four-story mansion, a young millionaire, a 32-carat diamond and a handsome apology—a story that in its wide ramifications includes an Italian boxer and the Titanic disaster," wrote the *Miami Daily News Record*.

The invitations had been engraved by Tiffany. There were five hundred people inside the church, which was filled to capacity. Outside a crowd of one thousand people had assembled. There was private security to augment the local police, who had to push people out of the streets to allow cars through.

On the day of the wedding, the wedding party and guests had to run a gauntlet of moving picture cameras, reporters, and spectators as they entered the Newport church. Many went through a side door to avoid the crush of publicity. On the right side of the church in the front pew was Madeleine Astor Fiermonte, attired in a gown of blue organdy in cape effect with a large hat. She was escorted to her seat and later out of the church by her son William. With her was Caroline Astor Wilson. Aunt Katherine's family occupied one pew, and in another sat Madeleine's second husband, William Dick, and their son John Henry. Mrs. Force was also present. The arrival of Adolf Hitler's personal aide caused one of the first audible gasps.

The engagement ring John Astor gave to Ellen French was not the same one given to Eileen Gillespie, who cleared out of Newport and sailed for Europe the day before the ceremony. The Astor wedding would take place an hour and a half after they had boarded the ship. The Gillespie family had to run through a crowd of reporters and cameramen to board. Mrs. Gillespie called the day of John Astor's wedding to Ellen Tuck the "luckiest day of my daughter's life."

"Yes, and I think so, too," echoed Eileen.

* * *

The rift over attendance at John's wedding seemed to be the rift that sent the Fiermontes on their separate ways, at least for the time being. Madeleine was reported to be planning a voyage after the wedding, though she would not say where she was going. Her friends hinted that her travels would land her within handy distance of the friendly divorce courts of Paris, France.

In New York, Enzo met with a lawyer, hoping to appeal his case to the New York Boxing Commission for his chance to face Slapsie Maxie Rosenbloom in the ring for the championship belt. Reporters had fun with the story, with one reporter asking hypothetically, "Is the boxing board discriminating against him because he is an Italian? Are the members afraid he will take the title to Italy. . . . Does the boxing commission object personally to (A) Enzo's curly black hair, (B) his profile or (C) the fact that he is the husband of the former Mrs. Madeleine Force Astor Dick?

"Enzo then will rip off his shirt, expose his chest, biceps, limbs and ask the members of the Commission to feel his muscles. He will then demand his legal right the privilege of exchanging slaps with Slapsie Maxie.

"After that the boxing board is expected to say 'Go get a reputation.'"

* * *

November 1934 saw one of the most dramatic events in the life of Madeleine Talmage Force Astor Dick Fiermonte. Though she had felt her share of societal rejection, society would officially reject Madeleine Astor when her name was dropped from the New York Social Register.

While Mrs. Caroline Astor's "Four Hundred" was an unofficial society list, the Social Register was the official bible. First published in the 1880s, the yearly publication historically was a directory of the names of the "old money" families from the northeastern United States. Most of these families descended from early American settler families. The publication is still in existence today. The "old money" publication was not easy to get into, and arriving there was more important than being invited to one of Mrs. Caroline Astor's balls. The decision regarding who was added and excluded from the Social Register (also called the Blue Book) was made by a board of selectors as part of an anonymous advisory group. Reasons for exclusion were opaque, but keeping one's personal life out of the newspapers seemed to be a key.

Among the other names erased that year were those of Elliot and Anna Roosevelt, the children of President Franklin Roosevelt, along with actress Jane Wyatt, who would go on to play the beloved mother in the popular 1950s television series *Father Knows Best* (not to be confused with Jane Wyman). Jane Wyatt was from prominent Pennsylvania society but had begun acting in Hollywood, which would be the cause of her exclusion from the register.

Also gone was the name of Madeleine Talmage Force Astor Dick Fiermonte, once the presumed leader of society.

"Running an eraser over the names of a number of hitherto elite, the board of selectors of the New York Social Register has caused a sensation with its eliminations in the new Blue Book," wrote the *New York Times*.

* * *

There was little Madeleine Astor could do about her exclusion from the Social Register, but she did have some control over her marriage. She took dramatic steps to salvage what she could.

Madeleine would go on her sea voyage after John and Ellen's wedding, though no divorce was filed for. Unsuccessful with the Boxing

Commission, Enzo would travel to Hollywood to try a new career as an actor. A screen test had been arranged before he arrived. Though Hollywood thrived on publicity, and Enzo had not been entirely shy of publicity, the newspapers noted that there was much secrecy surrounding Fiermonte's arrival by train in Hollywood. He was in the company of Adela Rogers St. Johns, a married magazine writer. On their arrival, Enzo and Mrs. St. Johns were noted together at various events. Mr. Fiermonte was asked by reporters about the location and intentions of his wife.

"I don't know where Mrs. Force is, and I don't care. If she wants to get a divorce, that's all right with me. If she doesn't, maybe I will."

While Enzo Fiermonte would find moderate success in Hollywood in later years, for now the trip yielded no immediate results. While making the rounds there, Enzo would sign with a new boxing manager.

In November, a picture ran of Enzo in Mexico. Reporters noted that he found solace from his separation from Mrs. Fiermonte and the loss of his boxing career by taking long walks at Agua Caliente.

"Correspondents suggest romance may lurk there for Enzo," one newspaper reported.

By now, according to Enzo, he had filed for divorce, but Madeleine was refusing to sign the papers. With everything in America at a standstill for him, Enzo secretly booked passage aboard the Italian steamship *Roma* for his defeated return home. Though his plans had been secret, reporters greeted him at the pier. Enzo declared to reporters that he was "glad to be free."

* * *

Shortly after the *Roma* left the dock in New York, reporters following Enzo noticed a woman who slipped aboard the liner just before sailing, presenting her passport to the ship's purser. She gave the name of Mrs. Enzo Fiermonte and bore a striking resemblance to the highly public Madeleine Astor. As soon as she was settled in her first-class cabin, the woman sent a note to Enzo Fiermonte, delivered to his cabin by a steward. On receiving the note, Enzo wired a friend, "Wife's aboard, God help me." That friend released the wireless message to reporters, and soon the story was international news.

According to passengers aboard the *Roma*, Mrs. Fiermonte continue to write notes to Enzo, which were carried by stewards to his cabin on B deck from her cabin on A deck. This routine went on for hours. At last Enzo agreed to meet Madeleine, who, he said, looked ill and pathetic. Enzo felt guilty for the pain he was causing her. By the end of the evening, the two were reconciled and sharing Madeleine's cabin. Enzo would issue a statement confirming the reunification.

"In spite of previous statements in the papers I am glad to say that Mrs. Fiermonte and I are reconciled," read a telegram signed by Enzo Fiermonte.

On board the ship, Madeleine and Enzo were soon inundated with telegrams from the press with questions about their reconciliation. They decided to issue a joint statement, hoping reporters would leave them alone. They did not.

Madeleine wanted to leave ship in France. Enzo said he was going to continue his trip to Rome to visit his family. Madeleine insisted on joining Enzo on the visit, but Enzo said no, assuring her that he would join her in Naples. She agreed. He telegraphed Tosca to meet him in Genoa with their son, Gianni.

Enzo reportedly had tears in his eyes when he saw Gianni from the ship in Genoa. The newspapers featured separate pictures of father and son. "He's a little rascal—just like my mother says I was when I was his age," Enzo told reporters.

* * *

While Enzo traveled to visit his family, Madeleine was met in Naples by a flock of reporters. She went straight to the hotel and at first refused to speak to them. Later Madeleine told reporters that American girls were too bold toward her husband and that she would protect him from them once she had gotten him safely away from Italy. She likened Enzo to a god or a Greek statue, calling him her "lovely boy."

Enzo's short visit with his family while Madeleine waited at a hotel went as planned, and in a few days Enzo was traveling to Naples to be with Madeleine. Enzo had just joined his wife in her room when they were interrupted by a knock at the door from the Italian police, who requested Enzo join them and another official downstairs. Enzo complied, and the officials confiscated his passport, informing Enzo he could not leave Italy for the time being. They said the police needed time to investigate his divorce and remarriage, which Enzo had obtained in Reno, Nevada, but reportedly never registered with the Italian government.

Madeleine Fiermonte had put herself in legal jeopardy with the trip to Italy. Because the Italian government did not recognize Enzo's divorce, Madeleine was warned by her lawyer that she might face bigamy charges while on Italian soil. She was advised she could face one to five years in jail. Her lawyer also warned her about people trying to take advantage of her while she was in Italy, telling reporters he had "instructed her not to pay any money to anyone without consulting me."

To avoid further legal complications, Enzo would go to stay with his mother, in addition to spending more time with Tosca and Gianni. Followed by reporters, Enzo's movements were reported in the newspapers, which Madeleine spent her waiting time reading. She was now suffering from insomnia and reportedly on the verge of nervous collapse. Enzo made brief visits to Madeleine at her hotel but was allowed to stay there after the issuance of a special identity card. Shortly thereafter, he appeared in the hotel's salon in immaculate evening dress with Madeleine on his arm. One of these visits was reported on by *Time* in its February 25, 1935, edition: "Fresh from a visit to his first wife, Enzo Fiermonte, occasional prizefighter, taxied up to a Naples hotel, hastened in to calm his tearful wife, Mrs. Madeleine Force Astor Dick Fiermonte, widow of John Jacob Astor II, mother of John Jacob Astor III. Hotel men, eavesdropping, heard sounds of a quarrel. After an hour, Enzo Fiermonte left to spend the night with his first wife's brother. Next morning he was off to Rome on the third lap of a wife-to-wife shuttling trip which began three weeks ago when he left the U.S. for a visit with Tosca, only to find Madeleine Force had tagged along. In Rome he visited Tosca, played with their young son. At Naples Mrs. Madeleine Force had a cold, could see no one except a lawyer. . . . Said Enzo's aged mother: 'My son really loves the American lady a great deal.' Last week newshawks rumored that Enzo might be conscripted to fight Abyssinia. Said one official: 'He is not considered desirable to represent Italy abroad.'"

* * *

The entire matter seemed to be settled over tea. In late February, Madeleine Astor Fiermonte would host Enzo Fiermonte's first wife and his mother in her hotel suite.

The *New York Times* described Tosca Fiermonte as his "sturdy, black-haired first wife, who comes from Italian peasant stock." The three women were joined at tea by Madeleine's lawyer, who helped arrange for Tosca to receive $10,000 at the time she signed the official Italian divorce papers, along with 500 lire a month for the support of Gianni.

"My son's wife is a dear," Enzo's white-haired mother told reporters after returning to her "humble apartment in a congested quarter." "She's older than Enzo, but together they seem like two young people of the same age in love with each other."

Tosca Fiermonte expressed her hope that Enzo would return to her and their son one day.

"I still love him, and I think he really loves me, too. I hope he'll come back to me, but I'm afraid it won't be very soon," she told reporters.

* * *

With their Italian legal troubles settled, Enzo's passport was returned, and he and Madeleine were soon sailing for France. They would call this trip their honeymoon. They spent their mornings riding horseback, the afternoons riding in a $300 car, "which was about as inconspicuous as a mobile soda fountain," wrote one newspaper. At one point they visited Monte Carlo, where Mr. Fiermonte enjoyed gambling in the casino.

The honeymoon would take a dark turn, however, when Enzo Fiermonte's name would be drawn into a custody suit reported across the country. When Enzo had gone to Hollywood after losing both Madeleine and his boxing career several months earlier, he was accompanied by a married woman named Adela St. Johns, a magazine writer who was going to help guide Enzo through the Hollywood system. Now, as the Fiermontes were reuniting in Italy, Mrs. St. Johns's husband was testifying in a custody suit that the friendship of his ex-wife with Mr. Fiermonte had made her an improper person to care for their son, who was six years old. He alleged indiscretions between Mrs. St. Johns and a "Richard Roe," who remained unidentified in court proceedings.

Mrs. St. Johns testified that she had associated frequently with Enzo Fiermonte, referencing the transcontinental auto trip with him, but said that their relationship was professional. She testified that her role was as Enzo's manager, that she had wired ahead across Hollywood for opportunities for movie studio executives to meet and see Enzo Fiermonte, and that she had intended to make him into another Rudolph Valentino.

In the end, Mrs. St. Johns retained custody of her son.

* * *

Returning to New York, Madeleine and Enzo would find new pressures added to their already rocky relationship. Enzo made plans to go into private business, which fell through. With the stock market again rocky, a career in that field was no longer an option, nor was boxing or Hollywood for the time being. Another conflict arose within the marriage when Madeleine confronted Enzo about a ride home he had given a young woman one evening. Within a month of returning to the United States, Enzo was miserable and lonely, and Madeleine sensed it. She suggested they travel to South Carolina.

It was there that Madeleine and Enzo discovered Dixie Plantation. Located on 25,000 acres of ground, the magnificent red-brick house was approached through an avenue of magnificent oak trees. The outside of the main house reflected its history, and the inside, while still rustic, had been modernized and was livable. Sixty acres of the expansive grounds of the plantation were under cultivation with a vegetable garden, and the rest of the property was wild. The surrounding forests abounded with game. The following day, the Fiermontes purchased the estate, paying $45,000.

Madeleine furnished the mansion with exquisite taste, regardless of expense. She and Enzo moved into the home, hiring twenty servants for the farm. In a symbol of the turmoil of the Fiermonte marriage, three days after moving in Madeleine fired the staff, according to Enzo, and told him they were going back to New York. In New York, a trip was planned for Newport, where Madeleine and Enzo would stay with her sister, Katherine. On the trip there, Madeleine told Enzo she did not know how Newport would react to their marriage.

The trip of the Fiermontes to Newport during the summer of 1935 for the christening of Madeleine's first grandchild seemed to be a temporarily unifying event for the fractured Astor family. All eyes turned to Newport for the arrival of Jack and Ellen's first child, the first baby of the *Titanic* Baby. Special accommodations had been made in the maternity ward at the hospital there for Ellen Astor.

"Stork Hovers Over Astors," read the headline in the *Biddeford* (Maine) *Daily Journal.*

Part of the interest in the baby had to do with the Astor fortune. By now Vincent Astor was forty-four years old and had no children. It was said that he had been stricken with mumps just before his first wedding, which reportedly rendered him sterile. This was an open secret, and the whispered question in society was what would happen to the Astor fortune when Vincent passed. The family tradition had been to leave the fortune to the oldest male. John's unborn child, if it was a male (and it was), would be the next logical heir. The Astor fortune was estimated to be worth $60–$100 million, lessened by Vincent's charitable business decisions, but still quite formidable, still worth billions in today's money. If John's son were to inherit the Astor fortune from Vincent, that would also make up for the incredible disparity in Colonel John Jacob Astor's will bequests to his two sons. The Astor fortune and its fate had always been a favorite storyline of the newspapers and its readers. The birth of John and Ellen Astor's baby was important in many ways.

After William Astor was born, John and Ellen Astor invited the entire family to their home in Newport for the christening. With the Lindbergh baby having been kidnapped just a few years before, six armed guards stood outside the door of the Chetwode cottage in Newport for the reunion.

The family visiting to see the new grandchild brought the Astor family together, if just temporarily. This occasion also gave the press an opportunity to bring up again the storyline of Madeleine marrying outside of society and her break with tradition.

"Why Newport Smiles on the Handsome Young Prize-Fighter and His Multi-million Dollar 'Grandson,'" read the headline of the syndicated news story about the family reunion.

"It's a Far Cry from the era of THE Mrs. Astor, who'd have called for her smelling salts if she had foreseen the goings on in her famous family at the present day. If Carolus Duran's portrait of THE Mrs. Astor is still extant—the one beneath which she used to sit at her stuffy dinner parties in the not-really-so-gay nineties—it must be wearing a slightly pained and definitely puzzled expression."

Madeleine and Enzo were at Chetwode for the event but had been staying at Katherine Spencer's home as her guests. Vincent Astor and his wife also came to the christening. Though there had been a rift between John and Vincent, it reportedly was healing at this time. John Astor was noted as having spent a number of years largely in getting on the front pages by dint of his escapades. By the time of the christening, John had gone to work for a company of which Vincent was a director, the International Mercantile Marine, also the owners of *Titanic*. John Astor was earning $25 a week.

* * *

While staying at Katherine's Chastellux, Enzo played tennis at the Newport Casino, and he and Madeleine spent time on the beach.

Though it was William's christening that brought Madeleine and Enzo to Newport, they soon were finding some level of acceptance there, perhaps mixed with a little curiosity. During one of Enzo and Madeleine's visits to the beach, they seemed to be offered a welcome. A woman walked up to Enzo on the beach, which was crowded with members of Newport society at the height of summer.

"Good morning, Mr. Fiermonte. I am Mrs. Cornelius Vanderbilt. I am so glad you have come here, and I hope we shall see more of you."

There was a silence as the whole beach seemed to stop and gape. People stared at Mrs. Vanderbilt. Enzo was amused.

Madeleine and Enzo were photographed on the sands of Baxley's Beach, called the playground of society. "Society Thaws to Fiermontes," read the headline.

"My sweet lamb—you're made here!" exclaimed Madeleine after the encounter. "Now that Mrs. Vanderbilt has spoken to you everyone will want to know you."

From there the couple started off with an invitation to a lunch party attended by forty members of Newport society. According to Enzo, Madeleine was overjoyed at being accepted back in the fold. After that there was a lunch party every day. Enzo said he enjoyed the balls and dances because he could dance with others and Madeleine had to just smile and accept it lest she risk the rejection that would come from causing a scene.

However, the conflicts within their marriage—Madeleine's jealousy and Enzo's flirtatious nature—would complicate Madeleine's reported desire to remain a member of the Newport society that had finally warmed to her. At Newport's White Elephant Ball that season, which was a costume dance for charity, Madeleine attended dressed as a naval officer with Enzo dressed as a sailor. All of Newport was there. At one point Enzo purposely danced with a young woman, and Madeleine was furious. The morning after the ball, according to Enzo, he received a lecture from Katherine, who had not been at the ball herself. Enzo told Katherine to mind her own business.

Soon Madeleine and Enzo were beginning to arrive late to social functions and leave early. At the functions they would dance less and less. Their fights were becoming a byword in the smart set, and people were afraid to extend them invitations. Enzo said people would issue him invitations to attend functions alone, but he declined them.

The Fiermontes' marital and social failures in Newport may have further caused a conflict between the Force sisters. Enzo would give a description of his sister-in-law, Katherine, a few years later: "She seemed to have the same kind of nerves as Madeleine. She would light three cigarettes, one after the other, and threw them away. She got up early, whereas Madeleine stayed in bed until very late after having been out the night before. Mrs. Spencer was a strong type. She played tennis like a man, and loved to gamble, whether it was in gaming rooms or in Wall Street. She seemed to affect Madeleine, with her ten-minute enthusiasms."

The couple left Newport and were soon headed back to Dixie Plantation, which they saw as their last chance at happiness. Being more remote, away from social obligations, there was much less chance for jealousy. Madeleine and Enzo decided to make Dixie Plantation their permanent residence. Soon they were drawing up plans for improvement of the plantation. Enzo said he was amazed to see how happy Madeleine was there. She would superintend the farm workers gathering vegetables in the gardens. Her health improved, her cheeks took on a natural color, and she smoked less. They saw and talked about Madeleine's family very little.

Madeleine wanted to play tennis as soon as possible and had a tennis court built on the grounds. Because of the lack of social contacts in South Carolina, they hired a tennis professional to play with them. Madeleine and Enzo would also spend time riding in automobiles and shooting rifles.

This life of marital contentment would be brief at Dixie Planation, lasting approximately four months. Madeleine suddenly took ill. A doctor was flown in from New York, who said the Southern climate was bad for Madeleine's health. Soon Madeleine and Enzo returned to New York, where Madeleine stayed in bed for two months. Trying to find a way to make his wife happy, Enzo spent that time studying Madeleine Astor.

Enzo Fiermonte saw a woman who spent her time reading current news clippings about herself. She never had a maid because she always had a nurse and would not spend money on both, although she seemed to be able to afford the expense. Thus, Madeleine's wardrobe, already scanty because of her aversion to going to shopping in public stores, had not been taken care of.

"Worry and lack of interest in life had combined to sap her physical strength. She was never happy. I used to watch her sometimes as I sat in her room whiling away the evenings. She would be reading, but her mind would be elsewhere, and all at once she would throw the book down in despair. Madeleine had reached the age when she had lived too much, and done too much."

Enzo continued to pursue his desire for an outside occupation, to which Madeleine would respond that she did not know why a man would want to work. Enzo wanted a child, but forty-two-year-old Madeleine's doctor disapproved. Enzo soon found himself restless, jittery, and bored.

One morning Enzo would be arrested on an outstanding warrant from a motor offense on Long Island two years previously when he had been training at the Hamptons. In court he was confronted by an array of cameras and reporters. One newspaper cameraman snapped a picture, and Enzo punched him. Enzo was jailed at the notorious Rikers Island. Madeleine's lawyer would soon arrive and tell Enzo that Madeleine would be there but that she was having trouble getting through the hotel lobby, which was packed with reporters. Enzo would spend five days incarcerated.

* * *

Madeleine and Enzo would give their marriage one more try, leaving New York and traveling to Europe. Enzo urged Madeleine to leave the doctor and nurse behind, and Madeleine compromised, leaving behind the doctor. When they arrived in France, Madeleine promptly hired a new doctor. While in Europe, Madeleine would accuse Enzo of being with a young girl, they had a fight, and for two days she refused to see him. A frustrated Enzo sent Madeleine an ultimatum, saying he would leave if she did not talk to him. Madeleine sent back a message telling him to settle his hotel bill before he left.

Both Madeleine and Enzo would end up back in New York, where reporters did not know they had separated. The couple talked on the phone to work out a story for the press and make other arrangements. They agreed to deny divorce rumors. Madeleine left for Florida to establish residency so that she could divorce him. A free man, Enzo stayed in New York and started to hit the town.

* * *

Madeleine and Enzo Fiermonte's marriage would continue to go from good to bad over the next two years, until 1938, when the divorce Madeleine had filed for was granted on June 11, after a long estrangement. The grounds she charged were extreme cruelty. Enzo did not contest the divorce.

On the day the divorce decree was issued, Enzo Fiermonte and three women with him were in an automobile accident in France, with the car Enzo was driving hitting a tree and overturning. One woman was injured. When police responded, Enzo quickly identified himself.

"I am the husband of Mrs. Astor."

The Fiermonte divorce was noted in *Time magazine*'s Milestones section: "Divorced. Onetime Pugilist Enzo Fiermonte, 30; by Madeline Force Astor Dick Fiermonte, 45, in West Palm Beach, Fla. Grounds: On various occasions he had 1) knocked her down, 2) broke her wrist, 3) hit her with his fist after a dance; been 'exceedingly unpleasant.'"

Enzo Fiermonte reportedly received a $125,000 divorce settlement from Madeleine. When he sailed for Europe one week before the divorce was filed, Enzo was met at the pier by reporters. They noted that Enzo was given a farewell kiss by Carol Leiper, a young Philadelphia society woman. Ms. Leiper explained to watching reporters that it was just a customary bon voyage kiss. This time Madeleine Astor did not follow him.

Enzo Fiermonte would later remarry his first wife, Tosca.

* * *

Having already lost her social position because of her marriage to Enzo Fiermonte, the following year Madeleine would suffer the final humiliation when Enzo Fiermonte sold the story of that marriage to a magazine called *True Story*. The monthly publication, a tamer version of today's *National Enquirer*, printed sensational stories that often related to current events or subjects.

"Kept Husband," was the name of the series, which ran for six issues.

"She gave Enzo up—what was she seeking?

"Here is the whole amazing story told by Enzo Fiermonte himself—one of the most startling and illuminating commentaries on life among the idle rich ever written.

"The story behind the headlines of the tempestuous marriage of Enzo Fiermonte into the Astor's millions is now told for the first time—and by Enzo Fiermonte himself. Don't miss the adventures of this former boxer in the world of the idle rich. Start it in February's True Story."

Enzo's exact motivation for selling his story is not known. He was still attempting a career in Hollywood and needed to tell his side of the story regarding many parts of his time with Madeleine Astor, including the broken arm he had caused. The details in the story were quite tame and far from sordid. The invasion of privacy, however, was the true insult. In the final of the six installments, published less than a year before Madeleine died, Enzo spoke directly to her in print in front of the entire country.

"Do you remember how you came aboard the Roma under an assumed name when I was running away because our life together was crushing my soul?

"If I had beaten you, as you alleged, you would not have come. No, Madeline, you came because you loved me. You risked publicity, everything to be with me, and you followed me to Rome for the same reason—not to be beaten. You were not happy with any one else, no one gave you the sense of being protected that I did. You came because I was good to you, because I was always a gentleman—a quality you appreciated more in a man than anything else—at least you told me so once. I was a gentleman to the end, even to allowing you to divorce me without bothering to defend my name. Why weren't you as sportsmanlike?

"I still cannot believe that you intended to proclaim me a villain, from the housetops. You could not be so cruel, unless perhaps you really meant what you said that day in the Savoy Plaza. Do you remember how you told me that when you had finished with me I would never be accepted in New York society? That one day, perhaps, you would throw me back into the gutter where you found me? Well, I am back there, but it is a gutter of sunshine on the roadside of true happiness, and I would that you could enjoy one moment of it.

"Only today I heard from some one who had seen you recently that you rarely laugh now, Madeleine. It is not too late to laugh. Sunshine is for all. Share it, and be happy."

Chapter 10

Little to Tell

As teenagers my older brother Billy and I would beg her for stories connected with the disaster. She had little to tell.

—John Henry Dick, youngest son of Madeleine Astor, in his book *Other Edens*

A month after the publication of the final *True Story* installment, Madeleine Astor's seventy-five-year-old mother was dead. Katherine Force died at Chastellux, her daughter Katherine's Newport home. The ailing Mrs. Force had been brought there a month before. In her obituary, Madeleine is listed as Mrs. Madeleine Force Dick. "Among her grandsons is John Jacob Astor," noted the *New York Times* obituary, the headline reading, "The Grandmother of John Jacob Astor Dies in Newport."

* * *

Madeleine would spend the rest of her short time on Earth "living in strict retirement in South Carolina." She now preferred to be called Mrs. Force-Dick. The press described her as tall and distinguished looking at age forty-seven. She would travel some, spending time in Palm Beach, where John, Ellen, and the baby, William, were also vacationing.

Madeleine would leave Palm Beach that spring, heading back to Dixie Plantation. The trip there was particularly bad for her. While on the train ride to South Carolina, she was robbed of jewelry valued at

$100,000. A female traveling companion reported the theft and added that most of the jewelry had been recovered, but around $800 worth was still missing.

During her trip to South Carolina, Madeleine received the news that Dixie Plantation had burned to the ground while being prepared for her arrival. The fire apparently started in the coal furnace that had been kindled during the morning for the first time since the previous winter. Workers rushed from nearby residences to help remove contents, but the blaze spread rapidly, and they were able to save only a small part of the furnishings. Dixie Plantation was in ruins when Madeleine Astor arrived.

Madeleine returned to Palm Beach, where she leased a home called Villa Invernale on Jungle Road, located near the ocean. Much like the previous few years, she did not socialize while there.

At 7:30 p.m. on March 27, 1940, Madeleine Force Astor died at Villa Invernale of a heart attack. Her middle son, William Dick Jr., by now in his late twenties, was with her.

Madeleine's cousin Lyndon Dodge flew to Florida the following morning to make preparations to have Madeleine's body moved back to New York. John Astor and John Henry Dick stayed in New York to await the arrival of their mother's body, which was accompanied by William. Members of the household staff made the announcement, which was not released until the following day. She had been ill for several months, they said.

When informed of his ex-wife's death, Enzo Fiermonte told reporters he did not know how to express sorrow. "I never expected this would happen," he said. "I knew she was suffering from heart disease, but never imagined her death would occur so unexpectedly. I always remember her with the greatest affection. Her death is a great blow."

Madeleine's death notice in the *New York Times* was listed as "Dick—Madeleine Talmage Force." Her funeral was held at St. Bartholomew's Protestant Episcopal Church in New York. There were fifteen hundred people in attendance, with another five hundred onlookers standing in the street outside the church. A choir of sixty people provided musical accompaniment. The coffin, which rested before the altar, was covered with a blanket of red roses and purple orchids. Flanking it on each side stood an eight-foot cross made of lilies.

Despite the frictions in Madeleine's family, everyone was there to say goodbye. Besides her three sons were sister Katherine, along with her three children, as well as cousin Lyndon Dodge. Caroline Astor Wilson was also in attendance. After a brief service, Madeleine Force Astor was buried at the Trinity Church Cemetery, where Colonel John Jacob Astor also lay at rest.

* * *

Madeleine's estate would be estimated to be worth $1 million, or $21 million when adjusted for inflation. She owed her second husband, William Dick Sr., $470,000 from four promissory notes given to her before their Reno divorce. Mr. Dick settled for $250,000.

Madeleine would leave her estate in trust to her two sons by William Dick, William and John Henry, both of Islip, Long Island, New York, noting that John Astor "has been heretofore amply provided for." She did leave John Astor a diamond ring valued at $50,000. Enzo Fiermonte received nothing.

Following Madeleine's death, a poem was printed in a Pennsylvania newspaper, the *Bristol Courier*, which reflected the nostalgia felt when thinking of the young Madeleine Force Astor, the times she symbolized, and the years that had passed since she was a young girl.

A GREAT SHIP

This week a memory stirs and sighs
The great *Titanic* rising once again—
Some of us remember those past days
When men still shuddered at the thought of pain.

Nineteen twelve, and all the world before us,
Unwritten pages spread, all white and clean,
The girls wore pigtails, boys said "Honor bright"—
And smiling Madeline Astor was eighteen!

What have we done with that great book of life?
The clean pages smeared with blood and tears.
Not all the waters pounding in the sea
Can ever wash that book of war-torn years.

Nineteen twelve! The fields of Flanders lay
Clean in the sun, sweet with the earth's good store.
Children played gaily; men shuddered still at death—
Nor heard him knocking loudly at the door.

So Madeline Astor Fiermonte is dead!—
She who was eighteen, young and sweat and dear;
Gallant he stood, that worldly man and said,
"I'll meet you in the morning, do not fear!"

The morning? Perhaps we've all been dreaming in the night?
We who wore pinafores when the waters rose—
When war clouds hung all black above our youth—
Will we awake, unharmed, do you suppose?

No, the book is there, the book that we have made,
Full of mistakes, wet with a thousand tears.
Behold the pages we have cruelly wrought
The highlighted fruit of nearly thirty years.

Give us some light to writ one clean, sweet page,
We who spent youth in serving armed might.
Give us some strength to leave one golden line
Girls who wore pigtails, boys who said "Honor bright!"

—Greta Drumm

* * *

Katherine Force had settled in a cottage named Chastellux on Halidon Hill in Newport, Rhode Island, after her marriage in 1922 to Major

Lorillard Spencer Jr. Katherine and Lorillard were prominent members of society there. The couple had one daughter, Katherine, and two sons, Stephen and William.

The year 1939 started out as a good one for Katherine Force Spencer, with the marriage of her son William Hurlbut Force Spencer being a blessed event. Sadly, the year worsened as it went on, with the loss of Katherine's husband, Lorillard Spencer, on June 10, 1939. The year would end in embarrassment as the *True Story* article series was released, with Katherine being mentioned in an unflattering manner in the final issues, followed by the death of her mother. The next year, her sister Madeleine was dead.

The widowhood of Katherine at age forty-two did not send her into early obscurity, however. Katherine Force Spencer was not a rich, idle woman of society like those before her. Instead, she returned to work, back in the real estate field, a move that had shocked society fifteen years previously. She would also take an interest in municipal affairs, serving on the Newport Zoning Commission, and continue to remain athletic, maintaining her proficiency on the tennis court.

Katherine Force Spencer would die on September 8, 1956, at the age of sixty-five at her home in Newport following a heart attack. Katherine's estate was estimated to be worth $410,000, roughly $5 million when adjusted for inflation, which she left to her children.

* * *

A Gold Star Mother—a mother who lost a child in the armed forces during war—wrote a letter to the *Newport Daily News* five days after Katherine Force Spencer's death.

"I wish to express my deep appreciation and that of all Gold Star Mothers to Miss Kay Spencer for the beautiful white floral cross and other flowers placed on the Honor Roll at City Hall in memory of her mother, Mrs. Lorillard Spencer, for our boys who gave their lives in World War II," wrote Mrs. Elmer Cudworth. "It is the most beautiful display that has ever been put on the memorial and I am sure all Gold Star Mothers who have seen this will feel as I do."

* * *

Eight years after his divorce from Madeleine Astor, the year after she died, William Dick Sr. married Virginia Keniston Connor of Akron, Ohio. The couple would have two children, a daughter and a son. They maintained a town house at 1 Beekman Place in New York City, as well as an estate at Islip, Long Island, where Mr. Dick died four years after Madeleine.

* * *

Enzo Fiermonte would pursue his career in Hollywood after Madeleine's death. He would find modest success there, generally in supporting roles, appearing in at least 116 films. Whenever his name was mentioned in the newspapers, Madeleine's generally was also. In the column "Walter Winchell on Broadway," the noted gossip columnist mentioned Enzo in 1948, ten years after Enzo and Madeleine's divorce: "Enzo Fiermonte, a former prizefighter who made headlines in America when he married the late Madeline Dick (formerly Mrs. John Jacob Astor), is doing well as an actor. His latest is 'Loves and Poisons.'"

The following year, Igor Cassini would write a story, syndicated in the country's newspapers, titled "Mister Cinderella." The story was about poor men who had married rich women. Madeleine Astor and Enzo Fiermonte were the first couple mentioned.

Enzo's movie career would alternate between Italy and Hollywood, finding modest success in both places. In 1953, while being considered for a movie role, Enzo Fiermonte was mentioned by Cholly Knickerbocker, a syndicated society columnist: "Enzo Fiermonte, the handsome Italian pugilist who was wed to Jack Astor's mother, the late Madeleine Force Astor Dick, has become very palsy with Roberto Rossellini. Enzo, who has been reduced to playing bit parts in Roman films, may get his first big meal ticket."

One high point of Enzo's modest film career was his appearance in the American movie *Romeo and Juliet*. Filmed in Italy, the movie would often be rebroadcast on American television. This would lead to small supporting roles on American television. Enzo was noted in Dorothy

Kilgallen's "The Voice of Broadway" column on January 6, 1955: "Enzo Fiermonte, quite a little headline-maker when he was cruising the U.S. (among other things, he married Madeline Force Astor), may return to this country. He's been getting nibbles from several Hollywood producers as a result of his appearance as Tybalt in the prize-winning 'Romeo and Juliet' cinema."

Seven years later, in 1962, Enzo would go on to appear in the classic American movie *Sodom and Gomorrah*, and the following year saw him in Metro-Goldwyn-Mayer's *The Slave*, filmed in Egypt. With his name starting to appear a bit more steadily in the headlines, the Astor–Fiermonte story still made good newspaper copy. Enough time had passed since *Titanic* sank (fifty years) and the Astor–Fiermonte divorce (twenty-three years) that a new generation would need a quick primer to remind them of why the names were important. This was true in the syndicated newspaper column "Hollywood" by famed columnist Louella Parsons: "Enzo's Back."

"It took me back in the yellowed pages of the Social Register to learn that Enzo Fiermonte has been cast for the role of the general in 'Dubious Patriots' with Bobby Darin, Raf Vallone, Mickey Rooney and Edd Byrnes.

"Maybe you are too young to remember the furor Fiermonte kicked up when he, a boxer, married Madeleine Astor of THE Astors. Although Enzo gave up his boxing career, Madeleine was dropped from the Social Register because of the marriage. It did not turn out happily and they were divorced to the tune of 'I told you so' from her family. In recent years Enzo has been living in his native Italy and the Corman Brothers, producers of the film, cable me that he has appeared in 80 foreign films."

Among other movies during that active time was *Grand Prix*, still seen occasionally on television. "Enzo is still a dashing figure on the Riviera, where he broke the bank at Monte Carlo in 1935," wrote Hollywood columnist Florabel Muir.

In the middle of Enzo's success in the early 1960s, a reporter visited him in Italy. The headline of the syndicated news story was "Boxing's Rudolph Valentino," with a sub-headline of "Prizefighter and the Lady."

"The good life for Enzo Fiermonte once meant Deauville and Monte Carlo in the spring and fall, Southampton in the summer and Palm Beach in the winter.

"Not bad for a pug with one tin ear."

At the time, Enzo was maintaining a small bachelor apartment on the Via Topino in Rome and a two-acre farm twenty kilometers outside of town, in Mentana, where chickens walked through the streets. The fifty-eight-year-old Enzo Fiermonte was described by the reporter as looking forty-five, "with a flat stomach and the discerning eye of a gay boulevardier," wrote the reporter. "Maybe the curly hair on top's gone, but you can tell Enzo was a good-looking guy."

The story recounted how Enzo had been in line for a shot at the middleweight championship of the world before he married "the Lady," who made him quit the ring, divorce his wife, and marry her instead.

"She hurt me, and she help," Enzo said to the reporter, shrugging his shoulders. "I got no education. I was work since I was 12 years old. I couldna do not'ing else."

Enzo talked about how he had wanted some type of career for himself, to support himself, for a chance at success. Every idea he had was vetoed by his wife due to her jealousy, Enzo told the reporter. She would refuse to back his business ideas. "To her, $25,000 was like one dollar to you."

Enzo said he had been down to his last 200 lire ($300) when he was cast in the movie *Grand Prix*. He told the reporter his plans for what to do with the money he earned from the movie, including building a house on his farm.

At the top of the news story were two pictures, a smaller one of Enzo from his prizefighting days and a larger one of him when the interview was conducted. With a cap on his head, the current Enzo was smoking a cigarette, his face wrinkled but still with hints of youth.

"Still a dashing figure is Enzo Fiermonte the prizefighter who dazzled the lady a generation ago and became the sensation of the tabloids."

* * *

Enzo Fiermonte would die in 1993.

* * *

Madeleine's second son, William Dick Jr., graduated from Trinity College, class of 1941, where he was a member of the Epsilon chapter of the Delta Psi fraternity. He initially went to work for his father at the National Sugar Refining Company, but shortly thereafter he was drafted into service for World War II. His younger brother, John Henry, would report for service six weeks later, after he finished his studies at Yale. Their mother had been dead for only a year.

After the war, William was discharged with the rank of first lieutenant. He would make his way to Jamaica, making that country his legal residence.

The saga that William's brother John had endured to marry current wife Ellen French Astor took a fresh twist seven years later when it was announced that John's half brother William Dick Jr. would be marrying Virginia French, the sister of John's wife. They were married on December 18, 1941. John's wife acted as maid of honor, while John was an usher. William's other brother, John Henry Dick, served as best man. The couple would make their home in Islip, Long Island.

Three years later, and one year after the divorce of John and Ellen French Astor, William and Virginia Dick divorced. Within a year of each other, Ellen French Astor and then Virginia French Dick established residency in Reno, Nevada, at the Tumbling D-W Ranch. Both women claimed "mental cruelty." Ellen French Astor would receive a flat $1 million divorce settlement, while Virginia settled for monthly payments.

"The recent Reno divorce of the former Virginia French from her husband, William Force Dick, son of a wealthy sugar magnate, has severed the last remaining strands of society's handsomest double love knots," read the syndicated news story.

* * *

Five years later, William would be the victim of a bizarre kidnapping and robbery.

William Dick Jr. reported to the Suffolk County sheriff that on November 10, 1946, he had been kidnapped and robbed while driving from his father's home in Islip at 10:30 p.m. He was headed to the South Side Sportsmen's Club in Oakdale, Long Island.

On the Montauk highway in Islip, said Mr. Dick, three young men wearing parts of army uniforms waved to him, and he stopped. One produced a pistol and ordered him to drive them to New York. On the way they forced him to hand over his wallet, containing $230. They crossed the Triborough Bridge and got out of the car in Harlem, returning the empty wallet and 50¢ to buy gasoline.

The following day, William phoned the sheriff and told him the story. The sheriff told reporters he had informed the New York police of the incident and that he was continuing the search for the three men.

* * *

William Dick Jr. would die at his home in Port Maria, Jamaica, on December 4, 1961. The *New York Times* described him as having been prominent in society there. He was forty-four and the first of Madeleine Astor's children to die.

* * *

Madeleine Astor's youngest son was John Henry Dick. A renowned and talented painter of birds, he wrote a book in 1979 that discussed his professional interests. His story also provided glimpses into the time when Madeleine Astor was Mrs. Dick.

Both of John Henry's parents came from active families who enjoyed the outdoors. In his book *Other Edens*, John Henry talked about the times the Dick family spent at their vacation home in Islip, New York. John Henry would spend some of that time hunting with his air rifle.

"Hunting for sport was as much a part of my background as the tall house on 84th Street in New York City, the succession of nannies with odd accents, the variety of tutors," wrote John Henry.

He talked of a childhood that he described as being otherwise darkened by family conflicts, poor performance at school, and a painful shyness. He said the happiest part of his childhood was spent in the wilderness surrounding the Dicks' Islip country home: "Here I felt an unprecedented freedom. Here I found a wild world of order and beauty that captivated and confirmed me."

Some of that time spent in New York's wilderness was with his father, William Dick. The two would hunt the four acres of the South Side Sportsmen's Club, its woods filled with pine and oak trees, its ponds and clear streams stocked with trout. Father and son would spend time in the blinds, watching black ducks flying in the late afternoon, feeling the thrill and suspense of the hunt. He described the moments they spent there hunting as the closest moments he had with his father.

"It was here, too, that I knew the closest moments with my father. In this setting I ceased to be the disappointing son and he the autocrat," wrote Dick. "We were companions."

Because of frequent absences, John Henry described his time at preparatory school, a private high school, as something of a nightmare. He said the absences were not his fault, although he did not elaborate. His grades were "disastrous." John Henry credited the perception and kindness of the school's headmaster for his graduation. To mitigate the absences and bad grades, the headmaster required that John Henry paint a mural of local seasonal birds for the wall of the school's dining hall. The mural hung there for thirty years before being moved to the school's art department.

John Henry Dick would go on to Yale, and during that time he visited his mother at her recently acquired Dixie Plantation, twenty miles south of Charleston, South Carolina, during the winter of 1937–1938. Shortly after his mother's death, John Henry was drafted into the Army Air Force, immediately after his brother William had been drafted. He was stationed at several bases in the United States before being stationed at Oahu, Guam, and then Saipan. He described this time, 1941 to 1945, as a time of compulsory tedium. He was stationed at Iwo Jima when the war ended.

"The fighting over, I was free to explore the island's devastated landscape and the labyrinths of Japanese tunnels. Many 'inhabitants,' fully uniformed and now badly decomposed, lay about, some still sitting with backs against the walk like discarded mannequins," wrote John Henry.

By the time John Henry separated from the military, he had inherited the remains of his mother's Dixie Plantation in South Carolina. He left Islip, New York, and built a new home in 1947 on his mother's land, on a slight rise looking out on miles of tidal salt marsh, meadows, wetlands, and forest nestled along the Stono River.

"I began painting in earnest, made new friends, and soon was building a collection of captive waterfowl," wrote John Henry.

John Henry would go on to become a respected bird painter, conservationist, global explorer, author, and photographer. He described himself as an "artist naturalist." He would spend time exploring the world. At one point John Henry Dick found himself on an exploratory ship in the middle of the North Atlantic. Seeing icebergs far away along the western horizon close to the area where *Titanic* sank in 1912 brought his mother's story as a young woman home to John Henry.

"Among the survivors was my mother, who was returning from a year-long European honeymoon. She was then 18 years old and five months pregnant. As teenagers my older brother Billy and I would beg her for stories connected with the disaster," wrote John Henry. "She had little to tell."

When his mother left the sinking ship, the full impact of the impending nightmare had not yet spread among the passengers, John Henry recounted his mother saying. The *Titanic* was "unsinkable." Only those left on board during that last hour would realize the irony of that claim, he wrote.

* * *

John Henry Dick would die in 1995, placing a conservation easement on the property of Dixie Plantation. The property was left to the College of Charleston Foundation, which currently holds classes there.

Of Madeleine's three sons, John Henry appeared to be the one who most escaped the family history and legacies. With the financial resources left him by both parents, he lived a quiet life, avoiding the social pages.

"In a world where so many people seem caught in a frantic search for identity and meaning, I've come to feel enormously blessed. Perhaps under other circumstances I might have found satisfaction in selling bonds, practicing law or medicine. But, fortunate enough to have a degree of economic security, I was able to pursue my first love—the study and painting of birds."

John Henry Dick was a godfather to Mary Jacqueline Astor, the daughter of his brother John Astor. In a guestbook John Henry kept at his home at Dixie Plantation, Jackie and her father, John Astor, have left signatures.

* * *

Madeleine Astor's visits to Bar Harbor had effectively ended in 1916, after marrying William Dick. Vincent Astor would continue his father's tradition of visiting Bar Harbor every summer aboard his yacht. With the Kane family still occupying Breakwater in Bar Harbor, Vincent would eventually spread the Astor name to the other side of Mount Desert Island.

In his adult years, Vincent Astor would join the Navy Reserves during World War II. He would also donate the *Nourmahal* to the United States for use by the military.

The year Madeleine died, Vincent and his first wife, Helen, were divorced after twenty-six years of marriage. Helen Astor was granted the divorce on grounds of mental cruelty. The property settlement was kept secret.

Acquaintances of Vincent Astor said his unhappy childhood growing up in an unhappy marriage seemed to leave him with depression and a suspicious nature. Vincent Astor adored his father, and immediately after the divorce they were together often. The toll taken on Vincent by the loss of his father on *Titanic* must have been incalculable. With the addition of Madeleine Astor (two years younger than Vincent) and the ensuing public firestorm that culminated in the *Titanic* tragedy, the situation must have felt so overwhelming to a man not yet of legal age with a billion-dollar company now his responsibility and the entire world watching.

Vincent Astor would be married three times, his last wedding being performed in Bar Harbor on October 8, 1953. Two years later, at the age of sixty-three, he and his wife, Brooke, would purchase a cottage in Northeast Harbor, located on a part of the island several miles away from Bar Harbor. Northeast Harbor was and continues to be called the "quiet side" of the island, where people with names as big as those in Bar Harbor still socialized but on a much quieter scale, without the public buildings such as the Casino and the Building of Arts.

The Astor property fronted on the Neighborhood Road and lay between that road and the South Shore Road, overlooking Gilpatrick Cove. The sale to the Astors was handled by the Knowles Company, still in existence today. Vincent and his wife Brooke named the property Cove's End.

The Astors were social with their Northeast Harbor neighbors, including the Rockefellers. Those two families, along with other prominent Mount Desert Island residents, often contributed to the Maine Republican Party. Though Maine was a seasonal home to them, it was still a home, and they took their civic duty seriously.

In 1955, after the death of Vincent's only sister, Muriel, in Europe, Vincent and Brooke brought her two daughters to the cottage in Northeast Harbor for the summer. The Astors became well known to the year-round people of the area, with Mrs. Astor going on to employ and become familiar with several generations of families there.

* * *

Vincent Astor would only have three seasons to enjoy Cove's End at Northeast Harbor. He died of a heart attack in his New York apartment early in 1959.

Vincent's funeral was impressive. Held at a church on New York's Madison Avenue, his coffin was blanketed with yellow jonquils and maidenhair fern. The altar rail was heavily banked by 140 elaborate floral pieces of many kinds and colors. Two uniformed sailors stood guard over the body of the veteran of both world wars. More than four hundred family, friends, and business associates attended the service.

The *Bar Harbor Times*, in its February 5, 1959, edition, described Vincent Astor as a prominent summer resident of Northeast Harbor at the Cove's End cottage. Those at the paper extended their sincere sympathy to Mrs. Astor and the other Astor relatives of New York City and Cove's End.

"He was active in all social functions in the community and will be greatly missed by his island friends," wrote the *Bar Harbor Times*.

Brooke Astor would own a second camp on Mount Desert Island, the more rustic August Moon on Indian Point. Brooke Astor loved the area, its scenery, and its people. "For Brooke, Maine had held out the promise of nature's beauty and rejuvenation for five decades. If she felt low, Cove's End lifted her spirits, and she treated the townspeople like extended family."

* * *

The passing of Vincent allowed all the years of private resentment between him and John to spill forth publicly. For generations, the Astor family tradition had been to keep the fortune together and to leave that fortune to the control of the oldest Astor son. Vincent Astor broke with tradition. He would leave the bulk of the Astor fortune to the Vincent Astor Foundation, which he set up to alleviate human suffering.

"Vincent Astor, who passed recently, knew that money is a wonderful servant and a terrible master," wrote popular newspaper columnist Walter Winchell after his death. "And he was aware that those who have fortunes owe a debt—to the community. Consequently, he spent millions of dollars to eradicate slums and fight disease and ignorance. Mr. Astor once pointed out that 'the satisfaction of doing good gives you something money cannot buy. In the final analysis, time is the greatest treasure.' Vincent Astor was worth $100 million—but he couldn't buy an extra minute."

The Vincent Astor Foundation was left in the control of his widow, Brooke Astor, Vincent's wife of three years. Vincent left nothing to his brother, John.

Some argued that because Vincent had no children, under Astor family tradition the bulk of the estate should have gone to John, and Brooke Astor should have been forced to live on a trust fund, as Madeleine had been. Vincent chose not to honor that family tradition, and once again John Astor was left empty-handed.

Had Vincent died without a valid will, under the law John would have been entitled to half the estate, while the other half would have gone to Vincent's widow. According to Vincent's lawyers, he had drawn up many wills in the past and none of them left anything to his younger brother. Within a month of his brother's death, John Astor filed an objection in court to Vincent Astor's will. He requested the document be examined by an expert. The court granted the request.

Martin K. Tytell of New York scrutinized the twenty-page will with his eyes, ultraviolet light, and other special instruments, looking for erasures, delineations, and insertions. John Astor's lawyers told reporters that the examination was conducted to preserve their client's legal rights in the case of any future action and did not necessarily indicate an intention to try to legally break Vincent's will.

Reporters for newspaper, radio, and now television news knew that a messy court battle involving the two sons of Colonel John Jacob Astor would make for great interest. This would be another chapter in the Astor–Force tragic romance story. One syndicated news story reported that "portly John Jacob Astor III" had begun "what may be a full-scale court battle over one of America's largest fortunes. . . . While Vincent always had been regarded as serious and thoughtful about the responsibilities of great wealth, John, now in Florida, has been involved in several marital battles."

John Astor filed formal suit to break Vincent's will in July. John claimed that Vincent was mentally ill when he signed the will on July 26, 1958, six months before his death. John said that Vincent was suffering from senility and arteriosclerosis, or a narrowing of the arteries limiting the blood flow to his brain, "and was thereby rendered mentally deficient and totally lacking in testamentary capacity." John claimed his brother was "incompetent to make a will."

Reporters would get the messiness they wanted when John also charged that the will was not executed freely and voluntarily but "caused and procured by the improper conduct and undue influence of the widow," Brooke Astor, together with two other administrators. John requested that the suit be heard by a jury. As the case was heard in court, the accusations and responses became personal and hurtful. John argued that his brother, the conservative Vincent, was a drunkard and that he was drunk when the current will was signed. In response, Brooke's lawyers presented witnesses who said that Vincent was sober at the time of the signing. One of Vincent's attorneys testified that Vincent was alert "and knew fully well what he was doing" when he put his signature on the will. John S. Allee, a young Columbia University law student who was doing summer work with a law firm when he was called on to witness the will, testified that Astor didn't order a drink during the signing and that Allee himself was served a weak scotch and soda during the signing at the Astor home, though there were no refills offered.

* * *

When Brooke Astor took the stand, she seemed to be saying the words Vincent might have said to reporters had he not been such a discreet gentleman. Vincent had grown up with his father and grandparents instilling in him the responsibility and behavior that comes with a high social station. Young John Astor did not have that advantage. Though Vincent had been married three times, the divorces were as quiet as possible. In fairness, Vincent had also become a man at a time when the newspapers were also a bit more discreet with personal details of the people they were covering. By the time of Vincent's death, John had been married and divorced three times, with the second divorce being ruled by a court to be invalid—after John had married for a third time.

Brooke Astor, when it was her turn to testify, agreed that her late husband did drink a great deal, "but he was not a drunkard." She said her husband liked to drink, but he was "a large man and could hold it. He carried his liquor well. I have never seen him drunk." She said that Vincent's doctors had said that the drinking was permissible because it helped his circulatory disease. "It keeps his blood flowing," testified Brooke Astor.

Brooke was asked by one of John's lawyers whether she was aware that her husband had a bottle of liquor with him whenever he was in the hospital.

"Did you know that?" asked the lawyer.

"Of course I did. I took it to him," replied Brooke.

Brooke was prepared to fight back when it came to the attack on her late husband from his brother and the threat that John presented to her newly acquired Astor fortune. This was the first time in history that the Astor fortune had been out of the hands of the family, and Brooke was not prepared to relinquish the treasure easily. Brooke testified that Vincent knew what he was doing when he excluded John Jacob from the will and had done so purposely. She said John's exclusion was because Vincent regarded his younger brother as "notorious as an indolent playboy whose escapades were disgusting." She added that Vincent was determined against "diverting his wealth from worthy purposes to replenishing the fortune of one whose conduct was offensive to his personal and family ideals." Vincent, she said, thought John "was the most useless and worthless member of society, and he despised him because he was a slacker and draft evader."

* * *

Before any more nastiness could be spilled publicly, the suit was settled for a quarter of a million dollars, worth approximately $2.5 million when adjusted for inflation.

* * *

For many years, the Astors were on two sides of Mount Desert Island, with the Kanes at Breakwater in Bar Harbor and Brooke Astor entertaining in Northeast Harbor.

At Annie Kane's death in 1926, Breakwater would be passed to Peter Augustus Jay (a nephew through John Kane's brother DeLancey) and Peter's wife Susan Alexander McCook. Susan would leave Breakwater to their daughter, Susan Mary Alsop. Breakwater has passed out of the Astor family hands but still stands in existence along Bar Harbor's famed Shore Path. Breakwater was listed on the National Register of Historic Places in 1992.

St. Saviour's Church in Bar Harbor, where Madeleine Astor's dramatic second wedding was held, was benefited by John and Annie Kane. They left a financial fund to the church, where there continue to be four stained glass windows in honor of the Astor cousins who contributed so much to the town. One window is dedicated to John Innes Kane, with three windows dedicated to Annie.

In 1915, two years after John Kane's death, a recreational path outside Bar Harbor village funded by Mrs. Annie Kane in honor of her late husband was completed. The trail is now part of Acadia National Park. A memorial plaque was set in rock near the mouth of the Tarn to mark the trail's entrance.

Several decades later, in 1990, a group of volunteers cleaning a portion of Acadia National Park uncovered a monument to Annie Schermerhorn Kane and her sister, Mrs. Fanny Bridgham, also a Bar Harbor summer colonist.

Located at Lake Wood in Hulls Cove, the monument is made of granite with chiseled letters. Near the forgotten monument, the volunteers also discovered the remains of a small stone footbridge, presumably part of the Schermerhorn sisters' monument. Because the area was remote from the nearby foot trail to a public swimming spot, the overlooked monument and footbridge had been overtaken by a thicket of alders and vines. Fallen deadwood floating on the water's surface battered the footbridge into pieces over the years. The footbridge is believed to have been designed by noted landscape architect Beatrix Farrand, whose brilliant yet simplistic work was in evidence all over Mount Desert Island during Bar Harbor's Golden Age.

"[T]he monument serves as a reminder of the role of early supporters who set aside land for the national park," wrote the *Bangor Daily News* in 1990. "As the monument and bridge are uncovered—in what was undoubtedly a well-manicured landscape years ago—another page in the architectural history of the park may eventually be complete."

* * *

Vincent's widow, Brooke, would continue the Astors' Mount Desert Island legacy in Northeast Harbor. Mrs. Astor's one hundredth birthday party, held in New York, was hosted by her Northeast Harbor neighbor and friend David Rockefeller.

Though Vincent Astor had only a few years to enjoy Cove's End in Northeast Harbor, Brooke would go on to make full use of the summer home, entertaining many famous and historical names there. After her death, Brooke Astor would leave contributions to several Mount Desert Island charitable organizations, and the Vincent Astor Foundation is still active in various forms.

* * *

Ironically, and sadly, the same questions that surrounded Vincent's will for the Astor fortune would surround Brooke Astor herself years later.

Brooke Astor, the first "outside" person to control the Astor fortune, was found in her older age living in her own filth in New York City. She had signed control of the Astor fortune to her son, Anthony Marshall. The stories of how Brooke signed the fortune over were comparable to John Astor's contentions about the signing of Vincent's will, maintaining that the signature was coerced from someone who was physically incapable of saying no.

* * *

In addition to plundering the Astor fortune, Brooke Astor's son apparently tried to steal the family's *Titanic* heritage. When Colonel John Jacob Astor's body had been recovered from the Atlantic, one of the personal effects that helped in his identification was the gold watch he carried, his initial "A" lavishly etched on the front. Vincent Astor took possession of the watch at the time of his father's death.

In 1935, Vincent Astor would present the watch to his new godson, William Dobbyn V, the son of both John and Vincent Astor's longtime private secretary, William Dobbyn IV, who had been at so many of the historic Astor family events. It was from the Dobbyn estate that the watch was acquired by a museum in California.

In 2013, after Anthony Marshall had been convicted of swindling the bulk of the Astor fortune from his mother, and while awaiting sentencing, he and his wife, Charlene, made a rare public appearance at a lavish party for a new cruise ship that was being planned, *Titanic II*. At the party, Mr. Marshall was reportedly showing a watch to other guests and offering to sell it for $1 million. He said that the watch was the one worn by Colonel Astor on *Titanic* and that Vincent had given the watch to him as a gift.

This was the ilk of the people for whom Vincent Astor forsook his own brother.

* * *

Enzo Fiermonte first met his future stepson after he began his relationship with Madeleine Astor in 1933. John was not yet twenty-one, at which age he would have control over the interest accumulated from the $3 million trust fund left to him by his father. John was living at Madeleine's New York City home at the time. Enzo described John as lackadaisical and said his bedroom floor was littered with the pieces of fifteen formal suits, all gray, lying about.

Enzo, athletic all his life, found John Astor to be a new experience. Enzo had never met a youngster who did not like sports of any kind. He said John could not swim and rarely walked anywhere, instead preferring to ride or drive in a closed automobile. John gave Enzo the impression of never really having enjoyed anything in his life.

"He had too much money, a poor little rich boy, if ever there was one. I liked him from the first, and I felt sorry for him. But he was hopeless as a companion. He had too much cash to throw away, and too much time in which to do it," said Enzo. "He was a strange boy."

Though John lived in Madeleine's home, he and his mother did not see much of each other. John was at an age when he was out with different girls much of the time. He had a great interest in automobiles but not much else, said Enzo. He looked forward to receiving his inheritance and felt that his monthly allowance was not enough. He would say that when the money was his, he would own ten luxury automobiles.

Enzo said that Madeleine worried what would happen when John took control of his fortune. He would come to her for advances against his inheritance, which she would deny. He would then make arrangements with someone else to borrow the money until his twenty-first birthday. For the past twenty years, the country had read about the worth of John Jacob Astor III at his twenty-first birthday. They knew he was good for it.

* * *

John Jacob Astor's marriage to Ellen French would be his first of four. A year after their marriage, in 1935, John's name made headlines when he began a $25 a week job working for his older brother, Vincent. The company was the International Mercantile Marine, the company that had owned *Titanic*. Vincent Astor was now vice president of the IMM, and he offered his younger brother the job.

The *New York Times* ran a story on John Astor's new position. He was to start as an assistant to Captain Fred Fender, assistant marine superintendent for the IMM. Clad in a gray suit with faint pencil stripes, heavy brown shoes, and a gray Homburg hat, the twenty-two-year-old John Astor was found by the *New York Times* reporter on the bridge of the ship, along with Captain Fender. They were inspecting the ship's overhauling job, which had been ongoing for several days. John's white shirt collar was rumpled, and his blue and gray tie was askew. The reporter said John Astor had the appearance of a man who had done a hard day's work. John told the reporter his new job represented the fulfillment of his purpose to enter some business and learn it from the bottom.

"I can merely tell you what I told the others," he said, "and that is that I determined some time ago to learn some business thoroughly, and this is it. My job here is to do whatever work Captain Fender finds for me."

Mr. Astor drove to work that day in his small roadster. His hours were 9:00 a.m. to 5:00 p.m.

"Five-day week?" John was asked by reporters.

"Five and a half, I hope," he replied.

"Six days," said Captain Fender firmly.

In the middle of July, John's son William was born, whose christening temporarily brought the Astor family together in Newport. Less than two months later, John and Ellen Astor were almost killed in an explosion aboard John's newly acquired secondhand yacht.

John had purchased the *Laurion* that spring and had the craft reconditioned. On September 5, 1935, while cruising in Narragansett Bay with three guests, two boiler tubes on the *Laurion* blew out, causing a powerful explosion. The Astor party was just finishing luncheon at the time. The party and the crew of seven narrowly escaped injury, though the yacht was disabled in the water. Two powerboats sped to the yacht, one of which brought the party safely to shore, the other towing the disabled yacht to port. When asked by a friend why he had bought a boat built in the nineteenth century, John Astor is reported to have replied that coal and steam were good enough for his father and would do for him.

In December of that year, John and Ellen hosted a grand ball at John's New York town house, decorated with poinsettias, evergreens, laurel, and other Christmas flowers and greens. Madeleine and Enzo hosted a dinner for some of the older friends of Mr. and Mrs. Astor at the same time. The event was the social debut of Ellen's sister, Virginia French.

A month later, at the end of January 1936, John resigned from his job with the International Mercantile Marine. He had tried his hand at various departments throughout the company and was in the position of assisting the general manager at IMM's Broadway office when he announced his resignation. John Astor had been a working man for less than a year. John told reporters he liked the hands-on work and found it interesting but found the monotony of the office work irksome.

"What was the reason for abandoning your career as a shipping man?" he was asked by a reporter.

"Now, let me see, what was the reason? Well, for one thing, it took too much of my time. The eight hours a day I worked didn't allow me time to look after my other interests. I didn't finish work until 5 o'clock and by the time I got uptown it was 6. And then I had to get up early in the morning. You understand that I have business of my own to look after, and in times like these you have to watch things pretty closely. It developed that I did not have enough time to devote to my own affairs."

After announcing that the job took too much of his time, he and Ellen boarded a ship to enjoy a six-week holiday in Paris.

* * *

John would face occasional challenges with his father-in-law, as he had with the invitation of Hitler's aide to his wedding. This time it was a book written by William French titled *The Yankee Shield Bearer*. Mr. French said the book "is the simple story of a man who sees society for what it is, and I have never minced words."

John Astor "induced" his father-in-law to refrain from publishing the book, fearing the book's publication would be harmful to his wife and her sister. Though the terms of John's inducement not to publish the book were kept private, Mr. French was to have received $50,000 from the publisher.

The following years were spent between Newport and New York, with the marriage of John and Ellen Astor fracturing. In 1938, Ellen announced she was filing for divorce, though it did not take place. The couple reportedly spent their final years as a married couple apart, with Ellen taking up residence in Reno, Nevada, in the spring of 1943, preparatory to beginning a divorce action, according to a statement made at John Astor's office. Mr. Astor's secretary confirmed a report that Ellen Astor would receive an outright settlement of $1 million when the divorce was obtained, in return releasing any claims to John's possessions. The grounds of the divorce were extreme cruelty, mental in nature. The parents would split custody of their son, who was called Billy, each parent having him for six months of the year.

In the fall of that year, John would be embarrassed when the *New York Times* ran a story about a pig that reportedly had a residence in John Astor's penthouse.

"Ailing Pig No Astor Penthouse Resident, Just Undernourished Member of Litter."

John Astor was living at 998 Fifth Avenue, not too far from the site of the now-demolished Astor mansion. The first intimation that Mr. Astor owned a pig came in the form of a communique issued by the press agent for the Ellin Prince Speyer Hospital for Animals in New York, which asserted that the pig was female, named Silvia, about nine inches long, and had undergone an operation at the hospital for an abscess on the right hind foot. The communique also called the animal Mr. Astor's "pet pig" and declared that she was known at the hospital as "the penthouse pig," as the Astor butler, who they said brought her down, gave the pig's address as 998 Fifth Avenue.

A representative of John Astor emphatically said that the pig was no pet, had never lived at the town house, and was, indeed, merely one of a litter from Mr. Astor's farm at Basking Ridge, New Jersey. The pig had rickets, the representative said. A second Astor representative was even more emphatic in saying that the pig was not a pet and not a Fifth Avenue resident. He affirmed that Mr. Astor and his chauffeur had taken the pig from the farm because it was undernourished.

Veterinary hospital officials, informed of the turn of events, declared first that the abscess most certainly had existed and been operated on. Later a hospital spokesman, with great emphasis, said the first pronouncement had been "all wrong," that the pig never had been domiciled in a penthouse, never had lived on Fifth Avenue, never had been a pet of Mr. Astor, and never had been operated on. The pig, said the spokesman, was simply undernourished and in the institution for observation. All parties agreed that the pig was improving.

* * *

John Astor would marry again in the fall of 1944, a year and a half after his divorce from Ellen. His bride was Gertrude Gretsch, also of New York and Newport. The engagement had been rumored for some time. The wedding would be small, with no attendants. John's brother John Henry would serve as his best man. Soon there was a newspaper item in which an eighteen-year-old Philadelphia girl, Virginia Jacobs, announced that "Jackims" had been holding her in reserve as a possible successor to Gertrude in case the marriage did not work out. The nickname "Jackims" would stick with John Astor for the rest of his life.

John and Gertrude Astor would observe the Astor family tradition of attending the opening night of the Metropolitan Opera in New York as guests in box 3 of John's aunt Caroline Astor Wilson and Mrs. Cornelius Vanderbilt.

Three years later would see the loss of John Astor's Newport home, Chetwode, sold at auction. John said he was selling the five-acre estate as a matter of necessity. He had paid $150,000 for the mansion, with the auction yielding $71,000. After making the highest bid at the auction, James O'Donnell, a drugstore chain operator, would receive notice from

John Astor that he had decided not to sell Chetwode after all. John Astor said he was invoking his legal right to reject the offer within five days of the auction. Mr. O'Donnell threatened to sue John for $25,000 for breach of contract, saying the notice was given by Mr. Astor after the five-day waiting period had passed. Ultimately, Chetwode would be sold to Mr. O'Donnell.

The following month, one of John Astor's employees would charge him with withholding her pay. A cook in the Astor home on Fifth Avenue said John had failed to pay her $172 in wages, having been hired on October 1 and resigning on October 28. At John's office, it was said that a check had been sent the cook over the weekend.

* * *

Two months later, in January 1949, a daughter, Mary Jacqueline, was born to John and Gretchen Astor. Five years later, in July 1954, John filed for divorce in Mexico. The grounds were incompatibility. A month later, John Astor married his third wife.

Accompanied by family and friends, John married Miss Dolores Margaret Fullman of Miami Beach, Florida. They were married in Arlington, Virginia, where a marriage could take place the same day as the license was issued. The chaplain of the local police department performed the ten-minute ceremony. Dolly was divorced and twenty-six; John Astor was forty-two. No one from John's family was at the ceremony.

Less than a month later, John's second wife, Gretchen, filed suit in court asking for a declaratory judgment that she was John Astor's lawful wife and requesting the Mexican divorce that he obtained be declared void on the grounds that the divorce was obtained by proxy. By now John and Dolly were on their honeymoon in Switzerland. In December, the court ruled that John Astor's divorce action in Mexico was considered abandoned because of his use of a proxy, thereby making the divorce invalid. The court also ordered John to pay maintenance and child support. John contested the decision. Eventually the divorce was granted.

Less than a month after the court's decree in John Astor's second marriage, John was filing suit against his third wife, Dolly Fullman Astor, for annulment or divorce. He and Dolly had separated on their return from their European honeymoon. John Astor charged that she had "shoved" him into marriage knowing that his Mexican divorce from the second Mrs. Astor was invalid. Mr. Astor said that his third wife had "greed in her heart" but represented herself as "a white flower of purity" before their marriage. He said he had married her only after his "resistance was broken."

For her part, Dolly also sued John, claiming something "so intimate in nature she did not want to tell about it," reported the *New York Times*. Mr. Astor responded that the allegations against him were "scurrilous charges and innuendoes, smacking of a form of blackmail that is becoming all too prevalent in this country."

At this point, John's brother, Vincent, would die of a heart attack, leaving John out of his will. With all the matrimonial turmoil in John's well-covered life, Vincent's exclusion of his brother from his will was understandable, though whether it was justifiable, especially in terms of the fortune's final fate, is questionable.

John Astor's legal fight against Vincent's widow, Brooke, won him no popularity in the press. John had been followed by reporters since before he was born, with the public seeing the expensive toys he played with and hearing stories of unimaginable wealth and luxury, the mansions, the yacht, the travel. Combined with the details of John's three marriages and divorces (including technical bigamy), John Jacob Astor III did not have the sympathy he had enjoyed with the public as the *Titanic* Baby. John's lack of sympathy was not helped by inaccurate press reports that the Astor brothers had divided Colonel Astor's fortune equally on his death on the *Titanic*. The message of the story would read that Vincent had been thrifty, while John had been careless.

"Astor Says He's Really Poor Boy; Has $5 Million," read a headline for the United Press International. "The half-brothers inherited about 70 million dollars each from their father, Colonel John Jacob Astor, who went down with the *Titanic*. Vincent nearly tripled his inheritance by shrewd investment, but John Jacob, who was born four months after his father's death, is reported to have depleted his share. The 47-year-old playboy was not mentioned in his 67-year-old half-brother's will."

* * *

John Astor seemed to lie low after the loss of his brother and his three marriages. In 1959, he would become a grandfather for the first time. Eight years later, at a Newport event, John would cause much talk as he came face to face with two of his former wives and a former fiancée.

"The Astors Come Out for a Newport Party," read the *New York Times* headline.

"The dinner Mr. and Mrs. James H. Van Alen gave here last night looked a lot like an Astor family reunion, and in a way it was. John Jacob (Jackims) Astor 3rd was there along with his daughter, his son and two of his former wives. He didn't run into a former fiancée until later at the Tennis Ball.

"'We'd hoped John could be with us' said Mrs. Van Alen. 'He doesn't get here very often.'

"By his own choice, the elusive Mr. Astor rarely gets anywhere very social these days. He lives in Miami, where he's never been much for big formal parties and lots of small talk. And when he walked through the front door, accompanied by his first wife, Mrs. Ellen Tuck Guest, more than one of the Van Alens' friends were visibly but silently startled.

"The party was in honor of Mr. Astor's only daughter, pretty, blond Mary Jacqueline (Jackie) Astor, who made her debut on Long Island in June. And Miss Astor's mother, Mrs. Sonio Coletti-Perucca (the former Gertrude Gretsch—Mr. Astor's second wife), was in the receiving line.

"Mr. Astor kissed his daughter and shook hands with Mrs. Coletti-Perucca. And then he stood there, a tall, heavy-set man with spectacles, quietly talking with Mrs. Van Alen.

"His son, William Astor, an investment banker who commutes between Morristown, New Jersey and Wall Street, was off in the drawing room with his own wife, Charlotte.

"'I guess there are lots of us,' William Astor said later. 'It's hard to keep track.'

"Also included at the event were Stephen Spencer and Mrs. Joseph Daugherty, who are Astor cousins. The grandmother of the host, Mr. Van

Alen, was an Astor. [This was Colonel Astor's sister Helen, who died at age twenty-seven.]

"After dinner, which started at 9:40 pm, everyone went to the Tennis Ball at the Newport Casino. And it was there, beneath a giant ball of fresh flowers and little lights, that Mr. Astor encountered Mrs. John Jermain Slocum, the former Eileen Gillespie. She was engaged to him before he married Mrs. Guest, who was supposed to have been only a bridesmaid."

* * *

The famous Empress Eugénie engagement ring that had caused so much trouble between John Astor and Eileen Gillespie made its way back into the news in 1974. John filed suit against a bank in whose safe deposit box the ring was kept. A former attorney for John Astor testified that he had transported $500,000 worth of jewels to the bank for John Astor twenty years earlier, during one of John's divorce proceedings. The importance of that ring was again emphasized, as this would have been during the period that John's second wife, Gretchen, had frozen all his assets in her suit against him, claiming his Mexican divorce to be invalid. The jewels that John Astor had deposited in the bank at that time included the thirty-two-carat diamond Empress Eugénie ring, along with two diamond necklaces and a brooch. According to John Astor's suit, the jewels were missing when he went to claim them years later. John told how the red safety deposit box now contained a tear-shaped piece of glass with a hole in it instead of the historic ring, indicating it might have come from a chandelier. One of the diamond necklaces also had nine pendants missing.

* * *

John Astor married his fourth and final wife, Sue Sandford, in 1956; she died in 1985. He would remain a widower until his death in 1992 at the age of seventy-nine.

* * *

The last years of Mr. Astor's life were spent at his large home on Pinetree Drive in Miami Beach, Florida. His death was reported by two of his cousins: R. Thornton Wilson, son of aunt Caroline Astor Wilson, and Stephen Spencer, son of aunt Katherine Force Spencer.

* * *

John's marital adventures were noted by popular syndicated columnist Charles Van Deusen at the time of John's fourth marriage.

"Poor Mr. Astor's Costly Urges," read the headline. The story noted how John Astor, for whom they used the nickname "Jackims," seemed to divorce and remarry every ten years.

"Oddly enough, his mother, the late Madeleine Force Astor Dick, met and also summarily married a 26-year-old when she, too, had entered her 40's. The groom was an Italian prizefighter named Enzo Fiermonte, and the marriage ended in divorce.

"So Jackims' itch may be inherited.

"As a result, he now finds himself skating on the thinnest social ice any Astor has ventured upon since his mother married a prizefighter," wrote Van Deusen.

Conclusion

The portrait of Madeleine Force Astor that emerges from her biography is largely based on the opinions and experiences of each individual reader. What emerges is not a simple, one-dimensional person. The newspapers would often try to fit Madeleine's continuing story into a simple, preconceived storyline, but she was much more complex than that.

Madeleine Force Astor cannot be seen entirely as either a victim or a champion; she was a little bit of both. She was a victim of a changing society, and yet she effected some of the changes that society would see during that transition period of the early 1900s. As the public read of Madeleine's experiences, they reflected on the antiquated system of the dowry, the need for a widow to wear black mourning clothes for the remainder of her life, and the injustice of a widow forfeiting her inheritance because of a desire to remarry and enjoy life again after a period of tragedy.

It might be argued that in her courtship with Colonel Astor and the arrangements of the dowry, Madeleine was not so much the victim of her parents but more the victim of a changing society. Where the amount of the dowry had been important to Madeleine's mother's generation, Madeleine herself was caught between that generation and a generation of younger women who were starting to question and reject a financial price being put on them.

Also emerging from Madeleine Force Astor's biography is a woman of strength and determination, at least during her Bar Harbor years. The Bar Harbor that Madeleine Force arrived at for the first time in 1907 was Colonel John Jacob Astor's Bar Harbor. By the time she left there in 1916, she had made Bar Harbor her own. Testimony to Madeleine Force

Astor's strength and determination can be seen not only with her championships on the tennis courts of the Bar Harbor Swimming Club but also in her experience during and after the *Titanic* tragedy. In her lifeboat, Madeleine was both victim and champion; her mind seemed to be a temporary victim of the tragedy, but she still worked hard to save the lives of herself, her unborn child, her fellow Bar Harbor summer colonists, and even a few other people in the water.

After the *Titanic* disaster, Madeleine took care of her son on her own for four years before remarrying. Despite the mental and physical strain of her recent *Titanic* experience, along with crowds of loud onlookers in the summer heat of New York City, Madeleine Astor was able to keep herself together and deliver a healthy son, even with a city bus crashing into her home just days before the baby's delivery. Had Madeleine Force Astor been a less strong person, her story easily could have ended during the *Titanic* period.

* * *

One might argue that Madeleine Force Astor's decision to leave Bar Harbor after her remarriage to William Dick in 1916 was one of the biggest mistakes she made. Why she left, exactly, is not known. Perhaps during their courtship her second husband had promised more of a presence there, only to backtrack on any such promise after seeing the circus that was made of his wedding ceremony. Perhaps Madeleine was looking for the escape and security that her new husband's rejection of Bar Harbor society offered. The Bar Harbor to which the widowed Madeleine Astor and her son returned was one that was increasingly threatened by World War I every season. After her return there with baby John, Madeleine could not go anywhere without crowds of people instantly forming outside whatever club she was attending. William Dick, and the secure, private life he offered, must have been tempting for Madeleine Astor after all she had been through. Madeleine Astor's third husband, Enzo Fiermonte, reported that Madeleine had said marrying Mr. Dick was a mistake. Whether she meant the man himself or the life she left behind to be with him is not known.

* * *

What gets lost in Madeleine Astor's story is the romance of her time with John Jacob Astor. Colonel Astor had the world at his fingertips and had been recently released from many predetermined obligations. His romance with Madeleine seemed to be a rejection of the society into which his position as Mrs. Caroline Astor's son and Ava Astor's husband had forced him. With his daughter in the care of her mother and his son now off in college, Colonel Astor was free of the immediate obligations of family. His long-protected name and reputation had been publicly sullied through the divorce action. But he still had his money, and he had nothing left to lose when he set eyes on the beautiful, young Madeleine Force on the tennis courts in Bar Harbor with the stunning Frenchman Bay as the backdrop. Madeleine and John seemed to meet at a time when they both needed to fulfill a youthful spirit. Bar Harbor was the perfect setting.

Perhaps it is Bar Harbor's ability to nurture a youthful spirit that made the area so desirable to Madeleine Force Astor. She excelled there as a young woman and returned there after an intense period of personal attack and tragedy. It was there as a girl that she first came to life, and it was there as a young woman that she later came back to life. It was in Bar Harbor that Madeleine Force added her own unique identity to the continuing role of *The* Mrs. Astor. She stayed later and later every year in Bar Harbor as each season became more active for "the girl widow."

As Madeleine Force Astor was a symbol of a changing society, she was also a symbol of a changing Bar Harbor. Her removal from Bar Harbor on her remarriage coincided with the very beginning of the end of Bar Harbor's Golden Age. The world was changing as a result of its first world war. In addition to depressions and stock market crashes, the country had a new personal income tax, which led to the curtailing of the opulent wealth that had built the golden Bar Harbor of the late 1800s. It is easy to think of the Fire of 1947 and the resultant loss of many of the grand cottages as the end of Bar Harbor's Golden Age. By the time of the fire, however, many of those cottages had been sitting empty for a long time, the victims of long-lost family fortunes, remnants of a time gone by.

When Madeleine Force Astor left Bar Harbor, she seems to have lost the spirit that Bar Harbor continues to offer. Sadly, the Golden Age of Bar Harbor, too, lost a little of its luster when Madeleine Force Astor departed its rocky shores.

Bibliography

A Journey in Other Worlds: A Romance of the Future, John Jacob Astor IV (1894)

Auburn Democrat-Argus (newspaper)

Bangor Daily News (newspaper)

Bar Harbor Historical Society, Bar Harbor, Maine

Bar Harbor Record (newspaper)

Bar Harbor Times (newspaper)

Biddeford Daily Journal (newspaper)

Boston Globe (newspaper)

Bristol Courier (newspaper)

Brooklyn Daily Eagle (newspaper)

Brooklyn Times (newspaper)

Canton Commercial Advertiser (newspaper)

Chicago Examiner (newspaper)

Cincinnati Commercial Tribune (newspaper)

Daily Kennebec Journal (newspaper)

Disaster at the Bar Harbor Ferry, Mac Smith (Down East Books, 2022)

Harper's Bazaar (magazine)

Herald and News (newspaper)

Hudson Columbia Republican (newspaper)

Indianapolis Times (newspaper)

Jesup Memorial Library, Bar Harbor, Maine

Mainers on the Titanic, Mac Smith (Down East Books, 2014)

Meriden Morning Record/Record-Journal (newspaper)

Miami Daily News Record (newspaper)

Mount Desert Herald (newspaper)

New England Resorter (magazine)

Newport Daily News (newspaper)

New York Evening Post (newspaper)

New York Evening World (newspaper)

New York Herald (newspaper)

New York Morning Journal (newspaper)

New York Sun (newspaper)

New York Times (newspaper)

New York Tribune (newspaper)

New York World (newspaper)

Oakland Tribune (newspaper)

Other Edens: The Sketchbook of an Artist Naturalist, John Henry Dick (Old Greenwich, CT: Devin-Adair Company, 1979)

Philadelphia Inquirer (newspaper)

Placerville Mountain Democrat (newspaper)

Portland Daily Press (newspaper)

Portland Evening Express (newspaper)

Rhinelander Daily News (newspaper)

Rochester Catholic Journal (newspaper)

San Antonio Light (newspaper)

Syracuse Herald (newspaper)

Syracuse Post Standard (newspaper)

Time (magazine)

True Story (magazine)

Utica Herald Dispatch (newspaper)

Washington Herald (newspaper)

Washington Times (newspaper)

Waterville Sentinel (newspaper)